FEMINIST
GENERATIONS

In the series

WOMEN IN THE POLITICAL ECONOMY,

EDITED BY RONNIE J. STEINBERG

FEMINIST
GENERATIONS

THE PERSISTENCE OF THE
RADICAL WOMEN'S MOVEMENT

NANCY WHITTIER

TEMPLE UNIVERSITY PRESS
Philadelphia

Temple University Press, Philadelphia 19122
Copyright © 1995 by Temple University. All rights reserved
Published 1995
Printed in the United States of America

♾ The paper used in this book meets the requirements of the
American National Standard for Information Sciences—Permanence of
Paper for Printed Library Materials, ANSI Z39.48-1984

Text design by Chiquita S. Babb

Library of Congress Cataloging-in-Publication Data
Whittier, Nancy, 1966–
    Feminist generations : the persistence of the radical women's
movement / Nancy Whittier.
        p.   cm. — (Women in the political economy)
    Includes bibliographical references (p.   ) and index.
    ISBN 1-56639-281-0 (cloth : alk. paper). — ISBN 1-56639-282-9
(pbk. : alk. paper)
    1. Feminism—United States.   2. Radicalism—United States.
I. Title.   II. Series.
HQ1154.W49   1995
305.42′0973—dc20   94-26260

CONTENTS

Acknowledgments vii

Introduction 1

1 :: Radical Feminism in Columbus, Ohio 26

2 :: The Evolution of Radical Feminist Identity 55

3 :: Changers and the Changed: Radical Feminists
in the Reagan Years 80

4 :: Keeping the Faith: Working for Social Change 116

5 :: United We Stand: The Impact of the Women's
Movement on Other Social Movements 155

6 :: Feminists in the "Postfeminist" Age:
The Women's Movement in the 1980s 191

7 :: The Next Wave 225

Conclusion: The Persistence and Transformation of
Social Movements 245

Appendix: Women's Movement Organizations and Dates,
Columbus, Ohio 259

Notes 263

Index 301

ACKNOWLEDGMENTS

MANY PEOPLE have contributed to this work. When I began the project as my dissertation, Verta Taylor, J. Craig Jenkins, and Laurel Richardson each provided helpful guidance, comments, and critiques. As I reworked the manuscript, Kim Dill, Myra Marx Ferree, Patricia Yancey Martin, David Meyer, Jo Reger, and Kate Weigand read portions and contributed thoughtful comments about both substance and organization. I am especially grateful to Sally Kennedy, Carol Mueller, Leila Rupp, Ronnie Steinberg, and Verta Taylor, who read the entire manuscript (in some cases more than once) and have contributed greatly to its coherence. Michael Ames at Temple University Press provided consistent encouragement and direction. I also appreciate Jane Barry's expert copy-editing. My students at Smith College have been a source of insight and inspiration; I particularly appreciate the comments and (often hilarious) title suggestions from students in my seminar Gender and Social Change. Verta Taylor has been indispensable to the project all along; I greatly appreciate her intellectual engagement and emotional support. All errors of logic or fact are, of course, my own.

I am deeply grateful to the women I interviewed, who were generous with both their time and their insight. The Ohio Historical Society gave me access to its collection of documents from the Women's Action Collective; I thank the staff for their assistance. Bertha Ihnat, of the Ohio State University Archives, was very helpful in tracking down relevant material. I also thank Debbie Chalfie, Chris Guarnieri, Mary Haller, Crindi Loschenkohl, Caroline Sparks, and Teri Wehausen for giving me access to their personal collections of documents from the women's movement. Kim Dill very kindly let me see interviews she had conducted with young feminists.

Portions of Chapter 2 appeared in somewhat different form in "Turning It Over: Personnel Change in the Columbus, Ohio, Women's Movement, 1969–1984," in *Feminist Organizations: Harvest of the New Women's Movement,* ed. Myra Marx Ferree and Patricia Yancey Martin (Philadelphia: Temple University Press, 1995).

The research was supported by a Women's Studies Small Grant from the Center for Women's Studies at The Ohio State University and by the Committee on Faculty Compensation and Development at Smith College. A Presidential Fellowship from The Ohio State University provided me with a much-needed year away from teaching obligations to finish the dissertation. Michelle Byrne and Gretchen Ulrich, my research assistants at Smith College, were expert, efficient, and long-suffering as they helped with tracking down references, collecting information, reading microfilm, and checking endnotes; they also provided me with useful feedback on the manuscript.

On a more personal note, I appreciate the support and encouragement provided by Kim Dill, Barbara Edgar, Jane Ellsworth, David Meyer, Joanne Reger, and Rick Tewksbury. Bill, Cecil, and Dupree were indispensable feline assistants, helping with such matters as lap-sitting, paper shuffling, and keyboard-jumping. Finally, I thank my partner, Kate Weigand, for her emotional and intellectual support. She has been patient with my stress and grumpiness and has helped me both to make this book as clear and interesting as possible and to maintain a balanced life away from the research.

INTRODUCTION

THE WOMEN'S MOVEMENT of the 1960s and 1970s transformed American society and the lives of many individuals.
Electrifying both to participants and to onlookers, feminist activism challenged what was taken for granted, articulated what
was unspoken, and left an indelible mark on a generation.
Thousands of women participated in radical feminist organizations across the country.[1] They talked to each other about their
most personal experiences in consciousness-raising groups and
began to think about their lives in new ways. They discussed
issues, argued with each other, picketed, protested, and created
a new definition of what it could mean to be a woman: to be
independent and strong, to take oneself and other women seriously, and to challenge the restrictions placed on women in a
male-dominated society. They established organizations, such as
rape crisis centers, battered women's shelters, feminist bookstores, and women's studies programs, that aimed both to improve women's lives in the present and to lay the groundwork
for more sweeping social transformation in the future. Such activities thrived throughout much of the 1970s, and many par-

ticipants expected, as one put it, to continue "making feminist revolution" into the 1980s and beyond.

But the 1980s proved to be hard times for radical feminists, as for participants in many other social movements of the Left. Widely described as a "postfeminist" era, the 1980s saw the election of an overtly antifeminist President, Ronald Reagan, budget cuts for social service and social change organizations alike, and the rise of a grassroots Religious Right.[2] Much writing and discussion in feminist circles focused on an antifeminist "backlash" as feminists lost ground on abortion rights, conservative efforts defeated the Equal Rights Amendment (ERA) and promoted a narrow model of "family values," and "feminist" came to connote a humorless, unattractive, hairy-legged, man-hating, lesbian anachronism.[3]

Just as damaging to the women's movement as these concrete setbacks was the myth, spread by both popular authors and scholars, of the "postfeminist" 1980s as an era of political apathy during which former activists traded in their political commitments for career mobility and Cuisinarts and young adults single-mindedly pursued career goals.[4] With a collective sigh of relief, conservative commentators heralded the end of the protests and disruptions of the sixties and the emergence of the "yuppies," painting student protestors against the war in Vietnam, for civil rights, student rights, and women's liberation as misled by the excesses of youth. As they matured, the myth goes, activists recognized the errors of their intemperate youth and settled down to raise families, build careers, and pursue change (if at all) through institutionalized means such as electoral politics.[5]

The same myth that depicted longtime activists as leaving behind their feminist commitments also contended that younger women were uninterested in feminism and the women's movement even as they reaped the benefits of women's expanded access to education and careers. To this "postfeminist generation," the women's movement had been necessary ten years earlier, but was outmoded by the 1980s because of its own success. Accordingly, "postfeminist" women happily entered formerly male colleges and universities, pursued previously male-dominated careers, and were unhindered by any remaining limits for women. Women who persisted in calling attention to sexism or raising feminist issues, according to the myth, were needlessly fighting old battles.[6]

The postfeminist myth, then, hinged on two assumptions. First, the conservative shift in the 1980s stemmed in part from former activists' abandonment of radical politics in favor of more mature and traditional goals and priorities. And, second, the 1980s drove a generational wedge between the women who had organized feminist groups and protests during the 1960s and 1970s and their younger counterparts, who came of age in an era that was simultaneously more hostile to feminism and less restrictive of women.

Like most myths, this one contains a kernel of truth. The 1980s did mark a turning point for individual feminists, who searched for new ways to be activists in the face of mounting opposition, financial difficulty, and their own aging. Yet women who had been activists in the 1960s and 1970s never abandoned their political commitments, and the radical women's movement not only survived the 1980s but began to grow again in the 1990s. Admittedly, as the social and political climate grew more conservative, the grassroots women's movement became smaller and less visible; but, as activists have known all along, neither the movement nor feminist individuals vanished.

It is also true that a generational divide emerged between older and younger women, and even between older and younger feminists. But this divide was neither absolute nor based on the younger generation's wholesale rejection of feminist values. Many younger women were uninterested in feminist protest, just as many women of their mothers' generation sat out the feminist upheavals of the 1960s and 1970s. Other younger women, however, organized and agitated on behalf of women. Because women who came of age in the 1980s had sharply different experiences from those who came of age ten or twenty years earlier, however, they redefined priorities and reconceptualized the meaning of feminism.[7] Generational politics, then, are more relevant to the resulting debates and shifts within the women's movement than to young women's decisions to become feminists in the first place.

Even among the women who mobilized the radical feminist movement of the 1960s and 1970s there were subtle, but important, differences among those who became feminists at different times, as well as divisions of race, class, and sexual orientation. Although they all faced the same hostile context in the 1980s and felt the same mix of pride and disappointment at the actions of younger feminists, veterans of the 1960s and 1970s movement are by no means a unified "generation." Nevertheless, generational politics contributed to the redefinitions of radical feminism in the 1980s and the conflicts surrounding them. Combined with longtime feminists' turn toward less militant forms of activism, this lent credence to the idea that the radical feminist movement was defunct by the 1980s.

In fact, both generational politics and the hostile climate of the 1980s affected the course of the women's movement, but neither caused its demise. On the contrary, a radical feminist challenge persisted throughout the 1980s and into the 1990s in many forms: women's movement organizations, the politicized actions of individuals in their daily lives, and within movements for other causes. Unlike women's groups that operated in the national political arena, such as the National Organization for Women (NOW), radical feminism survived mostly at the grassroots in cities and towns around the country. Longtime feminists—veterans of the thriving movement of the 1960s and 1970s—were central to the continuing struggle, but incoming activists also helped both to sustain and to transform radical feminism. Together, they carried the challenge, although not unchanged, into a new era.

The survival of radical feminism has been largely invisible to scholars precisely because the movement has never had a centralized or national organization but is based in grassroots, loosely organized groups. Any study of radical feminism is thus, by necessity, a local case study. I focus here on radical feminist organizing in Columbus, Ohio. A medium-sized, midwestern city, Columbus is the state capital and home to The Ohio State University. A radical feminist movement emerged in Columbus around 1969 and grew steadily throughout the 1970s. As in other locations, radical feminist organizations in Columbus decreased in number in the 1980s, but an informally organized feminist community, a handful of surviving organizations, and some new organizations kept the movement alive.

Organizations that identified themselves as radical feminist sought transformation rather than reform of existing social institutions. They built nonhierarchical organizational structures, eschewed most mixed-sex organizing, and usually operated outside mainstream politics. Members of these groups distinguished themselves from "liberal feminists" who engaged more directly with electoral politics, used more moderate tactics, and structured organizations more bureaucratically. The boundaries of radical feminism are blurry; activists and organizations cooperated across the line, and the wings of the movement have converged over time. Yet the distinction was meaningful to participants (in both wings) during the movement's peak and continues to be significant to their sense of self and their actions today. In referring to organizations as radical feminist, I have relied primarily on how they identified themselves and have used a broad definition. The category of radical feminist is more usefully understood as an identity that is constructed by activists, and is subject to debate and redefinition, than as a historically constant ideology. My concern is not to classify organizations and individuals according to whether they adhere to a particular definition of radical feminism but rather to understand the changing beliefs and activities associated with this sector of the women's movement.

Despite extensive feminist activity in medium-sized and midwestern cities, most researchers have focused on major cities such as New York, Washington, D.C., San Francisco, and Chicago.[8] Yet women in all areas of the country were engaged in feminist activism from the 1960s to the present; neither an exclusive focus on major cities nor a decontextualized account captures the concrete evolution of local movement communities. Columbus typifies the small or medium-sized midwestern cities, often state capitals or college towns, that were so important to the radical feminist movement and are still underdocumented by scholars. It is in such settings that the individuals and organizations of the second wave women's movement settled in for the long haul.[9]

THE PARTICIPANTS

In 1968, a college student at Ohio State University who had participated in campus demonstrations for civil rights and against the Vietnam War and the university's involvement in military industries since the mid-1960s heard about women in the New Left who were raising the issue of "women's liberation." The idea impressed her, and within a year she and others had founded a Women's Liberation group. She helped organize rap groups, where members talked about their experiences as women, and forged radical politics by participating in a militant student strike in 1970. Sometimes she thought of herself as a radical woman and sometimes as a women's liberationist and, despite frustration with and anger at male leftists, believed it was important to work in coalition with them.

In 1976, a young woman left her husband and moved to

nearby Columbus. Interested in volunteer work, she signed up to help out at a rape crisis center. Her next few weeks were full of one epiphany after another as she thought about women's experience and oppression and her own life in new ways, met dozens of committed feminists, and became part of a political community of women. Over the next five years, she found paid employment in the antirape organization and other women's movement groups and helped to organize countless programs and protests as part of a radical feminist organization. She also came out as a lesbian, stopped shaving her legs, and sought approval from other activists rather than from mainstream society. She thought of herself as a radical feminist and felt inspired by the energy and sisterhood she found in an all-women's organization, although the conflicts among her "sisters" were disturbing.

In 1988, a young lesbian entered Ohio State University. Her mother and her mother's friends had mentioned feminism, and so the idea was not new to her, but she was interested in learning more. She enrolled in an introductory women's studies course, where she was fascinated by the information and theoretical perspectives she encountered. She quickly became outspoken about women's rights and about lesbian rights and visibility, joined the Association of Women Students and the Gay and Lesbian Alliance on campus, and began, with others, to organize attention-getting actions such as a "Kiss-In" in a shopping mall. She called herself queer or a dyke and adopted an "in-your-face" sexuality that included public displays of affection, interest in lesbian pornography, and open admiration of other women's bodies. She was also an outspoken advocate of abortion rights and a leader in the student pro-choice organization.[10]

What do these three women have in common? All are part of what we call the women's movement, and all are concerned with some of the same basic goals. All three worked for social change outside established institutions rather than as state employees, social workers, politicians, or lobbyists. They all saw themselves as more radical (but not necessarily "better") than feminists who did work within such institutions, although the labels they chose for themselves—women's liberationist, radical feminist, dyke—varied. And all had contact with some of the same organizations, such as campus groups, a rape prevention and crisis center, and a feminist bookstore that survived over the years.

Despite their commonalities, however, these three women understand feminism and their experiences as women and as activists in very different ways. For the co-founder of the OSU Women's Liberation group, the women's movement was new and she was making it up as she went along. Her political perspective was shaped as much by her earlier experience in the New Left as by emerging feminist organizing. By the mid-1970s, the new entrant to the movement encountered a well-established feminist community in which she could quickly immerse herself. This thriving women's movement shaped her political perspective from the very beginning. Even more striking is the contrast between the women who led the second wave movement during the late 1960s and 1970s and those who came later. The young woman who took a women's studies class in 1988 benefited from years of feminist gains institutionalized within the university, as well as from the growing visibility possible for lesbians. Although the headiness of the early years of mass activism had subsided, she saw far more possibilities for herself as a woman and a lesbian, than did the first two women.

These three women's experiences raise three sets of questions. First, how are their experiences meaningful in the long run? In other words, how do the perspectives on the world that activists develop carry over into their later lives, after the movement recedes and they are no longer immersed in protest? Second, how can we understand the differences among these women? How do the social contexts of their different periods of activism shape how they define feminism and the actions they pursue?

Third, how do such differences among activists of different eras affect the persistence and transformation of the radical women's movement over time? More broadly, how do they reshape our view of social movements and our conceptualization of how challenges endure and change?

In order to answer these questions, I began by examining documents from radical feminist organizations in Columbus, Ohio, including the Women's Action Collective (WAC), a radical feminist organization founded in 1971 that brought together many of the key women's movement groups and individuals in Columbus, and organizations affiliated with The Ohio State University, including OSU Women's Liberation, the Center for Women's Studies, the Association of Women Students, the Office of Women's Services, and Central Ohio Lesbians. I also examined documents from feminist groups in Columbus that worked more closely within mainstream political institutions, such as the Ohio Task Force for the Implementation of the ERA, the International Women's Year Planning Committee, and the Ohio Commission on the Status of Women.[11]

I used these organizational records to identify women who were leaders or central activists in the radical feminist movement. Then, I set about tracking down as many of these women as possible. This was not an easy task. The Columbus telephone book yielded telephone numbers for some participants who had remained in the area, and personal contacts provided information about a handful of others. The first women I talked to were able to put me in touch with others, and some women contacted me after they heard about my research. I attempted to talk to participants in as many different organizations as possible, and I made a particular effort to locate individuals who had been on different sides of conflicts within the movement.

In the end, I interviewed 34 women who were core activists during the movement's heyday. Most, although not all, of these women identified themselves as radical rather than liberal feminists. All had entered the women's movement in Columbus before 1977, and their sense of themselves as feminists was rooted in those heady years. I talked with them in their homes or offices for between 45 minutes and four hours about their activist histories, their present lives, how they have changed over the years, and their views of the contemporary women's movement. I also spoke with participants in 10 women's movement organizations of the 1990s, including all the organizations in Columbus that (to my knowledge) have survived since the 1970s or grew directly out of feminist groups of the 1970s.[12] To flesh out the story of the most recent years of the movement, I have also drawn on my own participation in and observation of feminist events and organizations.

The women I interviewed were in some ways a cross-section of the women's movement of the period, and in other ways an overly homogeneous group. The longtime activists' ages at the time of the interviews (1991) ranged from 33 to 84 years, with an average age of 45. Thirty-three of the women interviewed are white (non-Hispanic), and one is Latina. They are a highly educated group: All but one have bachelor's degrees, and 74 percent have at least some postgraduate education.[13] Fifty-nine percent (20) identified themselves as lesbian, 26 percent (9) as heterosexual, and 12 percent (4) as bisexual; one did not disclose her sexual orientation. At the time of the interview, all but one of the respondents were employed, the vast majority (32), in professional or managerial occupations.[14] Approximately two-thirds of the sample described themselves as being from middle-class backgrounds; one-third said they came from working-class or poor backgrounds.

To a large extent, these characteristics reflect the composition of Columbus women's movement organizations of the 1960s and 1970s. Because it drew on a university community, the women's movement in Columbus had a large number of college graduates, and it is not surprising that so many are now in professional occupations. Like the national movement, the women's movement in Columbus was also predominantly white and middle-class, and most women I interviewed commented on how homogeneous their organizations had been. Although I made a particular effort to locate and interview the handful of African American and Latina women who participated in Columbus radical feminist organizations during the 1970s, I identified the names of only four women who were part of the movement before 1977 and was able to find a current phone number for only one woman, whom I interviewed. Notably, many of the white women I interviewed had not kept in touch with women of color and were not able to give me their addresses or phone numbers. By the mid-1980s, more African American women in particular were part of feminist groups in Columbus, and three of the women I talked to about contemporary organizations were African American.

The experiences of women of color in the feminist movement differed from white women's experiences both because of their marginality within the white-dominated movement and their connections to racial and ethnic communities. In addition, many women of color participated throughout the 1970s, 1980s, and 1990s in the growing women's and mixed-gender movements of African Americans, Latinas, Asian Americans, Native Americans, and other racial and ethnic minorities. As a result, we cannot simply generalize to women of color from the experiences of the white women I interviewed, although many commonalities exist.

I promised the women I interviewed that their identities would remain confidential and that I would not use quotations in a way that would allow the speaker to be identified, even by other members of the Columbus women's movement. This has proven a difficult task. I have sought to present as much of the richness and detail of women's stories as possible while preserving confidentiality. In some cases this has meant giving less than complete background information about particular quotations or giving only general information about speakers.[15]

I have attempted to let women speak in their own voices and

interpret their own experiences throughout the text. In accordance with feminist methodology, this has meant taking participants' perspectives on their lives and the larger women's movement seriously as I tried to understand how feminist individuals and groups survived and changed over time. By and large, I will present participants' own assessment of their continuing feminist activities and their impact. At the same time, I have not simply accepted women's comments at face value. Talking to many women who had similar experiences made it clear to me that what individuals often saw as personal choices and difficulties had social roots. I have tried to illuminate those roots and to put women's experiences in their larger context.

It was immediately clear when I began interviewing women that their experiences in the radical feminist movement had forever changed their lives and that they struggled to find ways to remain active feminists in the 1980s and beyond. This brings us back to the first of the three questions I raised earlier: How have their years as radical feminist activists shaped women's lives since then? How have they managed to remain committed and active feminists as the social and political climate grew more hostile?

LONGTERM COMMITMENTS

If someone asks me, "Who are you?" I'm a radical feminist. And I see radical feminism as my life's work.

I almost feel like my life has a theme. It's not just like I'm this little ant out there living and working with all the other ants on the anthill. There are things that I care really, really deeply about, and that sort of infuses my whole life with meaning.

Thousands of women participated in radical feminist activities across the country during the late 1960s and early 1970s. These comments by two such women were echoed by numerous others. Being part of the radical feminist movement was an important and transformative experience for most participants. The most intensely involved members—those who were leaders or otherwise immersed in radical feminist organizing—still believe in the perspectives and commitments they developed in the women's movement. Many continue to organize their lives around work for social change; all still feel the reverberations of their activism.

The early 1980s were a profoundly disorienting period for many longtime activists.[16] They came of age in a setting and time when politics were everything, and found themselves ten or twenty years later in a very different context. As the organized women's movement lost momentum, many participants dropped out of the organizations they had formed, returned to school, started working full time in professional jobs, or moved to other cities. They searched for ways to be politically active in a hostile environment while maintaining less marginal and stressful lives than they had led during the 1970s.

By seeking employment that allowed them to work for feminist goals, structuring their daily lives according to political principles, and carrying feminist concerns into other movements for social change, these women helped ensure that the women's movement would survive the 1980s and continue to influence public policy, culture, workplaces, and daily life. Yet many women I talked to now feel that they are somehow inadequate as activists, insufficiently involved with politics, too absorbed in the rest of their lives, or personally weak because they feel tired and demoralized after more than two decades of confronting "the system."

One of the key insights of the second wave of the women's movement was that personal circumstances and problems have political roots. The personal is still political in the 1990s. The difficulty that each longtime feminist faces in remaining politically active, her disillusionment with the current state of the women's movement, and her increasing turn toward work and daily life as avenues for social change are experiences shared by many other women and are due to larger, structural forces. The constriction of both political opportunities and economic resources in the 1980s destabilized women's movement organizations at the same time that the conservative culture and renewed emphasis on "traditional family values" made it unpopular to be a feminist. It is no wonder that veterans of the radical women's movement found it difficult to remain politically active and that they feel bad about themselves. But in fact, the actions of longtime radical feminists are an important part of the continuing women's movement. The existence of a large cohort of movement veterans who doggedly act on their political convictions in any way they can ensures the movement's survival.

Women who became feminists in the 1960s or 1970s remain the largest generation in the contemporary women's movement and energize much of the activism that occurs. Nevertheless, new recruits continued to enter women's movement organizations and communities and to identify themselves as feminist throughout the 1980s and early 1990s. They were recruited through women's studies classes, lesbian communities, and by feminist mothers and women's movement publications.[17] Not surprisingly, their understanding of feminism often departed from earlier definitions. These differences among women who entered the movement at different times bring us to the second set of questions I raised earlier. How can we understand such differences, and how are they shaped by the changing contexts in which activists operate?

FEMINIST GENERATIONS AND COLLECTIVE IDENTITY

The three women I described earlier illustrate the variations among women who entered the movement at different times.

The first two both became involved during the movement's peak years, in 1968 and 1976, yet they had different experiences as activists and each developed her own perspective on feminism. The third woman became a feminist during the more conservative 1980s, and her perspective diverged further still from her predecessors'. Of course, there are many factors that differentiate participants in social movements from each other. But one important factor, often overlooked, is *when* participants are politicized—in other words, their political generation. As activists have long taken for granted, what it means to call oneself "feminist" varies greatly over time, often leading to conflict over movement goals, values, ideology, strategy, or individual behavior. In other words, coming of political age at different times gives people different perspectives.[18]

Women who entered the women's movement together, at a particular point in the movement's history, came to share an understanding of what it meant to be a feminist. This common self-definition, or collective identity, is what connects them and what endures over the years to make their experiences in the women's movement meaningful in the long run. Collective identity is the "shared definition of a group that derives from members' common interests, experiences, and solidarity."[19] In the process of constructing a collective identity, challenging groups adopt labels for themselves (such as "feminist"), draw lines between insiders and outsiders, and develop interpretive frameworks, a political consciousness through which members understand the world. Of course, "collective identities" exist only as far as real people agree upon, enact, argue over, and internalize them; group definitions have no life of their own, and they are constantly changing rather than static.

If we look at political generations interactively, asking how women collectively proposed, debated, negotiated, and agreed and disagreed about what it meant to be a feminist, we can formulate new questions. How do individuals come to define themselves in politicized ways, in which their sense of self is linked to belonging to a group, advocating political change, and reinterpreting the meaning of the categories to which they belong, such as "woman"? How do individuals with diverse backgrounds and experiences come to see themselves as part of a group that shares central understandings and outlooks? How do many *I*'s become a *we*?[20]

Social theory about political generations offers some tools to help answer these questions about why activists of different eras construct distinct collective identities. Karl Mannheim first conceptualized a political generation as a group that experiences shared formative social conditions and, as a result, holds a common interpretive framework that is shaped by historical circumstances.[21] More than an age group, members of a political generation are bound together by shared transformative experiences that create enduring political commitments and worldviews. Mannheim viewed political generations as characterized by a common set of beliefs or worldview. In this vein, more recent studies conceptualize political generations in terms of the attitudes and beliefs that characterize a particular age group.[22] This approach has some important problems, however. It tends to view political generations and, by extension, social movement participation, as residing in the individual rather than in interaction and collective action. Further, it assumes a static model of political generations as consisting of fixed belief structures that are held by age strata.

But social movements are a fundamentally collective phenomenon. Understanding them requires us to examine commitment, identity, and generation at the *collective* level: culture, interaction, daily life, and collective identity. I conceptualize generational politics and collective identity as located in action and interaction—observable phenomena—rather than in individual self-conceptions, attitudes, or beliefs.[23] The hallmarks of generational difference, then, are interwoven into everyday life and the ways that individuals interact with each other and structure organizations. It is interaction within small groups—what some have termed "micro-mobilization contexts"—that shapes each generation's enduring perspective on the world.[24] The concrete, lived experience of organizing a challenge together, not an abstract "spirit of the times," is what gives participants a shared worldview.

Popular views of generations as characterized by a collective spirit or zeitgeist (such as "the Sixties generation" or "Generation X") gloss over subtle variations *within* political generations. In fact, women who came to radical feminism during its peak decade are not a homogeneous group: Groups of women who entered radical feminist organizations together, every year or two, shared similar experiences inside and outside the movement. As a result, many bonded together and saw themselves as distinct cohorts within the larger movement. These groups, which I term *micro-cohorts,* differed from each other, sometimes subtly, sometimes sharply, and provided a frame of reference for each other.

At the same time, veterans of the 1960s and 1970s radical feminist movement are also bound together by profound common experiences and perspectives that reverberate in their lives today. Women who were part of the radical feminist movement during its heyday, regardless of their micro-cohort, constructed a perspective on the world, their lives, and activism that is different from the outlook of women who entered the movement during the 1980s or 1990s. The shared experience of intense immersion in a *women's movement community* during the 1960s and 1970s linked together several micro-cohorts into one political generation that shares central elements of a collective identity, and set them apart from a later political generation of feminists (also containing several micro-cohorts) that carved out a feminist existence in more hostile surroundings.[25]

Because women who became feminists at different times saw

themselves and their movement differently, divisions among micro-cohorts or between political generations often led to conflicts and changes in the women's movement. Such conflicts are a major theme of this book. In internal debates, the underlying values and assumptions of different groups come to the fore, players negotiate collective identity more overtly than usual, and changes in the definition of feminism are thus apparent. Arguably, the presence and strength of conflicts over what it means to be a feminist and over appropriate feminist behavior and goals signify the continued vitality of the movement. A movement remains alive as long as there is struggle over its collective identity, or as long as calling oneself or one's organization "feminist" means something.[26]

Nevertheless, intergenerational and inter-cohort strife has been painful for all involved, in large part because it challenges what individuals take for granted, how they understand their own experiences, and even their sense of self. Coming of political age in the early 1980s, I, too, have experienced some of these conflicts. My understanding of feminism differs both from that of the 1960s–1970s generation and from that of young women entering the movement in the 1990s. While this gives me a useful vantage point on the clashes between these groups, it also makes my own generational perspective inescapable.

Such generational perspectives are powerful. Participants in the radical women's movement at its peak share a lasting legacy from those years. The political commitments women made fifteen or twenty-five years ago have endured, albeit not without change. This tenacious commitment fosters conflicts between longtime activists and newcomers, but it also has ensured the survival of the radical feminist movement across a hostile period. Attending to collective identity as it shifts and as it endures helps us to see the myriad places where a radical feminist challenge persists.

THE SURVIVAL OF THE
RADICAL FEMINIST MOVEMENT

Although veterans of the feminist upheavals of the 1970s have remained remarkably consistent in their politics over the past twenty-five years, the women's movement as a whole has changed sharply around them. The radical feminist, or women's liberation, wing of the movement emerged in the late 1960s with consciousness-raising (CR) or "rap" groups formed primarily by women active in the civil rights and New Left movements.[27] It flourished rapidly as rap groups multiplied and gave birth to zap action, publishing, and theory groups. Most of the first consciousness-raising groups formed in major urban centers, but within a year similar groups formed in cities of all sizes across the country. By the mid-1970s, many of the first radical feminist groups had grown into organizations with more formal structures. These new radical feminist organizations often provided services to women, such as rape crisis counseling, self-defense training, shelter for battered women, or childcare, as well as confronting external targets such as sexist employment policies, legislation, and the media. Many organizations that combined service with activism pulled in substantial grants from government and foundations, and a feminist community thrived around them.

These activities represented only part of the broad women's movement. Other activists, often termed "liberal feminists,"[28] also organized to lobby state and national governments, raise funds for candidates to elective office and legislative appeals, and mount court challenges. Such campaigns were organized primarily by large national organizations, such as the National Organization for Women (NOW), the Women's Equity Action League, and the National Abortion Rights Action League (NARAL), which by the mid-1970s relied on a sophisticated fundraising apparatus, paid leadership, and a federated structure of local chapters to mobilize resources and membership.[29]

Lesbian feminists and lesbian communities have been central to the women's movement—radical and liberal—all along. Activists began to raise lesbian concerns in the early 1970s, and over time lesbian issues became progressively more integrated into the movement's agenda. At the same time, lesbians came to represent a larger proportion of the movement's membership; by the early 1980s, the vast majority of Columbus radical feminists identified themselves as lesbians. There were some tensions between lesbians and heterosexual feminists, to be sure, but the "gay–straight split" in Columbus was much less intense than the conflicts other authors have described.[30] Further, the debates between lesbians and heterosexual women were not static; they played out in changing ways for members of each micro-cohort as the context changed and the parameters of lesbian feminist collective identity shifted. My focus here is less on conflicts between lesbians and heterosexual women per se, and more on the changing implications of lesbian feminist politics and sensibilities for the women's movement. My discussion of lesbian issues is woven throughout the book, rather than falling into a separate chapter or section, because lesbians and lesbian politics are integrated throughout the women's movement. In the hostile 1980s, as I will show, lesbians played an indispensable part in sustaining the movement.

For all parts of the women's movement, the 1980s were a period of retrenchment. By 1980, many organizations had dissolved, leaving a few struggling local groups and a handful of national organizations with little grassroots participation. In contrast to the national formally structured organizations that endured into the 1990s, such as NOW, many radical feminist groups of the 1970s no longer exist. The movement as a whole faced stiff opposition from an explicitly antifeminist Presidential administration, the growing New Right movement, and a popular culture generally hostile to feminism. But as women's movement organizations dissolved or cut back in the early

1980s, the movement took new, less visible, forms. While national feminist organizations built credibility in the political arena, radical feminists remained grounded in local communities, built bridges to other social movements, and maintained informal networks, service organizations, lesbian feminist institutions, cultural events, and assorted annual demonstrations. The radical wing of the women's movement, in other words, is far from dead. On the contrary, the feminist challenge survives in a variety of venues outside the traditional political arena where the centralized national organizations operate. Feminist individuals and groups continue the struggle at the grassroots, in workplaces, within other social movements, and in the rhythms of daily life, ensuring the continuity of a radical feminist challenge.[31]

In order to understand this challenge, and thus to understand the course of the women's movement, I view political participation and social movements through a broad lens. The women and organizations in local settings such as Columbus, Ohio, were not exclusively engaged in traditionally political activities. They did mount demonstrations, pressure government and university officials, perform zap actions, and organize other direct challenges to external authority. But they also sought new, politically guided ways of relating to each other, set up organizations to meet their own needs, developed a feminist culture, and generally integrated their political principles into most aspects of their daily lives. Their collective efforts for social change occurred in the realms of culture, identity, and everyday life as well as through direct engagement with the State.[32] Tracing the persistence and transformation of these individuals and organizations leads us to a new view of social movements.

RETHINKING SOCIAL MOVEMENTS

A broader definition of the political that is based on the case of grassroots radical feminism requires us to look at social movements in a new way. The radical women's movement contains many organizations, but it is more than the sum of those organizations. It is also made up of individual activists, communities, culture, and identity. It not only promotes legislative and institutional change but also seeks to transform mainstream culture, construct alternative feminist cultures, and change individuals' consciousness.

According to the "new social movements" approach advanced by European theorists, the broad goals and structure of the radical women's movement are typical of recent social movements in which the target or site of struggle is not an external structure, but identity.[33] Social movement actors, in other words, seek to redefine what it means to be a member of a particular group. The women's movement is an excellent example of this process because it has sought not only institutional transformation (the elimination of legal, political, and economic forms of gender inequality) but also new definitions of gender categories.

Feminists' overt challenges to conventional understandings of what it means to be a women are not new, of course. When suffragists and temperance advocates, for example, demanded that women be permitted to participate in public discourse, to enter the political sphere, they too were arguing that "women's place" should be redefined.[34] The recent women's movement, however, pays more widespread and explicit attention to meaning and self-definition because of its historical context. The rise of so-called "identity politics," argue theorists like Anthony Giddens, Jürgen Habermas, and Michel Foucault, results from structural changes in the late modern world that have lessened the influence of tradition on how groups and individuals define themselves and allowed collectivities to reconstruct and redefine themselves.[35] At the same time, state control has extended into previously "private" realms such as the family, reproduction, personal relations, and sexuality.[36] As a result, new arenas of conflict and challenge for social movements have opened up around identity and daily life. Social movements are one of the major contemporary agents of cultural change, redefining and making sense of social groups and cultural categories in part through collective identity processes.[37]

Even as feminists seek to rework cultural assumptions about what it means to be a woman, they also confront the State and other powerful institutions and acquire and wield influence in the political arena. In order to understand such actions, much work on social movements in the United States in recent years has focused on formal movement organizations, which are best equipped to engage the State directly.[38] At its core, however, the women's movement is not a collection of formal organizations—these ebb and flow over the years—but a broad perspective on the world and women's place in it. Individuals internalize this perspective, and individuals, communities, and social movement organizations put it into action.[39] Organizational dynamics and confrontations with the State also are critical to understanding the women's movement, of course. But if we focus too closely on a definition of social movements or political action based on formal organizations and direct engagement with the State, we miss much of radical feminism (and much of other social movements as well).

In order to tap the full range of women's movement activity and to recognize its continuity over time, I propose to define the women's movement in terms of the collective identity associated with it rather than in terms of its formal organizations. We see the movement, then, not just through the organizations it establishes, but also through its informal networks and communities and in the diaspora of feminist individuals who carry the concerns of the movement into other settings. What makes these organizations, networks, and individuals part of a social movement is their shared allegiance to a set of beliefs, practices, and ways of identifying oneself that constitute feminist collective identity. The concept of collective identity is central to understanding challenges, such as the women's movement, that do not limit themselves to institutional transformation. It allows us to detect the movement's continuity even as feminist organizations dissolve and re-form. The movement's continued vitality in a hostile climate is demonstrated by the actions and identities of individuals as much as by the existence of organizations. A focus on collective identity underscores the constantly changing nature of all social movements and recognizes that struggle occurs, not just in confrontations with the State, but in culture and daily life as well.

The women's movement has gone through cycles of rising and falling mobilization as its external context and internal dynamics have shifted.[40] In order to understand the endurance and transformation of feminism over time, I pay close attention to how feminist collective identity changes with generational turnover and to the implications of these shifts for the movement's tactical and organizational development and survival. In the end, the women's movement has survived the ups and downs because it encompasses multiple generations. Earlier members rarely drop out; in fact, core members usually remain active for their lifetimes.[41] But new participants continue to enter, keeping the movement vibrant and changing.[42]

When, in the cycle of protest, activists are politicized, they construct collective identities that are specific to their unique experiences and historical context; thus, they crystallize into a political generation. Political generations shape cycles of protest by their relative size; the large cohort of college-age people in the 1960s and 1970s helped prompt the wave of protest during that period, for example. In addition, the quality of intergenerational relations between movement founders and subsequent participants helps determine whether a wave of protest ends shortly after its crest or whether it sustains itself in multiple forms for a longer period, as the contemporary women's movement has done.

The "postfeminist" myth proclaims both the death of the feminist challenge and its rejection by a younger generation of women. In contrast, I suggest that the women's movement has both survived and changed because of the lasting commitments of longtime feminists and the continual infusion of new participants who simultaneously challenge and carry on the feminist legacy.

The aim of the women's movement has always been the transformation of both individuals and the social world. The movement's course has been shaped by the generation of women who came of political age at the movement's height in the late 1960s or 1970s and remain committed to social change. Their story and the story of the radical women's movement over the past twenty-five years are the story of the survival of political commitment in the face of opposition and of the persistence of a movement for women's liberation in multiple forms and locations over a quarter-century of ups and downs. They give us, I hope, both a clear picture of the difficulties of sustaining a political challenge over the long haul and the faith that it is possible to do so.

I :: RADICAL FEMINISM IN

COLUMBUS, OHIO

ORGANIZING AROUND women's issues in Columbus, Ohio, in the early days of the movement was much like the organizing that went on in many similar cities. Originating with New Left women who formed consciousness-raising groups, radical feminist organizations by the mid-1970s were developing feminist theory, providing services to women, and staging cultural events and frequent public protests. Housed in a shared space, women's movement organizations collaborated on projects, and participants lived within an extensive movement community.[1] In the late 1970s, although participation was decreasing, many organizations survived. But by the early 1980s, funds dried up and the groups that hung on had more limited resources. The women's movement community remained, however, and sustained a "submerged network" of feminist activities and institutions that periodically erupted into public protest.[2]

All along, visible, public confrontations with authorities have been grounded in the less dramatic daily rhythms of a community that fosters a feminist culture and collective identity as well as protest. That community is an informally organized network of individuals and groups that share feminist goals and a collective identity, and are held together by overlapping organizational memberships, movement institutions, and events.[3] In other words, cultural events have been integral to feminist organizing all along and are not a recent distraction from more important "political" work. The unfolding of the radical feminist movement shows that social movements are marked as much by collective identity and cultural strategies as by what we more often think of as political action.

ORIGINS

The women's movement in Columbus emerged from an ad hoc state commission on the status of women and the New Left, as happened in other states,[4] but it did so two to three years later than in larger cities. Periodization based on the national movement and on major cities does not, then, accurately describe the course of the movement at the grassroots level in smaller cities. Some of this difference between center and periphery is due to distance—the beginnings of feminist ferment in major cities did not immediately filter into smaller cities. But part of the difference is also due to the setting in which the movement emerged.

Columbus is the capital of Ohio and home of The Ohio State University (OSU), the largest land-grant university in the world, with sixty thousand students. A medium-sized city, Columbus has little industry and is dominated instead by service, government, and educational jobs. Its state government was controlled by conservative Republican governors throughout the 1960s and 1970s, with the exception of the one term served by John Gilligan (1971–1974), a Democrat. Governor James Rhodes, who served from 1963 to 1970 and from 1975 to 1982, was infamous for ordering the Ohio National Guard to the Kent State University campus, resulting in the shooting deaths of four students during a demonstration against the Vietnam War. Columbus was similarly governed by conservative Republicans for most of the 1960s and 1970s. As a result, most policy goals were out of reach for feminist activists. Activists sought in 1969 to establish an Ohio Commission on the Status of Women like those that existed around the country, but Governor Rhodes refused to authorize its creation, making Ohio the only state without an official commission. Instead, feminists formed an unofficial Ohio Commission on the Status of Women, which one member described as "self-anointed and self-appointed." The commission proceeded to research women's status in the state without governmental affiliation or resources. These feminists, who thought of themselves as "moderate" and whom more militant activists labeled "liberals," worked steadily on legislative and policy implementation issues, especially the ERA. But as a result of consistent opposition from elected officials, the most vital feminist organizing occurred outside the realm of the State, both in autonomous feminist organizations and in The Ohio State University, and took a more radical slant.

Women's Liberation emerged in Columbus in the context of student movements at OSU. As a result, the radical women's movement in Columbus was tied to the New Left and civil rights movement early on, as in many other locations. Activists initially focused on campus-based concerns, and only later did a radical women's movement establish itself off-campus. In the spring of 1970 a group of women who were associated with OSU, many of whom had been part of the civil rights, student, antiwar, and New Left movements, began holding consciousness-raising meetings and formed Columbus–OSU Women's Liberation (WL). An initial meeting drew several hundred women.[5] Shortly after that, campuses around the country erupted when the Ohio National Guard killed the four Kent State students. Columbus–OSU Women's Liberation was asked to join a coalition of striking groups at Ohio State. One member reported that leaders asked those present at the first organizational meeting to decide both whether they wanted to be part of Women's Liberation and whether the nascent organization should participate in the strike. Women's Liberation did participate, supported demands for "an end to discrimination against blacks, more student representation in the decision-making processes of the university, and an end to the university's involvement (through ROTC, government contracts, etc.) in the Viet Nam war," and contributed several demands of its own.[6]

These demands focused on issues affecting women on campus, and many seem modest by later feminist standards. They included the establishment of a free/low-cost childcare center that would be open to the children of both university-affiliated and unaffiliated parents; an on-campus Planned Parenthood Clinic; nondiscriminatory admissions and treatment of women in programs; nondiscrimination in university employment; an end to dual codes of conduct or dorm rules for women and men students; equal representation on all OSU committees; an end to stereotypes of women in university publications; and the establishment of an office of women's affairs with a woman director to begin a women's studies program and deal with grievances.[7] Women's Liberation expanded its demands the following year to include legalized abortion and abolition of the Student Health Center's policy of refusing to prescribe contraceptives for unmarried women.[8]

OSU students demonstrated, occupied buildings, and issued demands during the strike. Police and National Guard troops were called in, and persistent violence between police and demonstrators closed the university for several days. The women I interviewed who were active during this period recalled violent demonstrations in which police sprayed tear gas and sometimes blocked the only routes of escape. One woman described watching National Guard tanks roll down the street in front of her off-campus house, enforcing a dusk-to-dawn curfew. A new mother, she had to consult her physician about whether the tear-gas fumes hanging in the air would harm her newborn daughter. Other Women's Liberation members were part of negotiating teams that met with university officials. Although such negotiations yielded few immediate gains, they led to ongoing participation by students, including women's liberationists, in some university committees.

Participating in the strike consolidated Columbus–OSU Women's Liberation as an organization. Membership increased, the group developed an explicit statement of its goals, and the shared drama of the strike increased participants' sense of commitment to each other and to Women's Liberation. Some participants reported that Women's Liberation meetings in 1970 drew hundreds of women, many of whom were highly visible and active in the strike. Membership was informal, and most members were students, although "community women" also participated. Building on the New Left community that already existed, feminists formed their own alternative community with intense friendship networks and regular social events, a Women's Media Co-operative that trained women to make films, musical groups (the Women's Band and Lotta Crabtree), and a burgeoning number of feminist artists.

Activists promoted their goals through street theater, demonstrations, and negotiations with university officials. Daycare, equal educational facilities, and the provision of birth control services at the student health clinic were among the most visible issues. For example, in 1971 WL sponsored a "Child-In" in which participants brought hundreds[9] of children to campus and used the university grounds as a playground.[10] That same year, members protested against unequal athletic facilities by sitting in at the men's sauna. As the university administration began to address a number of the strike demands in the spring of 1970 and the following year, members of WL served on university committees to negotiate new policies. One such committee considered the establishment of a childcare center, and within two years agitation had led to the creation of an OSU Childcare Pilot Program.[11]

OSU Women's Liberation retained strong ties to New Left organizations. It co-sponsored demonstrations and actions with Students for a Democratic Society (SDS), attempted to build a coalition with a welfare rights organization, and met with North Vietnamese women as part of continuing opposition to the Vietnam War.[12] SDS, in turn, supported and publicized demonstrations like the Child-In. Although the gap between feminist and New Left organizations would grow, in the early years the groups frequently overlapped.[13]

The organization was also firmly linked to the university setting both because its demands centered on university policies and because it registered as a student organization, received university funding, and had an office on campus. An organizational base for women's activism already existed on campus in the form of the Women's Self-Government Association (WSGA). The WSGA was an official university organization to which all women students automatically belonged, and had the primary function of setting "women's rules," the codes of student conduct that differed for women and men. WL was not affiliated with the WSGA and in fact opposed women's rules as a form of discrimination against women students. Yet the WSGA was influenced by growing women's liberation activity and began discussing issues such as women's employment and women's changing roles. Because the WSGA had a sizable operational and programing budget, its interest in women's liberation was a boon to the movement. Yet as the WSGA began to allocate more programing resources to events dealing with employment opportunities or changing roles, it dropped some of its traditional fund-raisers, such as the "Golddiggers' Prom," and earned less from others, such as the annual Bridal Fair, which came under fire from women's liberationists. As a result, although appropriations from the university increased steadily between

1965 and 1971, the WSGA's total income from all sources dropped.[14] Ultimately, feminism was the WSGA's undoing: It declared in 1970 that women's rules were discriminatory and that its own judicial and legislative functions should therefore be abolished, thus eliminating the reason for its existence.[15] The WSGA in fact survived for two more years after the university dropped women's rules by focusing on programing. But by 1972 its budget appropriation from OSU had been cut in half.[16] The WSGA was replaced by the Association of Women Students, which remains active today but receives far less institutional funding than the WSGA.

WOMEN'S STUDIES

The effort to establish a women's studies program was a major focus of feminist activism on campus throughout the early 1970s. The campaign drew activists from a wide range of groups within the university, including faculty, staff, and students, and transcended divisions between "liberal" and "radical" feminism. The Women's Studies Ad Hoc Committee, the Women's Studies Caucus, and the Women's Caucus of the OSU Community, the main organizations behind the campaign, had largely overlapping memberships: One active participant indicated that the same women gave themselves a number of different organizational names in an effort to make their ranks appear larger. These groups drew up plans for a women's studies program and negotiated with university administration for its establishment. The groups were diverse, and they developed an effective negotiation strategy that played on radical feminists' ability to make moderates seem less threatening to university officials. One negotiator described this strategy as "good cop, bad cop."

> In the negotiating sessions we had it divided up by role. A couple of others were like good cops, and [one person] was the

young radical. . . . And they would move in and be concilia-
tory, more middle-of-the-road feminist. So that I and a couple of
others were seen by the university administration as just beyond
the pale, and then they could come in with something that was a
counterproposal. And it worked.

I do not mean to suggest that there were no differences between
women whom administrators perceived as "middle-of-the-road"
and those who were seen as "beyond the pale." Many students
had more affinity for disruptive tactics than did faculty members; there were at times genuine disagreements about both
goals and strategy; and the two groups of women often criticized and mistrusted each other. Yet the use of this negotiating
strategy illustrates that, at least on some issues, women who
were classified as liberal and radical feminists were not so far
apart. Women on both ends of the feminist spectrum made it
clear in interviews that their goals regarding women's studies
were the same and that they coordinated efforts with each other;
they deliberately appeared polarized for pragmatic reasons.

In addition to negotiations, advocates of women's studies
used other innovative tactics to call attention to their cause. For
example, the Women's Studies Caucus hired an airplane to fly
over the football stadium during the Homecoming game, tow-
ing a sign that read, "OSU—What about women?" When the
university president traveled to Japan, Caucus members located
a member of a Tokyo feminist organization by telephoning Japan and speaking their only Japanese phrase: "Hello, I am looking for the women's movement." At the group's request, the
Japanese woman picketed in front of a building where the president was lunching. The combination of negotiation and attention-getting tactics led to the creation of an Office of Women's
Studies in 1975, with funding that one member of the Women's
Studies Ad Hoc Committee described as "more than we ever
expected."

COMMUNITY RADICAL FEMINISM

In addition to university-affiliated groups, activists established many feminist organizations off-campus in 1972 and 1973. It is difficult to draw sharp distinctions between university and "community" organizing: Many off-campus groups relied on student members, university-affiliated organizations were open to nonstudents, and some off-campus groups formed university chapters in order to get funding as student organizations. Most of the groups were part of the Women's Action Collective (WAC), an umbrella organization that encompassed a variety of semiautonomous groups focusing on specific issues. In 1971 NOW established a Columbus chapter, which drew slightly older members. As in the campus-based organizations, most members were white, students or college-educated, and between the ages of 20 and 30.

WAC grew out of consciousness-raising groups organized by Columbus–OSU Women's Liberation. One such group, dubbed "Rap Group Number One," contained a core group of women who founded WAC and many of its original member organizations. In the fall of 1971, WAC organizers called a planning meeting at which participants listed their interests and skills. Interest groups grew around rape prevention, children's literature, auto mechanics, and other topics, and women began discussing and designing social change projects in their areas of interest and expertise. The founders of WAC wanted to do creative feminist organizing independent of the restrictions of the university, were interested in providing feminist services to women and establishing feminist businesses, and saw these tasks as steps toward social transformation.

Columbus–OSU Women's Liberation described its ideological outlook as "women's liberationist"; WAC called itself "radical feminist." It meant by this, as a member wrote in a paper about the organization, that it saw sexism as a primary form of oppression, sought social revolution rather than reform, and wished to provide separate spaces for women to gather and organize away from men.[17] WAC was also distinguished by a commitment to collective structure, making decisions by consensus and avoiding hierarchy within the organization.

By the fall of 1972, the collective was on its way to institutionalization as it formalized its structure, acquired resources, and expanded groups' ongoing activities. At this point its central groups included the Women's Community Development Fund, Women Against Rape, and the Women's Co-op Garage. The collective received its first grant of $1,000 and established a central treasurer who kept track of finances for all member groups.[18] Women Against Rape began analyzing rape and planning for a rape crisis hotline to begin in a member's home, while the Women's Co-op Garage acquired some tools and planned classes in auto mechanics. By 1973, the Women's Literature and Publishing Group, Prison Solidarity, Legal Action, Women's Support Group, the Women's Health Action Collective (later renamed the Women's Health Collective), the Share-A-Job Group, the Women's Center group, and the Women's Creative Arts Co-op were part of the WAC umbrella.[19]

The umbrella structure was typical of radical and socialist feminist organizations in many other cities, including the Chicago Women's Liberation Union, Twin Cities Women's Union and Twin Cities Female Liberation Group in Minneapolis/St. Paul, Iowa City's Women's Liberation Front, the Madison Women's Center, and Ann Arbor's Feminist House.[20] The umbrella structure allowed the same individuals to work on multiple projects in different member groups and linked projects with an external focus, such as protests against sexist advertising, with those that had a service focus, such as a rape crisis center, and those that had a cultural focus, such as producing feminist concerts.

ACQUIRING RESOURCES AND A HOME

The women's movement in Columbus grew rapidly in the mid-1970s, acquiring substantial resources and large numbers of new members. New organizations, both independent and part of WAC, proliferated, and existing organizations expanded as membership grew and resources poured in from outside. Similar growth occurred in cities around the country.[21] In the national political arena, the fight to ratify the ERA drew together feminists of different stripes.[22] In Ohio, however, the policy arena remained hostile. The Ohio legislature ratified the ERA in 1974 at the end of a one-term Democratic governorship, but during the remainder of the 1970s gains were few. Outside the policy arena, feminist service and cultural organizations flourished. New organizations founded in Columbus between 1974 and 1978 included Central Ohio Lesbians, a concert production company called the Women's Music Union, and four groups affiliated with WAC: the Single Mothers' Support Group, Women's Broadcasting Group, *Womansong* newspaper, and Fan the Flames Feminist Bookstore.

More striking than the emergence of new organizations was the expansion of existing ones. WAC became a nonprofit corporation in July 1974, established a formal structure with officers and trustees from each member organization, and adopted a statement of philosophy.[23] It continued to operate by a formal system of consensus, regularly rotating coordinators and meeting facilitators. Member organizations received tax-exempt status under the collective's "umbrella" incorporation and contributed a percentage of their income to the Women's Community Development Fund, which provided seed money for starting new organizations. Women Against Rape established a 24-hour hotline in a member's house in the fall of 1973, moved into an office in a local church in the winter of 1974, and in its first session trained around sixty volunteers to operate the crisis line.

The Women's Co-op Garage expanded by renting a garage and purchasing a wider selection of tools; in 1973 it had sixty members.[24] *Womansong* published feminist news, book reviews, theoretical articles, and poetry fairly regularly beginning in 1974. The Single Mothers' Support Group organized childcare exchanges and instituted the first shelters for battered women in Columbus, in members' homes. Lesbian Peer Support, which had formed in 1972 as Gay Women's Peer Counseling, affiliated with WAC in 1976 and continued conducting workshops and "coming out groups" for lesbians and women who were in the process of coming out. For an overview of these activities, see Table 1.

An influx of resources permitted much of this expansion. In 1976, WAC received a grant from the National Institutes of Mental Health for research on community rape prevention, a project entitled "Community Action Strategies to Stop Rape" (CASSR, pronounced "cass-er"). Members of Women Against Rape put together the grant application somewhat haphazardly and at the last minute. Building on discussion and study of the origins of rape in sexism, they designed a program to train women in self-defense and confrontation and stayed up all night before the proposal was due writing a grant they never dreamed the federal government would fund. The grant amounted to $425,000 over four years and included funding for indirect costs that went to WAC as the sponsoring organization. These resources enabled WAC to hire staff and rent a house that served as a geographic center for the feminist community and gave member organizations meeting space, access to office facilities, and a measure of legitimacy. For example, Fan the Flames Feminist Bookstore found a permanent home in the WAC house and greatly expanded its stock and business. At the same time, the expense of maintaining the WAC house required the group to spend more effort on fund-raising than it had in the early years.

TABLE 1: COLUMBUS, OHIO, RADICAL FEMINIST ORGANIZATIONS, 1970–1980: STRATEGIES AND TACTICS

Organization	Actions
Columbus–OSU Women's Liberation	Participated in OSU student strike, 1970. Consciousness-raising groups. Demonstrations and guerrilla theater. Meetings with university officials and serving on OSU committees.
Columbus Women's Media Co-operative	Put on workshops for women on how to use video, film, and photography equipment.
Women's Action Collective	Most activities were by member groups. WAC as a whole published a newsletter (1976–1982), held benefits (film festivals, dances, concerts), and conducted consciousness-raising groups and orientation sessions.
Women's Community Development Fund (WAC)	Provided seed money for start-up of new groups in WAC.
Women Against Rape, including Community Action Strategies to Stop Rape (WAC)	24-hour rape crisis line. Self-defense classes. Public speaking and education. Demonstrations. Boycott of sexist advertisers. "Whistle Alert" program distributed whistles for women to blow when attacked. "Courtwatch" observed and documented rape trials.
Lesbian Peer Support (WAC)	Peer counseling, support groups, and workshops for lesbians and women in the process of coming out. Speaking engagements. Published the *Purple Cow,* which included poetry, fiction, and announcements.
Womansong (WAC)	Feminist newspaper, published irregularly, ranging from eight to three times a year.
Women's Broadcasting Group (WAC)	Put on one-hour feminist radio program once a week, on public access radio station.

TABLE I—*Continued*

Organization	Actions
Women's Publishing Group (WAC)	Gathered titles and information on feminist books and publications.
Women's Co-op Garage (WAC)	Classes in auto mechanics. Garage space and tools available for members' use. Hired mechanic and trained members available for assistance.
Legal Action Group (WAC)	Gathered information about women and the law.
Women's Health Action Collective (WAC)	Gathered information and did education about women's health issues.
Single Mothers' Support Group (WAC)	Exchange of childcare, toys, and clothing. Support groups. Provided a 24-hour crisis line and shelter for battered women in members' homes. Wrote initial proposal for a battered women's shelter (1976).
Fan the Flames Feminist Book Collective (WAC)	Bookstore. Began sales at feminist events in 1974, and opened a store in the WAC house in 1976.
Central Ohio Lesbians	Sponsored Labor Day rallies for gay and lesbian rights in 1976 and 1977. Polled local politicians and judicial candidates on gay and lesbian issues, and publicized that information. Speaking engagements in OSU classes and local high schools. Campus education, including "Gay Blue Jeans Day." Published *Columbus Women's Calendar* (1977).
Women's Music Union	Produced concerts by local and national feminist artists.
Feminists in Self–Defense Training	Workouts for women martial artists with some experience. Later gave classes in martial arts and self-defense.

LESBIAN FEMINISM AND
THE "WOMEN'S COMMUNITY"

The mid-1970s were a period of extensive lesbian feminist organizing. Many of the members of WAC were lesbians, and member group Lesbian Peer Support was a visible presence. Outside WAC, lesbians organized at Ohio State University and in the community at large. Central Ohio Lesbians was the major lesbian organization that formed in this period. Established at the university in 1974 by a group of women who were dissatisfied with the direction of existing organizations, it took over the resources and office space that formerly belonged to WL by voting in their own officers as officers of WL, changing its name while continuing to receive university funding. Central Ohio Lesbians worked in close coalition with the other feminist student organization, the Association of Women Students.[25] Its actions included two successful lesbian and gay pride marches, the publication of a monthly Women's Calendar, and public speaking about lesbian issues. Although Central Ohio Lesbians was defunct by 1977, it helped lay the groundwork for the Stonewall Union, the gay and lesbian organization that emerged in the late 1970s.

Central Ohio Lesbians, Lesbian Peer Support, and the lesbian presence in other radical feminist groups also shaped the course of the broader women's movement. As distinctly lesbian organizations flourished and a growing proportion of the radical feminist membership in general were lesbians, what participants called "women's culture" took on a strongly lesbian tint. As early as 1970, feminist musicians, artists, and filmmakers were working in Columbus. Some of these musicians formed the Women's Music Union in 1976 in order to provide themselves with outlets for performing. The group quickly expanded from producing members' concerts to producing events with nationally known feminist performers. Lesbians were integral to the

Music Union, and concerts provided a place where lesbian sensibilities and sexuality were openly expressed and celebrated.

A women's movement community had existed all along, with cultural events and interpersonal networks alongside more overtly political activities. But it became institutionalized in Columbus during the mid-1970s.[26] The WAC house served as a central gathering place for the women's movement community. It was possible for women in Columbus between the mid-1970s and the early 1980s to spend virtually all their free time (and for many, their work time as well) in activities sponsored by feminist organizations. Every day of the week saw planning meetings for projects or demonstrations, impromptu "zap actions" (such as picketing a university record store that featured albums whose covers promoted violence against women), discussion groups, art exhibits, and concerts by feminist musicians. Although WAC was not uniformly lesbian, the majority of active members were lesbians, and the WAC house provided an environment where lesbianism was often taken for granted.

OSU also institutionalized extensive women's programming in the mid-1970s. Previously, Columbus–OSU Women's Liberation, the Women's Self-Government Association, and the Association of Women Students received funding from the university for women's programming. But events were sporadic and planned by activist groups rather than by the university itself. In 1975, the university responded to several years of agitation and funded a Center for Women's Studies, which served as a central gathering place for feminists on campus and, in its early years, took an active role in feminist programing as well as academic offerings. In the following year, the university established Women's Services, charged with "generat[ing] programs and services to meet the developmental needs of women students on campus."[27] The establishment of Women's Services took place amidst much controversy because it was linked to the campus Counseling and Consultation Services, and activists opposed the implication that women needed psychological help.[28] Its funding also was precarious, especially for the first years.[29] Nevertheless, the greater centralization and the continuity of paid staff in the office gave feminist programing a permanent and more visible place in the university. Women's Services, the Office of Women's Studies (later Center), and community feminist groups like WAC and the Women's Music Union often cosponsored events. The women's movement community did not, in other words, divide neatly into on- and off-campus segments. Instead, the institutionalization of feminist culture and services on campus complemented and strengthened the development of an alternative feminist culture off campus.

The institutionalization of the women's community occurred a couple of years later in Columbus than in some other cities. But Columbus and other midwestern college towns shared a central trait during the mid-1970s: the simultaneous flourishing of cultural events like feminist concerts and art exhibitions, services for women like auto mechanic classes and rape crisis counseling, and political action groups that protested publicly or confronted authorities with demands for change. In Minneapolis/St. Paul, for example, the Twin Cities Female Liberation Group engendered scores of other organizations, including, by 1972, a women's bookstore, counseling service, lesbian resource center, rape crisis center, food co-op, artists' group, several newsletters, and several direct-action political groups.[30] In Iowa City, the Women's Liberation Front was housed in a women's center at the university in 1971 and produced the widely circulated newsletter of midwestern feminism *Ain't I A Woman?*[31] Ann Arbor's Feminist House (established in 1972) encompassed the Women's Crisis Center, the Community School, which taught auto mechanics, women's history, self-defense, and other subjects, the Gay Awareness Women's Collective, which organized rap groups, and a self-help gynecological clinic. As in Columbus, these groups joined preexisting student and lesbian organizations associated with the state university.[32]

LIBERAL AND RADICAL

WAC's self-identification as a radical feminist organization, in addition to signaling its beliefs and strategies, set it apart from what members termed, somewhat disparagingly, "liberal feminism." In the view of many self-identified radical feminists, liberal feminists were overly willing to compromise or sell out, identified excessively with male standards of success and power, and sought reform rather than social transformation. Liberal feminists in turn saw radicals as incautious and likely to alienate potential supporters with their confrontational tactics. Although there were undeniable differences between the groups labeled liberal and radical, they were as much differences of style and strategy as of goals.[33] As in the battle for women's studies, liberal and radical feminist organizations often worked together on common goals. Nevertheless, activists in both camps distinguished themselves from each other and used the terms "liberal" and "radical" to describe their differences.

The feminist organizations that many WAC members saw as "liberal" operated within the state and local political arenas during the mid-1970s. These groups included the Coalition for the Implementation of the ERA, the Women's Research and Policy Development Center, NOW, and others. In other parts of the country, feminist organizations addressing the political process grew out of state and national commissions on the status of women. Although the Ohio Commission on the Status of Women was not state-sanctioned, it nevertheless laid the groundwork for later women's policy work. Forming organizations such as the Coalition for the Ratification of the ERA, these women lobbied the governor and state legislature and achieved the ratification of the ERA by the early 1970s. NOW formed a Columbus chapter in 1971 and joined the drive for state and federal ratification of the ERA as well as supporting campaigns of the radical women's movement. The Columbus chapter of NOW contained both militant and moderate elements all along, and experienced internal conflicts and factionalization over both goals and tactics throughout the 1970s and early 1980s. As a result, members of WAC saw NOW as overly conservative while other players in the policy arena saw NOW as too radical. Later in the 1970s, the moderate elements of NOW cooperated with the Women's Research and Policy Development Center, Ohio Women, Inc., and other organizations to pursue the formation of a women's center, the establishment of a program for displaced homemakers, and the implementation of the state ERA.

Despite their differences, radical and liberal feminist organizations formed coalitions at some points. In addition to Women's Studies, International Women's Year in 1977 brought together a coalition of radical and liberal feminists. Each state held a planning conference in 1977 in order to endorse a platform of women's concerns and elect delegates to an international conference sponsored by the United Nations and held in Houston. In most states, including Ohio, fundamentalist churches and antifeminist groups organized busloads of women to attend state conferences in order to elect antifeminist delegates and oppose inclusion of abortion rights, lesbian rights, and other feminist demands in the platform.

Although the planning committee for International Women's Year was dominated by moderate feminists who opposed the inclusion of lesbian delegates or issues, the threat from the Right forced a coalition between lesbian and liberal feminists. Radical feminists agreed to turn out in large numbers and vote for a slate of delegates that included radical and liberal feminists as well as open lesbians. Yet radical feminists I interviewed reported that when the slate of delegates was published, many of "their" delegates were not listed, and there was no mention of lesbianism. WAC members and other radical feminists refused to vote for the slate unless it was changed. In the end, a few feminist delegates, both radical and liberal, were elected from Ohio, but most of the state's delegates were conservatives.

The events surrounding International Women's Year left radical feminists feeling that they had been betrayed by the planning committee's last-minute exclusion of lesbians. Liberal feminists, on the other hand, felt that radicals' focus on the issue of lesbianism was divisive and allowed the Right to triumph. If radical feminists had supported more mainstream feminist issues, liberals believed, the Right would not have elected so many of its own delegates.

Setting off another conflict, the Women's Research and Policy Development Center proposed the formation of a centralized women's center to coordinate services for women citywide. When WAC and other radical feminist groups opposed such centralization, believing that more moderate politics would prevail and collective structure would be abandoned, the Women's Research and Policy Development Center commissioned a "needs assessment survey" that supported its own position. WAC remained opposed, however, and WAC members did not become involved in the efforts to establish the center. One woman who was instrumental in the effort believed that radical feminist opposition helped to undermine support for the center and contributed to its failure. Despite these conflicts, however, at no point were the divisions between liberal and radical feminist groups set in stone. Feminist organizations of varying ideological slants cooperated on specific issues far more extensively than a simplistic "two-wing" model of the women's movement implies.

ACTIVISM IN DECLINE

During the late 1970s and early 1980s, feminist mobilization in Columbus peaked and declined. While the radical women's movement was active, well-funded, and had many participants through 1978, organizations started disbanding in 1977. By 1980 membership had dropped drastically, funding was vanishing, and many organizations were defunct. A number of the core groups in WAC dissolved in the late 1970s, including the Women's Co-op Garage, the Single Mothers' Support Group, the Women's Health Collective, and *Womansong*. WAC as a whole and its member organizations had trouble keeping members active. Members were continually urged to take on more "collective responsibility,"[34] but with little success. Members voiced their concern about decreasing involvement in WAC activities in a 1979 newsletter.

> Is this apparent "malaise" at WAC just *our* problem, or symptomatic of a general "slow down" in activity in the women's movement at large? Are there actions we can take to turn things around or is it time to think about closing our doors? The question now is not, "How to raise more money," but "WHAT ARE WE FUNDRAISING FOR?"[35]

WAC went from plentiful funding in the late 1970s to shortages and financial insecurity by 1980 as the economic climate worsened. By early 1979 WAC was in its first major financial crisis, needing to raise $7,000 in six months in order to keep its house. In 1980 the rape prevention grant from the National Institute of Mental Health ran out. Since the grant essentially supported the WAC house and most of the activities of Women Against Rape, the latter cut back on many services and programs. In an attempt to make up for the lost income, WAC's house manager was forced to focus on fundraising, and her job was renamed "development coordinator."

Several short-lived study and support groups formed between 1978 and 1981; none lasted a full year. They included groups focusing on women and economics, international women, lesbianism, religion, radical feminism, the book *Fat Is a Feminist Issue,* heterosexual feminists, feminists in the workplace, pornography, lesbians who want children, substance abuse, and Jewish lesbians (see Table 2). These groups differed from earlier ones in that they were dedicated to discussion, reading, and

TABLE 2: SHORT-LIVED MEMBER ORGANIZATIONS OF THE WOMENS ACTION COLLECTIVE, 1978–1981

Organization	Dates	Major Activities
Women and Economics study group	November 1976	Study/discussion group
Herizon	October 1978	Women's coffeehouse
International women group	1978	Discussion and support group
Lesbianism study group	April 1978	Study/discussion group
Committee Against Sexist Advertising (CASA)	May 1978	Boycotts and pickets of record stores that sold albums with sexist covers; boycots and pickets of other sexist advertisers
Religion study group	May 1978	Study/discussion group
Radical feminism study group	December 1978	Study/discussion group
Women's Restaurant Collective	March 1979	Planned to open a women's restaurant; organized and served dinners before women's music events.
"Fat Is a Feminist Issue"	January 1980	Study/discussion group
Heterosexual feminists group	January 1980	Discussion and support group
Lesbian support group	February 1980	Support group

Continued on next page

TABLE 2—*Continued*

Organization	Dates	Major Activities
Feminists in the Workplace	March 1980	Study/discussion group
Pornography Task Force	March 1980	Study/discussion group; planned for action against pornography
Women's Education and Beautification Society (WEBS)	September 1980	Zap action group
Lesbians Who Want Children	1981	Discussion and support group
Slightly Older Lesbians	1981	Discussion and support group
Lesbian Association on Substance Abuse	April 1981	Discussion and support group
Jewish Lesbians	May 1981	Discussion and support group

support rather than protest and agitation and were more narrowly focused than earlier groups had been. A few longer-lasting organizations also formed between 1979 and 1981 and survived in various incarnations into the 1990s, including Feminists in Self-Defense Training (FIST), the Child Assault Prevention Project (CAP, which began as a task force of Women Against Rape and later became an independent organization), and Women's Outreach to Women (WOW), a 12-step program for recovery from substance abuse.

Although new organizations formed, those that disbanded in the late 1970s had been the mainstays of WAC. The Women's Co-op Garage was one of the first and largest organizations in the umbrella. The Single Mothers' Support Group and *Womansong* had been visible in the larger community, and their members and activities were interwoven with other groups; their analyses of feminist issues were influential, although both groups were somewhat disorganized and often criticized by WAC members. Lesbian Peer Support, which had existed in various incarnations since the early 1970s, had a spurt of activity as new members joined in early 1980, but this new core group "burned out and disbanded" in 1981.[36] Although the organization formed one more time with new members, it was defunct by 1983.

National feminist organizations like NOW continued to operate in the political arena, fighting for the ERA until its defeat in 1982 and engaging in other, lower-key campaigns after that.[37] In the local women's movement community of Columbus, cultural institutions and service-providing groups carried on even as other forms of organizing declined.[38] WAC, the Women's Music Union, and other organizations continued to sponsor cultural and social events, including dances, concerts, film festivals, and an annual event dubbed "Famous Feminist Day." By 1981 cultural events were arguably the most vital segment of the radical women's movement. Such events were not apolitical, however, nor were they new to the women's movement. The change in the face of the movement was a result of a decline in activism oriented toward external targets rather than an increase in cultural events.

The cultural and service-oriented groups that predominated in the late 1970s continued to define their purpose in political terms. WAC's by-laws, revised in 1977, made members' view of the connections between culture and social change clear.

> We will experiment with structures and organization that will allow us to develop our feminist consciousness, extend the independent women's movement, and create an alternative women's culture. Our goals as a collective are: to build a cooperative community of women with free space where we can learn to depend upon one another, work together, and live an alternative free of sexism; to create services for women that are responsive to

women's expressed needs; to create alternative jobs and new ways for us to support ourselves; to experiment in applying concepts of organization that we as feminists are interested in, such as small group organizing, sharing skills, work sharing, money sharing, and cooperative decision making and sharing of information and skills; to encourage innovation in any form that will move us closer to non-sexist relationships and institutions.[39]

For example, organizers defined the goals of self-defense classes broadly to include not only defense against attacks, but women's control over their own lives.

As feminists, we take an expansive view of self-defense, not limited only to physically dangerous situations, but as a means for women to regain control of our lives. We combine political discussion, mental and physical practice, to prepare women to handle any situation in which her autonomy, privacy, and space is violated.[40]

The goals of surviving radical feminist organizations were not limited to the provision of services, as this 1981 statement by a Women Against Rape coordinator about orientation of new members indicates.

My vision for [rape] prevention is one where, optimally, women get oriented to a feminist analysis of rape and how our socialization fits society's function for us. Then the women further question that socialization process, internalize the concepts and begin to live a feminist lifestyle. . . . As part of the radical branch of the movement, part of our responsibility as sisters is to provide resources, support, and concrete methods for sisters to become integrated in their area of interest. . . . It is through orientation that women will come to understand that WAR is not a small service providing agency, but rather an arm of a movement![41]

As antifeminism intensified in the early 1980s, feminist organizations from a variety of perspectives, including WAC, NOW, and the Women's Music Union, formed coalitions with each other. But although they were necessary as a defensive

measure, such coalitions brought conflict. For example, controversy erupted in 1979 between WAC, which opposed pornography, and the National Women's Political Caucus over the latter's acceptance of a donation from the Playboy Foundation.[42]
Other internal conflicts arose as women of color confronted racism within white-dominated feminist organizations and as organizations began to address new issues such as spirituality and
recovery which some veteran members saw as a diversion from
more important struggles. These conflicts are discussed in greater
depth in Chapter 2.

Coalitions were not enough. Women's movement organizations lost both tangible and intangible resources in the late
1970s. WAC moved to a smaller space in 1983, and was dismantled in 1984.[43] Only two of its member organizations,
Women Against Rape and Fan the Flames Feminist Bookstore,
survived (both WAR and Fan the Flames continue to operate
successfully in 1995). Outside WAC, the Women's Music Union
and programing at OSU ensured that feminism remained a visible presence in Columbus throughout the 1980s and early
1990s, albeit in a different form.

CULTURAL POLITICS

Popular wisdom in activist and academic circles holds that radical feminism declined in the mid-1970s as feminist groups
turned their attention away from political confrontation toward
building an alternative women's culture. This misconception
arises in part from Alice Echols' work on the radical feminist movement in New York City and Chicago, in which she
argues that "cultural feminism" had replaced radical feminism
by 1975.[44] In this view, cultural feminists failed to address external targets and reinforced dangerous gender stereotypes by
emphasizing essential differences between women and men.

The Columbus case suggests rather different conclusions

about the fate of radical feminism. Far from vanishing, the radical feminist movement remained active, large, and well-funded throughout the 1970s. It sponsored not only service projects and cultural events, but also zap actions, consciousness-raising groups, demonstrations, and other campaigns to confront sexist social structures. Although women's movement organizations established feminist institutions, services, and businesses in an attempt to construct a world apart from sexism, they simultaneously continued to confront the political system. It was not until 1980 that feminist organizations in Columbus really began to decline. Even then, feminist service and cultural organizations continued to define themselves as political and still confronted societal injustice.

In short, cultural events and institutions existed all along in the radical feminist movement, and participants saw culture as political in the early years as well as after 1980. Because "cultural feminist" activities have existed all along, we cannot reasonably blame them for the decrease in other forms of feminist activism. Instead, we need to recognize the influence of the external context, particularly more hostile political institutions and shrinking resource levels, and examine the connections between the cultural and the political more closely. As other social movements died down and the external context became more hostile, direct engagement with the State was difficult and infrequent. Cultural activities remained possible because they existed in a "free space" created by activists apart from dominant institutions.[45]

What would it have meant for radical feminists to remain "radical" in their tactics in the 1980s, given the overall decline of other social movements of the Left and the strength of opposition from policy-makers and social movements of the Right? Political engagement is difficult for radicals in a conservative context; without the support of mass protests by multiple social movements, the protests of radical feminists carried little weight with authorities. More institutionalized means of changing legislation or state policy, on the other hand, quickly stop appearing "radical" as activists move inside mainstream institutions in order to change them. Radical feminists in the late 1960s and early 1970s operated within the context of the larger New Left and engaged with other radicals, but their contacts with external authorities were limited to mass demonstrations, zap actions, and more moderate efforts to alter university policy by representing feminist students' interests on committees or to change courtroom treatment of rape victims by observing and reporting on trials. Do such tactics really represent greater engagement with external authorities than their successors' work with policy-makers and university officials about such diverse issues as the treatment of rape survivors, childcare, and public images of lesbians?

Were participants in the women's movement community deluding themselves in thinking that a feminist concert, for instance, was a political event? Did feminist culture instead represent a retreat from political engagement? The construction of a social movement community is political for two reasons. Cultural institutions had served all along to recruit new members, rejuvenate old members, and connect participants in different women's movement organizations to each other. They continued to do so even as the overall level of activism dropped. Thus "women's culture" helped sustain commitment through a hostile period and provided a setting that fostered collective action when the climate permitted.[46] In addition, feminist culture is directly political because it poses a challenge to hegemonic understandings of women's natures and relationships. By redefining what it means to be a woman, participants in the women's movement community not only change their own consciousness, but provide a model of an alternative way of being female. Because cultural hegemony triumphs by making nondominant points of view invisible or unthinkable, the establishment of a visible, institutionalized culture that promotes an oppositional reality is certainly a form of social change.[47]

These questions are, at their core, about what constitutes "politics" and what qualifies as "radical."[48] These are, of course, questions that have no objective answers. Rather, the political implications of particular actions depend on their context, including external authorities and structures, other social movements, and internal movement dynamics.

Radical feminism in Columbus and elsewhere changed over the years and saw a great deal of debate over shifting definitions of politics and feminism. These changes were partially a response to dropping resource levels and lack of receptiveness to feminist demands on the part of local and national political institutions. But the changes were not all due to the external environment. They were also shaped by participants' notions of what the movement was and where it should be going. Participants did not always agree about these questions, and their differences, conflicts, and compromises, within external constraints, shaped the course of the women's movement. Although some of these debates are revealed in the rise and fall of organizations, others are less immediately apparent. They require a close examination of the internal movement culture, dialogues among members, and the shifting collective identities that defined the movement and its participants from year to year. Whereas this chapter focuses on organizational dynamics and the impact of the external context on the changing radical feminist movement, the next chapter revisits the movement's heyday years with attention to collective identity and generational politics.

2 :: THE EVOLUTION

OF RADICAL

FEMINIST IDENTITY

THE WOMEN'S MOVEMENT in Columbus led to the creation of many new organizations and a constant stream of events that promoted feminist causes. But the experience of working for social change is about more than organizations and events. It is about the amazement of new insights, adrenaline and exhaustion, camaraderie and conflict, and, at least for awhile, it colors everything in your life. What it meant to be a woman, a feminist, or a lesbian was critical to the forms that radical feminist mobilization took and to participants' interactions and experiences. These definitions were neither self-evident nor clear-cut. Rather, they were constructed and negotiated among participants—sometimes explicitly, often implicitly—and were often a source of conflict.

Columbus activists in 1969 and 1970, like those in other cities, were immersed in an intense and compelling confrontation with university, police, and military authorities. They saw themselves as revolutionaries who were challenging and rethinking the meaning of revolution to include women's liberation. By the mid-1970s, other feminists were wrapped up in a world of like-minded women, designing, funding, and implementing a

55

seemingly endless stream of successful challenges to women's subordination. In both times, women who joined feminist groups did not just adopt new beliefs and participate in new activities; they thought of themselves in new ways and identified as part of a group of similar women. Participants who entered the women's movement at different times saw social change and their own lives differently. In other words, the collective identity "feminist" is far from static. Participants in collective action do not come easily to agreement about such complicated matters as what it means to be a feminist or how feminists ought to act in their daily lives. The construction of a sense of "we" is changeable and highly contested as activists seek to delineate who "we" are (and are not). In fact, collective identities are continually being reformulated, discussed, and debated. These debates are so intense because group definitions affect the central questions of political and personal life; as such, they are a site for contests over sameness and difference, homogeneity and diversity.

There are subtle variations in collective identity among *microcohorts* of women who became feminists at different times during the heyday of the movement between 1969 and 1984. A microcohort is a group with distinct formative experiences and collective identity that emerged at and shaped a particular phase of the women's movement. Each micro-cohort entered the women's movement at a specific point in its history, engaged in different activities, had a characteristic political culture, and modified feminist collective identity. Each defined the type of people, issues, language, tactics, or organizational structures that "qualified" as feminist differently. Presentation of self, use of language, and participation in political culture help to identify individuals with their micro-cohorts. Participants recognized the existence of micro-cohorts and identified as belonging to a common group with those who entered the movement at around the same time. As one participant in the formation of Women's Studies at OSU commented about another activist from the early 1970s, "[She] and I, we're of the same age group. We have a history that I just don't have with some of these younger women, a history that goes way back."

Turnover in membership helps explain both organizational change and conflict over collective identity in Columbus between the late 1960s and the early 1980s. As we will see in this chapter, incoming activists sometimes began new organizations and contributed to changes in existing ones. As successive waves of activists with distinct perspectives on gender inequality and the women's movement gained influence, each used different language and analysis to understand the social world and feminism. The varying outlooks of feminists who entered the women's movement at different times meant that interactions among micro-cohorts were sometimes conflict-ridden. In fact, I will suggest that micro-cohort differences were a major source of conflicts within the women's movement, although of course schisms emerged around other divisions as well.

The central difference among micro-cohorts was how members defined themselves, as women and as feminists. Group definitions—with implications for individuals' views of themselves—are what make up collective identity. In the process of constructing a collective definition of the group, activists define group boundaries, or whom they consider insiders and outsiders, and the traits of each. Participants analyze the world relative to themselves and their group, politicizing their beliefs and understandings about events and placing their personal life histories into a larger political narrative of oppression, commonality, and resistance. To become a feminist is to see yourself as part of "a group called women,"[1] feel a bond with other women whom you may think of as your "sisters," and reframe your past and present experiences in terms of oppression and resistance. Such understandings affect everyday life as feminists enact their identity.[2]

The notion of collective identity suggests that a group's common structural position is not sufficient to mobilize members into action. The mere fact that women share similar experiences in workplaces and families, for example, does not mean that they will act collectively to change their position or that they will agree on what changes are desirable. Rather, interaction among group members crystallizes their sense of collective interests and action.[3] Activists discuss their experiences, events in the outside world, their successes and failures, and construct collective identities that make sense of the demands of their social context, both within and outside movement organizations; in this way, social structure affects collective identity.

Women in different micro-cohorts constructed different collective identities because they were politicized at different times. It is not surprising that each micro-cohort made sense of the world in its own way, because each entered a changed world, a different context. During the 1970s, both the external environment within which feminists operated and the movement itself changed rapidly. Even a year or two made a significant difference in activists' outlook because of the rapid change in societal attitudes about gender, information about feminism, and dynamics within the movement itself (and its opposition). What an activist took for granted in 1970 was no longer necessarily true by 1973. Feminist groups in Columbus experienced rapid turnover in leadership and core membership throughout the 1970s, and as a result new micro-cohorts emerged every two to three years. Many feminist collectives, in order to prevent the formation of an elite, specified that key leadership positions could not be held by one individual for more than one or two years. Even in organizations that did not formally require the rotation of positions, leaders regularly "burned out" or were attacked and forced from their positions, thus creating a similar effect. In addition, a movement that is centered on a university, as in Columbus, has an almost automatic turnover in personnel as participants graduate or move on.

The course taken by the Columbus women's movement suggests four micro-cohorts. *Initiators* entered the women's movement as organizations were emerging in 1969 and 1970 and shaped them through 1971. *Founders* entered in late 1970 and 1971 as growth began and established lasting organizations in 1972 and 1973. *Joiners* entered the movement during its peak between 1974 and 1976 and, together with founders, were most influential through 1978. *Sustainers* entered women's movement organizations between 1977 and 1979 at the tail end of the movement's heyday, and maintained them from 1979 through 1984 as the movement declined. I will sketch out the central defining characteristics of each micro-cohort, the shifting context that shaped each one's perspective, and the major changes in women's movement organizations and collective identity that occurred on each micro-cohort's watch.

INITIATORS: 1969–1971

The years between 1969 and 1971 saw the beginning of the women's liberation movement in Columbus, with the establishment of Columbus–OSU Women's Liberation (WL). The first micro-cohort of activists, whom I have termed "initiators," developed and made visible a critique of the status quo, formed initial organizations and networks, and articulated the issues that initially mobilized feminists into action. Because initiators were first politicized in the New Left and civil rights movements, their collective identity reflected the links between the women's movement and the mixed-sex Left. Most activists described themselves as "women's liberationists," drawing on the terminology of the black liberation movement.[4] They viewed themselves as part of a broad struggle against oppression in all its forms and talked about themselves as "sisters" to all women, writing, for example, about the need to cooperate with "our sisters in the North Side Welfare Rights Organization."[5] The culture of WL emphasized militant tactics and "being willing to put your body on the line," and members' participation in

the 1970 student strike reinforced this perspective. An awareness of infiltration and surveillance by the Federal Bureau of
Investigation pervaded the consciousness of early feminists,
most of whom brought up the question of informants' presence
in WL during their interviews. Later entrants did not generally
share this culture; one woman who entered the movement in
late 1970 described the earliest activists as "too wild for me."
Early feminist Carol Anne Douglas suggests that this distinction
existed outside Columbus as well: "Those of us who were politicized in those years feel a depth of alienation, a sense of ourselves as revolutionaries, that seems a little different from the
feelings of many radical feminists who were politicized at a later
period. We were aware that state violence could be turned against
us."[6] The unrelated murders of two Columbus feminist activists
(apparently by their male companions) added to local feminists'
sense of being under attack by a male-dominated society.

The major conflicts in this period were over *how closely* (not
whether) WL should be linked to other struggles. In August
1970, a few months after WL was founded, some activists split
off to form a more "politically-oriented group." They criticized
WL for focusing excessively on "making life more comfortable
for white middle-class women," instead of liberating women of
all classes. The dissenters allied themselves more closely with
male-dominated New Left organizations than WL did and
quickly became absorbed into those organizations. This "poli-
tico–feminist" split mirrored conflicts in the women's movement nationally.[7]

The organizations begun in 1969 and 1970 were informally
structured and did not last beyond the first few years of the
movement. But rap groups organized by WL brought in a new
cohort of activists. While initiators were closely tied to the student movement and their demands focused on conditions for
women at the university, incoming activists were less willing to
work primarily within OSU because of the constraints the University imposed on student organizations; they were more inter-

ested in forming autonomous women's organizations. At the same time, many initiators moved out of town as they graduated or took other jobs, thus opening a space for newcomers to organize. Others remained active but took a backseat to incoming activists as women's movement organizations proliferated and became institutionalized in the early 1970s.

FOUNDERS: 1972–1973

In 1972 and 1973, members of a Women's Liberation rap group founded formally structured organizations that later became the mass organizations of the mid-1970s. Most of the new organizations were part of the Women's Action Collective (WAC), but these activists were also central to the burgeoning campaign to establish a Women's Studies program at OSU, joining women faculty and administrators. Many of the members of "Rap Group Number One" had participated in the actions surrounding the student strike in 1970 and 1971, but with few exceptions they had not been leaders in WL. One member of Rap Group Number One explained:

> Our CR group had a lot of people who had lots of leadership skills, and we tended to branch out and start projects. We met for about three and a half years once a week, and then we were activists the rest of the week.

These women saw themselves as a distinct group within the larger movement, according to one founder.

> It seemed like there was just one group of people who were starting everything. Maybe I'm misguided, but I don't think there was that much going on then other than the things that we were doing. There was the Music Union, there was the Action Collective, and Women Against Rape, and women's studies. . . . It was all sort of a cohort of people that were doing it all at once.

I have termed this micro-cohort of activists *founders*. They entered the movement after initial activism had begun, but before lasting institutions had developed. They transformed the ideas, dissatisfaction, and ad hoc organizations begun by initiators into lasting feminist institutions. Many of WL's initial demands, such as the availability of birth control to unmarried women at the student health center, the establishment of a campus daycare center, and legalization of abortion, were met or seemed to be well under way by 1972 or 1973. Incoming activists then moved on to a wide variety of issues, including the establishment of alternative institutions such as the rape crisis hotline, the Women's Co-op Garage, and the Women's Community Development Fund.

Although the women's movement remained politically aligned with the New Left on many issues during 1972 and 1973, it diverged culturally. Women-only events and activities increased, and although membership remained decidedly mixed in sexual orientation, lesbians became increasingly visible. Growing numbers of activists in women's movement organizations came out as lesbians; some had identified as lesbian before joining feminist groups, and others came out as an outgrowth of their feminist activism. Thus, lesbians were not limited to the founder micro-cohort, and the conflicts that arose between lesbian and heterosexual women (which were minimal in the early 1970s) did not split among micro-cohort lines. An explicitly lesbian organization, Gay Women's Peer Counseling, emerged in 1973. By running support and discussion groups and doing peer counseling, Gay Women's Peer Counseling helped politicize lesbians and encouraged feminists to be open about their lesbianism.

It was during these years that participants in Columbus began to use the term "radical feminist" to describe themselves and their organizations. This signified an important shift in collective identity from "women's liberationist," with its link to the New Left, to an emphasis on building an autonomous feminist movement and women's institutions. Founders envisioned WAC as a multi-organization coalition that would simultaneously confront women's oppression and provide for women's needs by, for example, publishing nonsexist children's books, teaching self-defense and car repair skills, and establishing rape crisis services. Gay Women's Peer Counseling, similarly, sought to confront lesbians' oppression through education and to provide support and encouragement to lesbians coming out in a hostile context. Such organizations, founders hoped, would establish a solid base for feminist organizing that was not linked to either the male-dominated New Left or to mainstream institutions.

The use of alternative institution building as a strategy, the increasing cultural distance between the women's movement and the New Left, and the growing lesbian presence in women's movement organizations all linked radical feminist collective identity more closely with separatism. As a result, WAC was poised for its subsequent growth into an extensive "women's world."

JOINERS: 1974–1978

In the mid-1970s the women's movement in Columbus, as elsewhere, expanded rapidly. Organizations grew, membership increased, and substantial resources poured in from outside sources.[8] Large numbers of new activists entered the women's movement between 1974 and 1976, usually by becoming part of existing organizations. I have called this micro-cohort *joiners,* because their primary role was to expand existing organizations. Although most founders continued to play central roles in the organizations they had begun, participants drew a distinction between the "Old Guard" or "founding mothers" and newer members.

Some joiners first learned about the women's movement from

feminist writings or the mass media; others made contact by volunteering in feminist organizations. For example, one woman signed up to train as a crisis hotline volunteer for Women Against Rape. She expected, she said, to be a "do-gooder"; instead, she was revolutionized. Like her, most of the joiners I interviewed first became politicized in the women's movement, unlike earlier members who often had been politicized in other social movements. As a result, joiners lacked some of the sense of having to fight for every gain that characterized women who had forged feminist organizations out of somewhat hostile New Left contexts. Joiners' frame of reference was established feminist organizations that were sufficiently successful to recruit and politicize them.

The hallmark of the women's movement during the mid-1970s was its success: Activists established organizations, acquired outside funding, won legalized abortion, pushed the ERA through Congress and many states, and achieved at least some decrease in the public acceptability of blatant sexism.[9] In Columbus, as we have seen, OSU funded an Office of Women's Studies in 1975 after five years of activist pressure. By this time, many core members also held paid positions in Women Against Rape, WAC, or Women's Studies, the movement's membership was growing rapidly, and Women Against Rape received its large grant from the federal government. Not surprisingly, women who were politicized during this period were optimistic about the possibility of achieving social-structural change on a large scale. Their goals were broad, and the scope of the organizations they joined and expanded was similarly far-reaching.

Participants continued to apply the label "radical feminist" to themselves and their organizations, but its meaning changed. Most strikingly, feminism was increasingly tied to lesbianism. Gay Women's Peer Counseling changed its name in 1976 to Lesbian Peer Support and joined WAC, signifying its self-definition as part of the women's movement rather than the mixed-sex gay liberation movement. Although not all WAC members were lesbians, the vast majority were, and a new lesbian organization also grew outside WAC. Central Ohio Lesbians, a campus-based group that lobbied for gay and lesbian legal rights, organized the first local gay pride march and provided a lesbian speakers' bureau. In keeping with theoretical developments in the larger women's movement,[10] members of WAC and Central Ohio Lesbians saw lesbianism as a challenge to male domination and an important component of women's liberation. At the beginning of the period, WAC's 1974 Statement of Philosophy noted:

> We recognize a woman's right to free discovery and expression of her sexuality. Lesbianism is a positive expression of women loving women which resolves splits that are present in our relationships is [*sic*] we cannot express ourselves physically and sexually with each other.[11]

Three years later, the link between lesbianism and feminism was much more explicit. A statement on lesbianism and lesbian rights adopted by WAC in 1977 framed lesbianism as an explicitly political rejection of male dominance.

> Lesbianism . . . affirms the process of challenging traditional institutions forced upon women and constitutes a primary commitment to women. The Women's Action Collective recognizes Lesbianism as a positive means for eliminating one facet of the power relationship of men over women. As such, Lesbianism is an integral part of the Women's Movement.[12]

At the same time that lesbianism became more closely tied up with feminism, radical feminist collective identity increasingly entailed separation from men. In 1972 and 1973 members saw forming alternative institutions for women outside the dominant culture primarily as a *strategy* for achieving social change, rather than as an end in itself. After 1974 separatism became a more central ideological principle. The 1974 WAC

Statement of Philosophy reflected the belief that the feminist movement was the preserve of women alone, although it was careful to avoid assuming *innate* differences between the genders.

> The work of the women's movement must be done by women. . . . No man can experience women's oppression; therefore, no man can be a spokesperson for the women's movement.[13]

Members argued that women needed "women-only space" to develop a strong opposition and to contradict the cultural devaluation of women, and they specified that the WAC house was, accordingly, "women's space."[14] At orientation sessions for new members that WAC began holding in 1977,[15] facilitators defined radical feminism as focusing on the connections between the personal and the political, including the concept of the lesbian as a "woman-identified woman."[16] In short, theories about the connections between women's personal experiences and their political roots cast both lesbianism and separatism as politically beneficial as well as personally preferable.

The growing women's movement community[17] expressed and expanded this developing "women-identified" culture. Feminist musicians and artists had exhibited and performed since the early 1970s, and in the mid-1970s feminist culture really flourished. Nationally known feminist musicians and artists toured Columbus, and the institutions that supported feminist culture developed. Locally, these included Fan the Flames Feminist Bookstore, which established its store in the WAC house during this period, and the Women's Music Union. Nationally, Olivia Records established the first feminist recording company, the Michigan Womyn's Music Festival began, and feminist publishing companies were formed. Joiners were unequivocal in viewing feminist culture as political; some founders and initiators, however, drew a sharper line between "cultural" and "political" activities even as they participated in both.

Because of the large influx into existing organizations, the period between 1974 and 1978 was characterized by conflict between more and less experienced members of organizations. These conflicts helped to shape the experiences and perspectives of joiners, who both admired their predecessors and sometimes resented their greater control over organizations. Members who had been around for longer sought to teach new members the skills necessary to participate fully in the organization, as one founding member of WAC explained.

> We were operating in a completely collective environment where supposedly everybody had equal access to decision making, but some of us were just damned skilled by that time. . . . We ran endless workshops to try to train women so they could still make competent decisions. But some of us still became known as sort of the kitchen cabinet of the Action Collective.

Such attempts, regardless of their success or failure in transmitting skills to incoming members, underscored the gap between experienced and new members. Conflict between core and peripheral members is not necessarily a result of micro-cohort differences. However, core members of WAC tended to be those who had been part of the organization for the longest time. One founder remarked that those who were perceived as elitist were often the founders of the organization.

> The folks who were on salary [with the CASSR project] I think were perceived to be some kind of an elite. And certainly they were the people with the longest history with the organization, and the people that had been around since the early seventies or maybe late sixties. So by virtue of their history with the organization, they had a fair amount of power. And I think eventually that some of the newer people chafed under that sort of thing.

Women who began the two new organizations established during this period, Central Ohio Lesbians and the Women's Music Union, explicitly stated that they founded new organizations because they felt closed out of WAC, not because of being lesbians (most WAC members were, too) but because of being newcomers. One founding member of Central Ohio Lesbians explained that she had not felt welcome to assume decision making in WAC.

> Some of the more older and established groups had very much their idea of how they wanted to run things, and it was our perception that no one was really to tread on that. And there was this vague invitation to provide input, but you never really got the impression that that input was going to be taken seriously or acted upon in any way.

On the other hand, more experienced women felt frustrated with what they perceived as incoming women's lack of political sophistication. One woman who joined Women Against Rape during the mid-1970s explained that her greater familiarity with feminism made her frustrated with newer members.

> I think the longer you were there the less patience you had with brand new women coming in. . . . There was always a continuum of women who had been there forever and ever and had read everything, and grappled with all these issues for so long, and the women who just joined. . . . And we were eons apart.

Some women who joined existing feminist organizations did not perceive such blocks to their participation as equals and their access to decision making. One woman who joined WAC in 1973 declared that she had no difficulty participating actively.

> What you did in the organization was pretty much up to you. And I certainly did not perceive any barriers to getting more involved with the organization. I didn't perceive any possessiveness or anything like that. So if you were willing to do the work and get involved, they were willing to let you in. And I can sort of remember conversations among the old-timers, talking about new people coming in. "Well, so-and-so has really come a long way." . . . And so people were really pleased when women began to develop more feminist consciousness.

Although she perceived the organization as open, it is clear from her comment that incoming members were expected to adopt the same definition of feminism as "old-timers" in order to be considered to have "come a long way."

Not surprisingly, founding members were concerned that incoming members not displace their ideas and goals for their organizations. One founding member of Women Against Rape recounted her anxiety as the group prepared to train its first new members.

> When we put together our training, we were very careful. It was like, we had this little group of seven, and we all knew each other, and now we're going to open it up to this group of sixty and we don't know what's going to happen now. . . . How we feel about things might get diluted, or altered, or misinterpreted.

Another group, Fan the Flames Feminist Book Collective, needed to replace two members in 1976 and approached the task with caution. A notice published in the *WAC Newsletter* asked for new collective members:

> We have never seen ourselves as just a business but a friendship group with shared politics and work. When we began in 1974, we had all known each other from other projects and knew we wanted to work together. . . . We want to add two collective members and want to do it in a way that allows our group to continue the spirit we began. We are nervous about how to do this because we have never done it before. . . . We definitely are looking for women with a history of political activism in the women's movement (our first preference is members of the WAC since we probably know you already) with a radical feminist outlook. . . . It would be nice to find people who have some knowledge of bookstore work. . . . Most important, of course, for us is to find comfortable friends to work with.[18]

On one hand, the collective's search for new members who shared the same understanding of politics and who would be "comfortable" made the group more cohesive and increased members' commitment. On the other hand, it insured homogeneity. In any case, their concerns indicate the importance of radical feminist collective identity to activists. Such concerns about how new members might redirect an organization indicate that participants recognized the potential of micro-cohort turnover to change the movement.

With such a large influx of new members, passing on information, experience, and perspectives became an important task for experienced activists. Orientation sessions served as an institutionalized means for experienced feminists to transmit ideology and movement history to incoming members. WAC began holding orientation sessions in 1977, and these were instrumental in the political socialization of new members. One new member reported that the bulk of the time in her orientation was spent defining radical feminism so that, as she perceived it, "we could see what we were supposed to be if we were going to be radical feminists." The women who entered WAC in 1977, 1978, and 1979 through these orientation sessions became the fourth micro-cohort. As often younger women entering a well-established organization in which the founders were still present, the incoming micro-cohort complained about their treatment by earlier members, as did this woman.

> We were all referred to as the baby feminists for a time, and I really hated that. I really wanted to be accepted simply as a feminist, WAC member, and for people not to just see me as this young person. . . . But there was a little bit of, I guess you'd call it maternalism.

Despite such resentment, orientation sessions provided a setting where new members read and discussed feminist tenets developed by earlier members and where they could establish a network among other newcomers to the organization.

Women who began feminist activism in the mid-1970s, in part because their large numbers swelled and strengthened the women's movement, led the growth of an alternative feminist culture and took for granted both that they would work outside the mainstream and that they could appropriate the resources of the State for feminist ends. This proved a powerful combination as long as resources remained available, but the decline of the nonprofit sector hit women's movement organizations and their personnel hard. As the 1970s gave way to the 1980s, the micro-cohort politicized in WAC's late-1970s orientation sessions took over leadership of the organization.

SUSTAINERS: 1979–1984

Women who entered WAC between 1977 and 1979 faced a difficult external environment. As the social and political climate became more conservative and feminist organizations foundered, activists struggled to redefine radical feminism in a way that was applicable to the changing times. Newcomers in the late 1970s were politicized by the substantial gains of the earlier women's movement. The movement's success in establishing a Center for Women's Studies at the university meant that students discovered feminism in college classes, and the institutionalization of WAC's orientation sessions opened another route for politicization. This micro-cohort became influential in 1979 and 1980 as earlier cohorts took less active roles. I have called them *sustainers* because one of their main tasks has been to pass on the ideas of the peak of the women's movement to the activists who entered the movement in the 1980s.

Sustainers modified radical feminist collective identity by further emphasizing lesbianism, emphasizing differences of race, ethnicity, religion, and class among women, and defining new issues, notably spirituality, as feminist. In sharp contrast to joiners, sustainers were largely pessimistic about the prospects for sweeping social change. The late 1970s and early 1980s were marked by internal conflict over these issues and the painful exits of longterm members. The conflicts did not break down neatly along micro-cohort lines. Although many advocates of new positions were sustainers, sustainers fell on both sides of conflicts. These conflicts and the growing external opposition to feminism were the defining experiences for sustainers.

All the women I interviewed who joined WAC between 1977 and 1979 were lesbians, as were the vast majority of other incoming members in the late 1970s. The predominance of lesbians was due to several factors: The flourishing lesbian feminist culture helped bring in new recruits, lesbians were less able to assimilate outside the women's movement and so maintained feminist commitment even in a hostile period, and heterosexual women felt uncomfortable in a largely lesbian movement. Because earlier micro-cohorts also contained many lesbians and saw lesbian and feminist politics as linked, sustainers' lesbianism did not cause conflicts between micro-cohorts. Rather, being part of an almost exclusively lesbian organization simply gave sustainers a different perspective from their predecessors. Yet even as the organization became more homogeneously lesbian, members debated the centrality of lesbianism to feminist identity. Some argued at a 1981 WAC meeting that the organization's Statement of Philosophy should state: "WAC believes that lesbianism is the lifestyle most consistent with radical feminist theory." Others countered that "we are feminists first and lesbians less obviously" and that heterosexual women should not be excluded from the women's movement.[19] Substantial debate ensued over whether WAC should attempt to appeal to heterosexual women, although in practice the organization was almost exclusively composed of lesbians by this point. The centrality of lesbianism to the definition of "feminist," in other words, was contested.

A second issue of increasing debate was racism and homogeneity within the women's movement. Earlier feminist theorists analyzed sexism as if all women were an undifferentiated "sex class." In the late 1970s women of color and Jewish women began to raise the question of differences among women; a number of books on the topic were published in the early 1980s, crystallizing discussions in many local communities.[20] Members hotly debated these issues within WAC at a series of meetings—dubbed "struggle sessions"—in 1981 and 1982 at which members concluded that WAC had been a white-dominated and racist organization and that white members should examine their own racism and classism in order to encourage minority women to join.[21] Participants in the struggle sessions noted that they should not simply try to recruit women of color to "their" organization, but should be willing to change in order to accommodate the needs and perspectives of minority women. At the same time, many members were concerned that WAC not "water down" its radical politics in order to attract a broader membership. These women argued that the group's role was more properly that of a "vanguard" organization rather than a mass movement. The upshot of all these discussions was that "racism and minority women's issues" were added to WAC orientations,[22] and WAC newsletters more frequently discussed issues of both race and class. Yet, as with the discussion of recruiting heterosexual women, the organization remained largely white. Many white WAC members genuinely had their consciousness raised about race and class through these discussions, but the immediate legacy of the discussions for white feminists was more guilt than organizational change.

A third area of conflict—feminist spirituality—also revolved around collective identity, or the definition of what constituted a feminist issue. In September 1982 the *WAC Newsletter* sported a new logo of a crescent moon with a women's symbol and a new title, "Womoon Rising." An accompanying letter from the newsletter committee explained the change.

As radical feminists we have all made the commitment to ending the patriarchy and re-establishing Matriarchy. One of the ways we do this is by claiming as our own the strong ties between ourselves and the Mother Spirit. In Prehistorical societies . . . the moon represented this Mother Spirit. We take the name WOMOON RISING because we are Womoon. And, although we may not yet be full, we are definitely rising."[23]

The change of name sparked controversy within WAC. Many members objected both to the name itself and to the way the decision to change the old name was made. A letter from eight active members of WAC, including sustainers, founders, and joiners, protested against the new name.

> What is a Womoon? No one knows, but it certainly doesn't sound like a political activist. . . . Equally disturbing is your reference to a "Mother Spirit. . . ." The whole concept, down to the name being capitalized is traditional in many ways.[24]

A subsequent letter from a more recent member countered that WAC ought to focus more attention on the issue of spirituality.

> I have seen this spelling [womoon] in popular womyn's literature for the past year, at least. Womyn's spirituality is a "hot" topic in the many, many womyn's journals nationwide and in many womyn's lives. The Women's (sic) ["sic" in original] Action Collective has been in the forefront of womyn's theorizing and the movement itself. WAC now seems, by our lack of forward progress, to be isolating ourself. . . . This is an issue WAC will need to deal with soon, as, unfortunately, WAC is becoming very mainstream feminist.[25]

The conflict over "womoon" was essentially a debate over whether to redefine what it meant to be a feminist. Advocates of "womoonhood," who were predominantly sustainers, defined feminism as including matriarchal spirituality and viewed personal transformation through a connection to a Mother Spirit as an important form of social change. In their view, an orientation toward external confrontation was "mainstream," and therefore undesirable. Their opponents, on the other hand, sought to maintain the previous definition of feminism that linked it to external political change and did not include what they saw as "flaky" spiritual concerns.

Participants' views of their role in the women's movement changed during this period. Two "struggle sessions" on whether WAC should be a mass movement organization or a radical vanguard that did not attempt to appeal to most women illustrated this shift. Earlier micro-cohorts had viewed the role of radical feminists as agitating for profound social transformation, using visible tactics that were likely to have an impact, spreading a radical feminist critique of society, and pushing the women's movement as a whole toward more radical stands. By the late 1970s, however, sustainers no longer held such an optimistic view of radical feminism. Rather, they were more likely to describe their purpose both in publications at the time and in later interviews as serving as the radical fringe of the women's movement that would make the liberal wing of feminism seem more acceptable to mainstream society. One woman explained:

> I don't disagree with the premise that you need a radical left to keep people pulled that way, that that helps balance things out. But I don't have an illusion that because you feel very strongly that your ideas and beliefs are right that you're going to be able to convince the whole rest of the world of this, and have some sort of revolution that's going to make radical change in the course of one person's lifetime. That kind of change happens much more slowly.

Although earlier activists also believed that their radicalism made moderate demands more likely to be met, they had grander hopes as well. Yet all of the sustainers I interviewed stated that they had never—or only very briefly—believed that they would see radical feminist social transformation in their lifetime. Although they appear to have been correct, it is not surprising that they became discouraged, their commitment waned, and many of them chose to pursue more moderate goals. Public hostility to feminism and decreasing political success made feminists who entered and staffed the women's movement between 1977 and 1981 inclined to be more pessimistic than earlier feminists about achieving their goals.

In addition to conflicts with generational undertones about race, class, and spirituality, direct conflicts raged between members of different micro-cohorts. Some sustainers criticized many longtime members of WAC for "power-tripping," elitism, and making decisions without consulting the collective. These were often vicious attacks that left the founders of the organization feeling hurt, angry, and bitter. Many members of both founder and joiner micro-cohorts moved out of town, either for unrelated personal reasons or because they were criticized and attacked. Those who stayed in Columbus adopted an advice-giving role and ceased to be active participants. For example, one founder of Women Against Rape described her relationship to the organization around 1980.

I was tired, basically, and I felt like I kind of sat around as the wise old lady who dispensed advice. Because I no longer had the energy to do anything. But I didn't mind talking to people about what they could do and how they should do it. [I said,] "Oh, yeah, we tried that, in 19-da-da-da." [*Laughs*]

The loss of large numbers of experienced members due to internal conflict, combined with shrinking resources and the increasingly hostile climate, left women's movement organizations foundering. Sustainers, already justifiably pessimistic about the likelihood of radical social change, had trouble maintaining their organizations in the face of such obstacles. As I describe in Chapter 1, most of WAC's member organizations were defunct by 1980, and the collective itself dissolved in 1984. By the 1980s, feminists increasingly pursued their goals within mainstream institutions such as social service and governmental agencies, the judicial system, colleges and universities, and the Democratic Party.[26]

CHANGE AND CONFLICT IN
THE WOMEN'S MOVEMENT

Social movements are made up of participants as well as organizations. Even when social movement organizations as a whole endure, different people staff those organizations over time. In the Columbus women's movement, organizations changed and experienced conflict as successive micro-cohorts entered and redefined the feminist collective identity.

Initiators raised the issues of women's liberation and established the first organizations, such as WL, even as they remained closely linked to the New Left. *Founders* built on initiators' gains and established formal, enduring organizations, such as WAC, that separated from the mixed-sex New Left and laid the groundwork for a large and independent cluster of women's movement organizations and culture. This developed in the mid-1970s as many women flocked to feminist organizations and events. These *joiners* led a shift that placed lesbianism more centrally in feminist collective identity and promoted the growth of a separate "women's community." At the same time, as we have seen, joiners fueled the expansion of WAC's member organizations and staffed influential projects on rape prevention, the treatment of rape cases in courts, education and awareness about homophobia and coming out, sexism in advertising, women's studies, and more. *Sustainers* entered while the women's movement community still thrived, and launched new debates about lesbianism, diversity within the movement, and spirituality. As they argued over these cleavages and fought stiff opposition, sustainers presided over the demise of many women's movement organizations in Columbus.

Internal conflicts among feminist activists sometimes crossed micro-cohort lines: Debates about spirituality, lesbianism, and contact with men or with other movements emerged within micro-cohorts as well as between them. Micro-cohorts were not homogeneous, and micro-cohort dynamics cannot explain all conflict in the women's movement. But conflicts between micro-cohorts, particularly the splits over core members' control of organizations and newcomers' influence that led to longtime members' being "trashed out" of their groups, were widespread. Their different conceptions of feminism meant that participants who entered the movement at different times took different points of view even in the conflicts that were not strictly between micro-cohorts, such as the debate over feminist spirituality. Micro-cohorts, then, or the time at which participants became feminists, shaped individuals' collective identity and, in turn, their position in internal debates. We cannot understand conflicts within women's movement organizations solely in terms of micro-cohorts, but we cannot fully understand the conflicts without examining micro-cohorts.

This look at micro-cohorts shows in a detailed way how women's contexts and concrete experiences influenced the collective identities they constructed. The conflicts that ripped through feminist organizations during the 1970s stemmed in part from the divergent politicizing experiences of different micro-cohorts and did not result solely from ideological disagreements. Change in women's movement organizations, like conflict, resulted in part from the continual entry and exit of micro-cohorts with varying collective identities. Many pivotal studies focus on the origins of the women's movement and thus describe radical feminists as having been initially politicized in the civil rights and New Left movements, and then building on those experiences in the feminist movement.[27] Yet joiners and sustainers entered radical feminist organizations without first having been part of the mixed-sex Left. Their perspectives were grounded instead in the women's movement and changed the course of the movement as a whole.

Despite their differences from one another, women who were part of the radical feminist movement between 1969 and the early 1980s shared an important experience that changed their lives. The conflicts among them underscore the importance of the meaning of "radical feminist" to participants' sense of themselves and the world. This collective identity proved enduring even when the organizations in which it flowered did not survive. In the following decade, the differences among micro-cohorts that seemed so critical in the 1970s paled in the face of a conservative sea-change in American politics and culture. Women from each micro-cohort retained their own unique perception of the 1970s women's movement and kept most closely in touch with other members of their own micro-cohort. Nevertheless, their shared participation in the heyday of radical feminism bound them together and set them apart in the conservative 1980s. In the next three chapters, I turn to their common experiences as radical feminists in that decade.

3 :: CHANGERS AND THE CHANGED: RADICAL FEMINISTS IN THE REAGAN YEARS

AN ANTIFEMINIST MOVEMENT gained strength throughout the 1970s and was bolstered by Ronald Reagan's election to the presidency in 1980. Reagan's presidency and the rise of the Religious Right were a watershed for the women's movement and other movements for social change. On one hand, the intense battles around the ERA, the attempt to pass a right-wing federal Family Protection Act, and attacks on abortion rights spurred feminists to increased efforts. On the other hand, cutbacks in funding for social services decimated feminist organizations, and American culture grew more hostile to feminists. Columbus was no exception to the national picture: Feminist gains of the 1970s eroded under funding pressure, opposition, and increased internal conflict in the early 1980s. Activists of the 1970s found themselves increasingly marginalized and demoralized in the 1980s.

Despite the antifeminist climate, veterans of the 1970s women's movement had been transformed by their experience. They could not simply turn away from their politics and step back into mainstream society. Instead they sought support from each other and found ways to sustain their commitment. We

have seen how each micro-cohort's definition of feminism shaped members' perceptions, daily lives, and conflicts during the movement's peak. Their commitment to feminism continued to shape participants' interactions after mobilization receded. Longtime feminists have changed without a large and vibrant movement to sustain them, but commitment to social change remains central to their sense of themselves, their peers, and the world as a political place. For core members this commitment has been exceedingly enduring.

Their lives help us understand how participation in collective action affects individuals' lives and how social movements endure and change over time. How are attitudes and behaviors established, and how do they continue to change throughout life? To what extent do individuals' beliefs and actions grow from historical circumstances, and when that context changes, how do individuals change as well? As members of one of the largest and most influential social movements of the twentieth century, participants in the second wave women's movement are an excellent illustration of both social movement continuity and the intersection of history and biography.[1]

In this chapter and the two following, I treat veterans of the 1960s–1970s women's movement not as members of four separate micro-cohorts but as members of one political generation. Recall that I define micro-cohorts as subsets of political generations. At some point, separate micro-cohorts cohere into a distinct political generation when the similarities among them outweigh their differences. For participants in the radical women's movement, this occurred in the early 1980s as a result of sharp changes in the external context. The differences among second wave micro-cohorts paled in the face of both the antifeminist climate and the divergent attitudes of younger feminists. To look at it another way, a political generation is made up of all the micro-cohorts that are active in one wave of a movement. When feminist organizing declined and lost ground in the 1980s, the women's movement passed into a new phase, and entering activists were part of a new political generation that differed sharply from all the earlier micro-cohorts. All four earlier micro-cohorts faced the same dilemma of making lives as feminists in a hostile climate, and they all went through similar processes of continuity and change. By the early 1980s their micro-cohort differences took second place to generational similarities; although veterans of the 1970s movement are not all alike, they share a generational perspective that sets them apart.

In the context of the 1980s, longtime feminists sustained their political consciousness and sense of group boundaries; in short, their collective identity proved enduring. The endurance of individuals' perspectives is fundamentally tied to their membership in a political generation. Just as collective identity is constructed through interaction, it is maintained through group processes. In other words, the radical feminist heyday created a context in which participants developed and enacted oppositional identities that served to sustain activism later, in other contexts.

THEORETICAL VIEWS OF POLITICAL GENERATIONS

There is no doubt that experiences in radical feminist organizations were central to participants' lives at the time. But how are these experiences meaningful years later? There are several possible courses that political commitment and actions might take over time, as individuals age and historical circumstances change. Three major perspectives on this question—lifecycle, period, and generational—have emerged. The lifecycle perspective views youth as the natural time for rebellion. Focusing on the effects of aging, theorists suggest that as individuals mature they settle into family and work roles and are more likely to be involved in mainstream politics rather than radical social change.[2] In the popular version of the lifecycle perspective, the media portray the commitment of 1960s activists as transitory, due more to youthful exuberance than to support for clearly defined goals of social change. This view has been used to discredit social movements by implying that activists outgrow their commitment.[3]

A second approach centers on the effects of the external environment on collective action, suggesting that the social and political context encourages or discourages activism regardless of the age of participants. This "period" perspective is consistent with resource mobilization and political process approaches that suggest that social movements develop when structural conditions are conducive to their growth and die down when the political climate changes. The 1960s, then, had the right combination of economic prosperity and political openness to foster mobilization. As the economy tightened in the early 1970s and the political climate became more conservative, social movement participants were unable to sustain their previous level of mobilization and turned to other pursuits. Resource mobilization and political process theories focus on the organizational and structural levels, however, and do not help understand the fate of individual participants after mobilization dies down.[4]

The generational perspective pays particular attention to those individuals. It suggests that activists who participate together in a social movement develop political commitments and networks that endure even as mobilization declines and external conditions change.[5] Members of a political generation share an identity[6] or an "aware[ness] of its uniqueness . . . a sense of solidarity, and [a] join[ing] together to work for social or political change," comparable to the concept of a class "for itself."[7] In other words, what characterizes a political generation is a broad and enduring collective identity.

Mannheim argued that experiences in adolescence or early adulthood are formative because they shape a "natural view of the world," a lens through which later experiences are interpreted.[8] However, a political generation need not be defined by age but instead may be defined as a group that has a common experience during the same period.[9] This common experience may be birth (for an age cohort) or other events such as completion of school, marriage, migration, or entry into the workforce.[10] In the case of social movements, the defining factor is the era or wave of the movement when individuals are initially politicized.[11] Thus members of a political generation have roughly the same "activist age," although their chronological ages may vary. Political generations are made up of multiple, overlapping micro-cohorts that enter the movement during the same era and share some commonalities. This definition of a generation does not include all members of an age group, unlike media-created stereotypes of the "baby boomers" or "Generation X." Instead, members of a political generation share experiences in collective action from which they construct enduring networks and commitments.

The overwhelming majority of empirical evidence supports the view that political generations' shared consciousness endures over time because it is grounded in common transformative experiences. Follow-up studies of civil rights activists,[12] participants in the Berkeley Free Speech Movement,[13] student protesters at the University of California at Santa Barbara,[14] participants in 1960s protest in general,[15] and members of the West German peace movement[16] show that former activists retained radical political beliefs and identification and are more politically active than nonactivists.[17] Their political participation remained more radical than the mainstream; for example, 61 percent of former civil rights activists reported in 1986 that they continued to participate in political activity that could lead to arrest.[18] In addition, participants in social movements of the 1960s are concentrated in teaching and service occupations[19] or governmental social service agencies,[20] earn less money than nonactivists,[21] and are less likely to be married than nonactivists.[22]

It is one thing to retain one's political commitments in a setting that reinforces that outlook, as the highly mobilized radical feminist community did for all micro-cohorts. It is quite another matter to hold to one's point of view in a hostile context. As "period" approaches recognize, mobilization is not simply a matter of participants' commitment. External factors influenced both the course of women's movement organizations and the ways that longtime radical feminists thought about and acted on their political commitments. Participants' oppositional consciousness and their sense of themselves as a group with shared boundaries still bear the imprint of their earlier years of activism.[23] But to be a radical feminist in the 1980s was a very different experience.

THE BACKLASH YEARS: POLITICAL OPPORTUNITIES, RESOURCES, AND CULTURE IN THE 1980S

To students of Left protest, "the Eighties" connotes a dismal period of intense opposition, social movement retrenchment, and loss of resources. Activists agreed with this assessment. One longtime feminist characterized the decade as "a time of this horrible backlash, a fear-producing, economically self-motivating time, when lots of stuff was driven out of the visible realm into the personal again." To what extent is this bleak picture accurate? We can answer this question on three inter-related levels: changes in resource levels, political opportunities, and mass culture. An economic recession, an antifeminist federal administration, funding cuts to social services, and cultural conservatism fed off each other and together caused the demise of many women's movement organizations.

Ronald Reagan was elected president in 1980 on a platform that emphasized cutting federal government programs and shifting responsibility for funding social services to state and local government and the private sector. Along with services for the poor, national women's movement organizations that had relied on federal funding (from the Equal Employment Opportunity Commission, the U.S. Civil Rights Commission, the Department of Labor, or the Department of State) quickly lost their funding base.[24] Such losses were significant. The Women's Equity Action League, for example, received half its 1980 budget from the federal government, and lost that entire appropriation.[25] In Columbus, WAC was largely supported by federal grant money from the National Institute of Mental Health. This dried up in 1980, and the organizations' subsequent attempts to get federal grants were fruitless. In addition, Reagan promptly abolished the Comprehensive Employment Training Act (CETA) program, which had funded staff for Women Against Rape.

The foundations and nonprofit organizations that were supposed to pick up the slack, according to Reagan policy, lost federal dollars themselves at the same time that their burdens increased.[26] Foundation grants to women's groups increased from $20 million in 1980 to $60 million in 1984, but still constituted only 3.69 percent of all foundation grants.[27] In the scramble to secure scarce foundation money, social movement organizations that had pre-existing relationships with foundations were the most successful.[28] Organizations that grew out of the women's movement had to emphasize service provision, minimize radicalism, and adopt a hierarchical organizational structure in order to receive funding from foundations or the United Way.[29]

Columbus radical feminist groups did not pursue this course and were critical of those who did. WAC members particularly criticized groups that accepted money from the Playboy Foundation, which frequently funded feminist projects in order, radical feminists believed, to quiet feminist criticism of pornography and emphasize First Amendment freedoms instead. Yet without foundation support, they suffered poverty. While national feminist organizations could augment their income with direct-mail fundraising appeals and membership contributions, grassroots groups had less success doing so.[30] Like many progressive movement organizations, Women Against Rape began a door-to-door canvass in 1979 that sustained the organization through lean years in the 1980s, but was never large or reliable enough to maintain earlier levels of activism. Instead of surviving on membership contributions or foundation grants, most feminist organizations in Columbus continued to apply unsuccessfully for federal money and sought income through fees for services and affiliation with The Ohio State University.

Nonprofit organizations around the country that provided social services, such as community mental health centers and soup kitchens, were forced to shift to a population that could pay for services and increase their fees; as a result, funding and services to low-income populations dropped sharply.[31] In Columbus, women's movement organizations garnered some funds by marketing services to agencies that could afford to pay. Women Against Rape was the most successful at doing so. It contracted to conduct training sessions for mental health professionals and police officers and used its longstanding chapter at OSU, the Rape Education and Prevention Project, to gain university funds for self-defense programs. After an alleged gang-rape in a campus residence hall in the early 1980s, the university funded a greatly expanded Rape Education and Prevention Project in response to student protests. But between 1980 and 1983, the situation looked bleak; groups had lost federal money, few could get foundation grants, and service contracts had yet to take hold. Even later in the 1980s, surviving women's movement organizations in Columbus and elsewhere operated with far fewer resources than they had during their peak in the 1970s.

Meanwhile, the public policy arena saw a mixture of gains and losses for feminists. At the federal level, the losses were heavy. The federal courts, sometimes sympathetic to feminist causes in the 1970s, ruled in 1984 to limit Title IX restrictions on sex discrimination in education and upheld limits on abortion rights in the 1989 *Webster* decision.[32] And despite the growth in the feminist lobby in Washington, legislative victories were few, and threats and losses multiplied.[33] The ERA was defeated and a Family Protection Act proposed in Congress. Further, women made up a shrinking proportion of fulltime executive appointments—9 percent under Reagan and 9.6 percent under Bush, a 50 percent decrease compared with 13.5 percent under Carter.[34] But despite the federal government's inhospitality, other political opportunities actually increased for feminists during the 1980s.

Foremost among these was the greater presence of women in state and local government. Women in state legislatures increased their numbers steadily, from 8 percent in 1975 to 18 percent in 1991; on county governing boards, women rose from 3 percent to 9 percent; and women were 10 percent of all mayors and members of municipal governing boards in 1981, compared with 4 percent in 1975.[35] In Ohio, women were 12.9 percent of state legislators, 9.5 percent of county board members, and 16.5 percent of mayors and municipal governing board members, all increases over a decade earlier.[36] Women in public office tended to be more liberal and supportive of social welfare than men, were more likely to take feminist stands, and were sometimes openly feminist; concretely, women state legislators introduced more bills dealing with women's issues.[37] Male elected officials also became somewhat more responsive to women's concerns as a "gender gap" in voting patterns appeared following the 1980 presidential election. As a result, women's issues took a larger role in the presidential campaigns of both Republicans and Democrats in 1984 and 1988.[38] The growing presence of elected officials sympathetic to feminism was a success of the women's movement; it also created openings and allies for the movement that shaped the goals and strategies activists chose.[39]

The growth in women's representation and influence at the state and local levels combined with women's movement organizations' shift to service provision to promote the development of women's policy networks.[40] As funding shifts encouraged feminist groups to seek contracts with service providers and municipal agencies, extragovernmental networks of activists, social service workers, and women in public office formed. In Columbus, these policy networks formed around the issues of violence against women, displaced homemakers, and women's mental health. In each case, existing movement organizations—such as the rape crisis center and the shelter for battered women—drew on university and state officials, contracts with municipal departments such as the police, and links with nonprofit agencies such as mental health centers and antipoverty groups. The resulting networks allowed feminist influence to penetrate into mainstream institutions.[41] Police officers did not become radical feminists, but they did receive training in how to deal with women who had been raped that was based on a radical feminist analysis. Such steps were significant and increased the influence of the women's movement in mainstream settings.

What was the impact of these changes, positive and negative, on participants? The loss of resources and resulting demise of organizations, combined with overt hostility at the federal level, were demoralizing. Even groups that successfully shifted their funding base to contract services and donations had to cut back on staff and projects and were unable to continue political advocacy at as high a level. And although public opinion polls showed continued support for feminist goals, the increasing reluctance of many women to identify as feminist and the media proclamation of the 1980s as a "postfeminist" decade left veteran activists feeling increasingly marginal.[42] "I've found the last ten years to be incredibly isolating," commented one. "[We]'ve found it very difficult to survive the Reagan years, and are just essentially holding on." Another woman who has remained an activist emphasized the fear that being an active feminist produced. She saw a retreat from politics as a safer solution, although not one she chose for herself.

> Right now, I think there's a lot of fear because of the economy, and because of the right-wing bent that the country seems to be taking. And it's much easier to closet yourself away. . . . It's like sinking into that ooze that Holly Near used to sing about. It's much easier to not rock the boat.

The declining acceptability of feminism not only affected participants' state of mind, but also made organizing more difficult. For example, a woman who works in an elementary school commented on how difficult she finds it to talk about the women's movement to her co-workers.

> You can't even talk to anybody about feminism anymore. Everybody has such a negative attitude toward the word. . . . I'm always having to say something like, "Aren't you for women's rights, equal rights?" [They say], "Yeah, I am." Well, that's what feminism's all about.

Such apathy or hostility toward the women's movement in the so-called "postfeminist" 1980s and 1990s proved demoralizing to many feminists.

In addition, the worsening economy, and in particular the recessions of the early 1980s and early 1990s, contributed to an overall reluctance to continue fulltime political activism. During the 1970s, participants were willing and able to survive on minimal earnings from employment in women's movement organizations. An employee of WAC during the late 1970s, when she earned 40 dollars a week, explained that in the 1980s, "with economic times being tough, folks [are] feeling that they can't afford to live on 40 dollars a week anymore. I think a lot of that has had a negative impact on rebuilding the movement." The shaky economic situation made individual feminists more concerned with their own financial security, and compelled them to spend more time earning a living and less time changing the world. In the face of these changes—shrinking resources, open hostility from the federal government, cultural marginalization—few of those who had been immersed in a radical feminist world during the 1970s could maintain that level of participation. Yet the radical feminist collective identity remained central to their politics and to their lives.

REMAINING RADICAL FEMINISTS

What does it mean to say that a political generation has retained a radical feminist collective identity? In terms of practices—women's real lives—it means that participants have kept in touch with each other, believe they have things in common that they do not share with others, hold fast to central tenets of feminist ideology, and think of themselves as "radical feminist" and therefore different from the mainstream. Virtually all the women I interviewed continue to identify with the term "feminist" and most with "radical feminist," and this identification remains important to them. "If someone asks me, 'Who are you?' I'm a radical feminist," declared a woman who now works for a public interest organization. "And I see radical feminism as my life's work, even though I'm spending most of my days, most of my weeks, most of my years, doing something else." Seeing oneself this way still sets women apart from the majority of the population. As one woman succinctly put it, "Like most radical feminists, I'm really odd wherever I go." This "oddness" stems from her beliefs or consciousness and from her membership in a distinct group of women's movement veterans. Radical feminists' political consciousness about the world and their construction of group boundaries both set them apart from others and bind them together. I will first discuss consciousness and how it has changed, then turn to group boundaries and their changes.

Feminist Consciousness

Developing feminist consciousness was, and is, a central task of the radical women's movement. Most movements possess a formal body of writings and scholarship that communicate interpretive frameworks and explain the group's position in the social structure, and members also interweave political under- standings into their daily life and interactions.[43] The radical women's movement of the 1970s took the meshing of politics and everyday life to a new height. In consciousness-raising groups and other settings, women discussed their experiences and politics with the aim of rethinking their understandings of the world. From this work grew elaborate theoretical frame- works that explained women's oppression, male dominance, and patriarchy, and politicized all aspects of life with the notion of the personal as political.[44]

In the late 1970s, WAC's orientation sessions were a politi- cal education for many women that included analyzing their own experiences through a feminist framework and constructing and learning theoretical analyses. As one woman explained, "It taught me everything I know about feminism, racism, class- ism." Whether individuals experienced "consciousness raising" through a consciousness-raising group, in the course of protest, or through a political orientation session, these transforming ex- periences forever changed the way a generation of feminist activ- ists looked at the world. As one succinctly put it, "It's like once you realize that the world is round, you can never again believe that it's flat."

Most women I interviewed were emphatic that the beliefs they formed during the women's movement had endured, al- though they were aware of the popular stereotype of 1960s radi- cals selling out. A woman who has not remained active in femi- nist organizations maintained that her feminist principles still exist, saying, "We continued to believe that a better world is possible, that we do need a creation of a new culture." Another woman, who became part of WAC in the mid-1970s, explained that the women's movement had a lasting and profound effect on how she looks at the world despite her belief that feminism is now in "the doldrums."

It helped me learn how to construct principles. . . . And that was in a sense the beginning of a real life for me, of choosing to live a principled life. . . . And so, even if the doldrums continue forever and ever, I am light years ahead of them, personally.

Participating in consciousness-raising groups, activist organizations, and political actions such as boycotts or pickets gave women a new interpretation of themselves and the events around them. A former member of WAC explained how her feminist framework grew from consciousness-raising groups.

Everything that happens in the world, I have a framework for understanding it. And that framework comes from the consciousness raising first, and understanding women's common experiences and my own experiences and the validity of that, and then seeing the rest of that through that validity. . . . If I didn't have a feminist framework to look at the world, I'd be, like most people, kind of adrift.

The women's movement developed highly complex interpretive frameworks. Feminist theory analyzes the sources and operation of patriarchy and male dominance, women's economic and social oppression, violence against women, the links between sexism and racism and classism, the role of homophobia in perpetuating female subordination, and a variety of other phenomena. Such analyses are widespread in written works but are not limited to the printed page. Women's movement organizations in Columbus and elsewhere discussed and refined feminist theory as part of their daily operation, and activists were sufficiently well-versed in feminist analysis to explain the reasons for a demonstration to the press, argue with each other, and interpret their own lives in light of feminist theory in consciousness-raising groups. The large number of discussion groups that emerged in the late 1970s around specific issues such as women and economics, the workplace, radical feminism, and white supremacy are a testimonial to the importance of theory to the women's movement.[45] An antirape activist explained the centrality of theory development to WAC strategy during the 1970s.

> In the [Women's Action] Collective when we were doing theory [we used the process of] trying to figure out what you are doing by starting with your metaprinciples, and then going down to your principles, and then your objectives, and your goals, and then your strategies, and then your tactics. Everything relates back up to your metaprinciple, which in the case of rape prevention was respect for persons. The easiest way to get rid of rape would be to kill all the men, but that's not respectful of persons, therefore you can't do it. You have to keep going up and down this, to try to figure out. Whatever you do is going to be principled.

Theory remained important. Many respondents reported forming discussion groups in the late 1980s and early 1990s on topics including feminist theory, women and economics, feminist art criticism, and "How do we keep hanging on?" in hard times.

Despite the complexity of feminist theory, the lasting beliefs that respondents attributed to their participation in the women's movement were a general ethic of personal responsibility, egalitarianism, skepticism, freedom, and a policy of treating others well. Just over half of the women I talked to spontaneously mentioned the Golden Rule ("Do unto others as you would have them do unto you") as part of their core values. Although the Golden Rule was part of feminist ideology earlier in the century,[46] its biblical origins make it widely known and consistent with mainstream culture. Yet longtime feminists translated it into a radical political context. The following statements by three different women illustrate the broad definitions of feminist principles.

> Just nonsexist, nonracist, nonclassist, treating people fairly, nonhomophobic, all those -isms. . . . Mostly, I just try to use the Golden Rule, I guess. I just try to treat people the same way I would want them to treat me.

That ethic of the sixties is very egalitarian, political, and realizing there's politics in everything personal. And not always believing what your government says, and questioning everything. And questioning authority above all.

I still have the same idealism. I'd still like people to be free to do what they want, and I'd still like people to have choices, and I'd like us all to be working on important issues. Bringing peace to the world, ending war.

Respondents have not forgotten or disregarded the more specific and complex elements of feminist consciousness over the years. Rather, they take for granted the application of feminist theory to specific topics. Feminist analyses of rape, for example, as an act of violence rather than sex, of sexual harassment, and of sexism in advertising, have become so intrinsic to participants' views of the world that they did not articulate them when I asked about their feminist principles.

Most respondents thought that their feminist beliefs have been a positive force in their lives, even in the 1980s and 1990s, when support for radical feminism made them increasingly politically marginal. One activist described the far-reaching effects.

I think it's made me stronger. I think it's made me really clear about who I am. It's made me very clear about what the problems are that women face in society. . . . I almost feel like my life has a theme. It's not just like I'm this little ant out there living and working with all the other ants on the anthill. There are things that I care really, really deeply about, and that sort of infuses my whole life with meaning. And I've retained that, and I think I always will.

Attributing the difficulties in one's life to structural rather than personal causes (seeing the personal as political) is an important component of oppositional consciousness and helps motivate people to participate in collective action aimed at changing their circumstances.[47] It also makes daily life easier for respondents and motivates activism, as one woman who is now a professor explained.

> If you really understand that the problems are out there, instead of blaming yourself, it makes you willing to take more risks. It makes you more motivated to fight the motherfuckers! . . . If I didn't have that base to latch onto, I would just go nuts.

A few respondents, however, felt that their feminist beliefs, although accurate, made their lives more difficult. As one woman who has not remained active in feminist organizations explained:

> From becoming active in the women's movement . . . I've gotten a different perspective on politics and how government is conducted, how business is conducted, almost everything that goes on in our society. And I don't like a lot of what I see. Much of what I see is extremely disturbing. Some of it frightens me or depresses me or angers me. And there are times that I wish I had never joined that first women's C R group and learned to look at the world differently.

Despite her regrets, she, too, has been changed irrevocably. Yet there have been some important changes in feminist consciousness as well as continuities over the past two decades.

Changes in Consciousness

Reflecting changes in the larger women's movement, respondents reported that they have become less concerned with "political correctness," or taking a strict political line on everything. Instead, they criticize some features of the 1960s–1970s movement, view feminism as broader and encompassing a variety of social reform issues, and are more aware of race and class differences. One woman articulated the declining significance of political correctness, commenting, "I don't look at life now in terms of feminism and what's politically correct and what's not." This remark must be placed in the larger social context of the 1990s, where a backlash against multiculturalism has taken the form of attacks on so-called mandated political correctness within universities.[48] It has become unfashionable and perhaps politically dangerous to appear to be overly concerned with language use, subtle forms of discrimination, verbal harassment, and the like.

Nevertheless, many participants reacted against what they perceived as the excesses and mistakes of the women's movement in the 1970s. Many singled out collective structure as an experiment they did not want to repeat. One former member of WAC proclaimed that she no longer believed in collective process.

> To be honest, we got really sick of consensual decision making. . . . Some of us feel like, I wouldn't go to a meeting if that was the way it was going to be! I don't want to be part of it, I have no patience with it.

Another WAC veteran commented in a similar vein:

> We did a lot of experimentation with the collective process, thinking that was the ideal structure, and found out that it wasn't. And now, I wouldn't be involved in a collective if you paid me a million bucks. Absolutely not!

Participants' reactions against perceived errors in the women's movement of the 1970s have led not only to disillusionment but to new and perhaps more effective organizational structures as well. "I've got to have radicals [on the board of directors] who at this point are so mellow on their own stuff that they're going to say to me, 'It's your vision, do what you want. Run with it . . . ,'" explained a woman who founded a feminist organization in the 1980s. "I wanted some way to counter the fact that we got so bound up by the end of the seventies. We've got to give

women the chance in their lifetimes to fly, and this is mine."
Further, some women commented that they simply wanted
their lives to be less serious than in the 1970s. "We had some
fun in the seventies, but we were also quite grim a lot of the
time," commented one woman about her changing approach to
activism. "And I want to have some good times for the rest of
my life. I want to do some fun things."

A second major change in the women's movement in the
1980s and 1990s has been an increase in attention to differences
among women, particularly to issues of race and class. As I
describe in Chapter 2, sustainers and others began discussing
race and class in the late 1970s. These discussions and feminist
writings by women of color changed the outlook of the entire
political generation. Longtime feminists reported a growing
awareness that women are not an undifferentiated group and
reflected critically on the race and class homogeneity of the
women's movement in the 1960s and 1970s. One woman described the changes in her consciousness as follows:

> Back in the Ohio days I would have described myself as a radical
> feminist and since then I'd describe myself as a socialist femi-
> nist. . . . [In the early 1980s] we started wondering why we
> were all white, and what was wrong. . . . So I had a heavy
> infusion of thinking about race and class. It means that instead
> of viewing women as this undifferentiated group that are op-
> pressed more or less equally by men, there are differences of class
> as well as race.

Only three of the women I interviewed reported that their identification had changed from radical to socialist feminist, but
most reported an increasing concern with race and class.

A third change is a broadening of the goals and analyses of
feminism. The women I interviewed increasingly define feminism as encompassing other struggles such as peace, environmental protection, animal rights, humanism, lesbian and gay
freedom, socialism, and human rights. One woman who has

become involved with the movement for recovery from addictions articulated the shift in her consciousness this way:

> I haven't forgotten the women's movement. But to me it's a piece of this larger issue, in which we need to think about how all people can be empowered, as who they are. It's the feminist criticism, I think, that has expanded our consciousness to the point where we can even see that there's a problem. But I guess I don't see feminism as my guiding call anymore. It's sort of part of the whole picture.

Another reflected on similar motivations for her increasing involvement in lesbian and gay and spiritual issues.

> I think that my feminism is more geared toward humanism at this point. . . . It's less geared specifically toward women. I mean, it's clearly related to those issues, that's my central focus.

Radical feminists view feminism and other issues as connected by larger principles of empowerment and respect for all people. One woman who now works in state government explained the connections she sees among such issues as feminism, the exploitation of workers, and animal rights.

> My philosophy is we're all in this together, and whatever you do to one hurts the other. You can take it down to a real narrow level that when women are not concerned about the plight of the blue-collar woman worker, the indignities they suffer hurt all of us. When you have people killing animals for sport, that hurts all of us, because that's something that a human being does that is to me wrong. And if they're capable of doing that, they're capable of having a callous soul.

Another woman who occasionally worked on environmental issues during the late 1980s explained the connection between feminism and environmental protection in practical terms.

> It doesn't matter if we make a dollar for every dollar they make if there isn't any clean water left. It doesn't matter if we have

clean water if we have to drop down to forty cents on the dollar to do it. One is not more important than the other, but they have to work together.

The broadening of concerns and the increasing incorporation of race and class issues do not signify a drastic or discontinuous shift in feminist consciousness for this generation. Rather, respondents are applying the basic principles of feminist consciousness to additional issues. In addition, women who came to the women's movement from the New Left are returning to some of their earlier concerns and examining them in a feminist light. When asked if her beliefs or view of the world had changed over the past twenty years, almost every interviewee first answered, "No," and then described some shifts. In other words, the core of feminist consciousness has remained consistent for this generation although there have been modifications. As one woman said, "I still retain my feminist principles absolutely, although they have evolved and changed."

Group Boundaries

Although participants construct their consciousness interactively in a movement context, individuals internalize it. Much of the foregoing evidence addresses this individual level. But collective identity is about far more than consciousness. At root it is about seeing oneself as part of a group, a collectivity. The mechanism by which this is accomplished is the construction of group boundaries, or symbolic and material distinctions between members of the collectivity and others.[49] Participants establish group boundaries through a symbolic system and by constructing an alternative culture or network that serves as a "world apart" from the dominant society. These manifestations of collective identity are visible in interactions among group members and in the actions of individuals; they are not limited to the attitudes or beliefs of individuals.

The notion of group boundaries may imply rigid delineation of who is permitted to be a feminist. But in fact it refers to a much more ambiguous process by which people try to make sense of their lives and of their similarities to and differences from others. Group boundaries can be rigid or permeable and vary in their importance. For longtime feminist activists, boundaries between themselves and others became less important in the 1980s even as their sense of self remained inextricably linked to feminism. Boundaries have both persisted and been transformed between feminists and nonfeminists, women and men, and different political generations. A network of relationships among feminist veterans helps them to maintain their collective identity.

Distinguishing feminists from nonfeminists. Despite rhetoric of sisterhood, the "we" defined by radical feminists twenty-five years ago did not include all women. The labels "feminist" and "radical feminist" distinguished between women who adopted such labels and those who did not. For participants, a transformed individual identity as a woman meant seeing oneself as a member of the collectivity "feminists"; adopting "feminist" or "radical feminist" as a public identity signified membership in the group of women who had experienced such a transformation.

Despite the continuing importance of feminism for self-definition, the distinction between feminists and nonfeminists has become less significant in two ways. First, many women I interviewed said that they are less likely to form negative impressions of people who do not identify publicly as feminists. As one woman who now leads workshops on sexual harassment put it:

> I'm much kinder to women who aren't feminists and who are deferring to men when it's clearly against their best interests. I'm much better in discussing it with her and helping her overcome that than I would have been five years ago. Fifteen years

ago I would have kind of jumped down her throat, and she would have had to avoid me. [*Laughs*]

Another woman, now a lawyer, remarked that she, too, is less critical of those who differ politically from her.

> I used to size people up in two minutes concerning their politics, and if their politics weren't right, I didn't have any use for them. I would cast them aside and be on my way. . . . And that was stupid, and I've stopped doing that.

In other words, the boundary between feminists and nonfeminists has become more permeable, and feminists are willing to cooperate more with those outside the group.

Second, many longtime feminists reported that they are less likely to see themselves as part of a common group with someone simply because she calls herself a feminist. As one professor of women's studies declared:

> One thing I know now is that just because someone calls herself, or himself, a feminist does not mean that person's values or behavior or way of operating in the world is going to be something that I identify with. . . . So I'm much less influenced by someone marching up to me and announcing they're a feminist. I'm much more wanting to watch how that person operates before I make a decision about whether I'm really in league with them.

Another state government employee commented similarly that she no longer trusts women simply because they call themselves feminists.

> I'm not saying that all feminists are wonderful. In fact I no longer accept people's self-definition of feminism, having had problems and having been stabbed in the back by professed feminists.

Their own adoption of the public identity of feminist remains important to these women, but their interactions with others are far less influenced than in the past by whether the others adopt a feminist label.

Language use is an additional marker of the boundary between feminists and nonfeminists. The women's movement developed a sweeping critique of sexism in language that brought about substantial change in language use.[50] Derogatory terms used to refer to women—chick, cunt, bitch, girl, and so forth—were a special target of feminists in the initial years of the movement and have remained so since then. Like the label "feminist," the use of language remains an important boundary marker, but, as one woman indicated, failure to conform to feminist terminology (indicating "outsider" status) carries fewer consequences than it did during the 1970s.

> I paid too much attention to language [in the 1970s] as a means to assess politics. I think language is important, and to this day I'd have real problems having a close personal friendship with somebody who referred to women as chicks. But it got to be so crazy, and if people didn't use your exact terminology they were an enemy.

Other feminists suggested that even their own use of language has changed to include terms that would previously have been used only by outsiders, as this lawyer commented:

> I can remember the time that my tongue would have rotted in my cheeks before I would have said the word "girl" in relation to a woman at all. And at least now I've gotten to the point where I can joke with some of my friends and at least use the word. But I can't even imagine being in a meeting and talking about a young woman as being a girl. That still would really make me nuts.

In short, what would previously have been a fairly serious boundary violation has become acceptable, but only within limits and in certain settings.

Distinguishing women from men. Another means by which radical feminists established boundaries in the 1970s was by emphasizing women's difference from men and denigrating many masculine traits. Some feminists made this argument in essentialist terms—the view that the differences between women and men reflected the sexes' innate natures. Many others, however, viewed the differences as a socially constructed product of socialization and structural position. One woman explained how being a feminist kept her from forming close relationships with men during the 1970s.

> It made it impossible to be close to men anymore, because . . . I was entering a universe that [they] couldn't come into. . . . All men became aliens when I realized that I didn't have to live as though I approved of patriarchy. They just can't relate.

Most feminist veterans reported that their close friendships and their political alliances are still primarily with women. Like other boundary markers, however, the division between women and men has lessened. Many lesbians reported increasing political work and a feeling of commonality with gay men. Both lesbian and heterosexual participants indicated a tension between a continuing view of men as untrustworthy and different from themselves and increasing cooperative contact with men. This woman's comment illustrates the ambivalence.

> I have to deal with men on a day-by-day basis, so I do deal with them. I'm not sure that I like them or I trust them any more than I did twenty years ago. But I've also learned that there are really some very, very good men out there who do try and are very supportive. And I don't think when I was truly involved with the women's movement that I would have admitted that, at all.

Like the distinction between feminists and nonfeminists, the boundary between women and men is more permeable than it was ten years ago.

Two kinds of changes can occur in how challenging groups construct their boundaries when their social movement falls on hard times. One model is illustrated by the National Woman's Party in the 1950s, which developed an elite-sustained structure.[51] Boundaries become rigidified, increasing the commitment of a small cadre of activists but keeping out new recruits and allies. The second possibility, which has occurred in the Columbus women's movement, is that boundaries may become more permeable and differences less salient. Although members still see radical feminists as a distinct group, they are more willing to cross the boundaries between their group and others, opening up the possibility for the coalitions that have developed in the 1980s.

Accompanying this development is a reframing of emotions, from anger to acceptance or openness. Almost everyone I interviewed said she felt an increasing "mellowness," more tolerance for people with different political views or lifestyles, less stridency, a growth in spirituality, and an increasing reluctance to be motivated by anger. One woman's comments were typical.

> In the early seventies, when I was eating and breathing and sleeping feminist activity, I was so angry! I was really fueled by fury a lot of the time. And at this point in my life, to be angry is too hard. I just can't do it. It doesn't feel good to be angry, and I also had the realization that I didn't like the way things went for me when I was angry. When you're angry, other people are intimidated and they don't want to do what you want them to do. It really sets up an opposition.

Relationships among feminists, once stormy, calmed somewhat for these women. "Now I'm much more into why can't we all get along, and getting people to deal more on a one-to-one or in small groups of people," explained one. Many women saw their changed attitudes as a function of age, as this woman did.

> When you reach your thirties and forties, you have a more overall view of life. I don't in any way think that I have become less radical or that I have mellowed, I think that's not a proper use of your greater age. It's just that I have a wider view of things

and I'm more tolerant of other people because I'm more compassionate now than I was then.

It is difficult to know how much of this change is actually due to age, but "mellowing" in political attitudes is not biologically determined. Years of experience and the need for unity in a hostile environment made feminists less angry and more willing to compromise.

Generational boundaries. Unlike the differences between feminists and nonfeminists and between women and men, which have been socially reconstructed and minimized, the women I interviewed perceived a variety of differences between themselves and people who did not share their experiences in the women's movement of the 1960s and 1970s because of age or politics. One woman who was very active in lesbian feminist protest during the mid- to late 1970s described her perception of younger lesbians who had not shared her experience in the women's movement.

> When I am involved with women who have not been through the experience I've been through, I feel a little bit sad for them. I feel that they have lost a major part of what it is to be a feminist, and to be a lesbian. . . . And it's hard to convey to them what feminism is, let alone what lesbian feminism is, in the sense that I learned it, and how encompassing it is.

Another veteran of the earliest days of W L, who now works in a mainstream corporation, felt that her social movement participation set her apart from people of different ages.

> I talk to some of these young kids at work, and it's like they don't know anything about the politics in El Salvador, they don't know anything about anything. They've just been yuppified. And they don't see the big political picture. Or people that are ten or fifteen years older. It's like [they say], "What's wrong with you?" when I start ranting about politics, or Bush, or Reagan.

Movement veterans symbolically underscore the importance of remaining true to one's political commitments by telling "cautionary tales" about women who were formerly radical feminists and have "sold out" in the 1980s and 1990s. One woman, who is employed by a nonprofit organization and owns a modest house, told such a tale.

> I'm not a big consumer or a real high materialist. But I know some women who went the other way. I know one woman who makes a lot of money, well over a hundred thousand dollars a year. And she used to be in WAC. . . . And now she's just very different.

Another told a similar story about a woman who "went from being a radical lesbian to being a Reagan Republican who wanted to get rich." A variation on this theme concerns a rumored social group for professional lesbians, including former radical feminists, that limits membership to women above a certain income. A sense of identity and commonality is reinforced by those who are different. Thus, stories of women who have sold out serve to support others' status as "dedicated feminists" and symbolically underscore the boundary between those who have retained commitment and those who have abandoned it.

Lesbian feminist identity. Throughout the 1970s lesbians became more visible in the radical women's movement; lesbian feminist ideology developed, and in practice activists often conflated the categories "lesbian" and "radical feminist." By the end of the decade, heterosexual women were a shrinking minority in radical feminist groups at the same time that a lesbian feminist subculture was growing. Large women's movement organizations embraced lesbian issues, but animosities remained between heterosexual and lesbian women. The new source of conflict was some heterosexual women's charge that lesbians dominated the movement. "I think that straight women have been pushed out of the women's movement by lesbian women," complained one heterosexual respondent, "and it's been pretty ugly. . . . The women's movement is the only place in the world where women have to come out of the closet as a heterosexual."[52] Most of the heterosexual women I interviewed did not share this sentiment, but many felt left out of a predominantly lesbian movement. During the 1970s, the celebration of womanhood had made heterosexual women welcome as part of the mostly lesbian "women's community." But by the 1980s and 1990s, lesbians were increasingly unwilling to soft-pedal either their sexuality or their political demands. Both lesbian and heterosexual identity became more salient in the radical women's movement as a result.

At the same time, divisions among lesbians diminished. In the early and mid-1970s, lesbian feminists were often critical of longtime lesbians for "mimicking heterosexuality" in butch–fem roles, viewing women as sex objects, and not participating in feminist activities. For example, a fundraising talent show in Columbus attempted to bring the bar and political worlds together. A humorous skit in which a woman adopted a "ditzy" feminine character, enjoyed by bar women, was loudly protested by political women, who disrupted the performance arguing that it parodied women. The talent show ended prematurely, and the alliance between the two groups stalled. By the late 1970s and early 1980s, however, the local lesbian bar, Summit Station (commonly known as "Jack's"), sometimes hosted feminist fundraisers and became more of a hangout for lesbian feminists. At the same time feminists softened critiques of traditional butch–fem relationships and subculture and increasingly recognized political resistance by lesbians outside the formal women's movement. One longtime lesbian activist described the changes in relations between lesbian feminists and other groups of lesbians.

[In the 1970s] the community was fairly well segregated, so that the political community was separate from the softball community and was separate from the community of teachers. . . . Over time those sort of walls came down, among those groups at least, as women aged. . . . [Now] there's a great deal of mix and less separation between and among those women that define themselves variously.

Conflicts between bar and political lesbians continued to decrease throughout the 1980s, although some divisions remain.

In addition to the lessening of distinctions among lesbians, the division between lesbians and gay men has become more permeable in the 1980s, particularly with the rise of acquired immune-deficiency syndrome (AIDS) and lesbians' extensive participation in the AIDS movement.[53] One woman who had been part of Lesbian Peer Support commented that she had become involved with a local AIDS organization because

> for the first time I identified that this is happening to my tribe. These are my people, and I need to stand with them now, because this is important.

"My people" means lesbians and gay men for her now, whereas in the 1970s it meant women. This is not simply a change in political activities, but a shift in sense of self; it represents a new view of who is like and unlike her. The same woman explained further that her new sense of "we" with gay men proved troubling at times.

> It feels pretty strange to be working and identifying with gay people instead of lesbians, or with feminist women. Sometimes I worry, maybe I should not be putting so much energy into this gay male thing. Because let's face it, lesbians are barely affected by AIDS.

Another woman who has been active on gay and lesbian issues since the 1970s explained her continuing identification with gay men.

> It doesn't have to do as much with an identity of being a woman as of being a gay and lesbian sort of outcast. . . . That's more

> direct and more related to my own set of things than other kinds of issues like childcare or abortion.

Seeing lesbianism, rather than womanhood, as the defining element of her identity is a significant change.

A final notable pattern is illustrated by three participants who identified as lesbian but reported having sexual relationships with men in the 1980s for the first time in two decades. Two of the three continued to identify themselves as lesbians, whereas the third identified as bisexual. One lesbian, who described her affair with a man as "totally peculiar," saw affairs with men as a widespread phenomenon, commenting that she has "discovered since that a whole lot of us, lesbians, went through a phase like that." This "phase" occurred as lesbian feminist identity became more fluid, permitting sexual experimentation without the stigma of political betrayal. At the same time, it may be that as the feminist community weakened in the early 1980s, the ideal of being "woman-identified" came to seem less real and more difficult to maintain. In the early 1990s the counterintuitive notion of "lesbians who sleep with men" spread: The lesbian writer Jan Clausen published an article in a gay publication about her relationship with a man, singer Holly Near wrote in her autobiography about being a lesbian but having sex with men, and students at OSU formed a support group for "lesbians who just happen to be in relationships with politically correct men."[54] Most of the women I interviewed still believed that sexuality was linked to politics and that the political implications of being a lesbian who slept with men were different from those of being a lesbian who did not. But the borders between lesbians and nonlesbians were undeniably blurred. The debate over whether one can identify as a lesbian and still be sexually involved with men is, at core, about collective identity: What behavior must one exhibit (or refrain from) in order to be considered a lesbian? A feminist?

The feminist network. Veterans of the Columbus women's movement have maintained an elaborate and meaningful network that makes them more than an abstract political generation; they are a community. The network is a material embodiment of group boundaries. Many participants kept in touch with each other, and even when they had not been in touch, often kept tabs on each other's locations and activities.[55] One woman, for example, told me that each year she checked the new phone book listing for another activist to make sure that she was still at the same address, although they had not talked in years. Of course, not all women who were active in the Columbus radical women's movement have kept in touch with each other. More peripheral members, those who have become conservative, former lesbians, and those who were "trashed out" are all less likely to have retained contacts with others. But even though the network is partial and has many broken links, many women are integrated into it in some way.

In part, the network exists because women's political commitments still make them inclined to work together on social change issues. One woman who recently ran for political office noted that a former member of the Women's Caucus at OSU was the first person to send a contribution to her campaign. Another woman contacted a fellow activist who had established a new feminist organization and took publicity about the new organization to a local conference. A national feminist organization founded in the 1980s by a veteran of the Columbus women's movement now has a board of directors that includes several women who participated in feminist organizations together in the 1970s.

In addition, the network remains important because of the emotional and intellectual closeness that grows from sharing a common important experience. Many longtime feminists reported that friendships they formed in the women's movement of the 1970s have remained important in the 1980s and 1990s. One woman explained the quality of such relationships.

Some of these people, I've known them for so long now that we can refer back to a certain event or series of events with just a word or two. It's that kind of communication you can have with someone you've known for a long time, so that we don't really discuss it, we know what we mean. And we get that kind of good feeling that you have with people that you've been through a lot with and you've known for so long.

Another woman described formalizing important relationships through the creation of what she terms "chosen kinship."

I've been working on my own chosen family . . . [and] I run workshops for women on kinship and chosen kinship. . . . At this point, I have a ritual and I take people in only if they seem to be really staying powers in my life. I don't do this lightly.

Although her chosen family is not limited to women with whom she was active in the 1970s, several such women are part of her network. The formality of the notion of chosen kinship emphasizes the importance of a network for establishing group boundaries.

Such relationships serve to sustain commitment to feminist politics and collective identity. One woman who works in a nonfeminist setting explained that in order to retain feminist commitment when social pressures urge her to be absorbed into the political mainstream, "I surround myself with all my friends . . . people that I think still have a political world ethic about them." Another woman who is in a committed relationship with a woman she met in the Columbus women's movement of the 1970s said simply:

Without each other I don't know how we'd be surviving. . . . One of the things we are for each other more than anything else is a reality check. Without the reality check, we could fall off the edge. In the 1980s, I certainly could have fallen off the edge if [she] hadn't been here.

Perhaps, in the end, the "reality check" is the most important contribution of the network: the reminder that, despite opposition and sometimes invisibility, feminists are neither crazy nor alone.

The women who were the furthest removed from the organized women's movement and whose feminist identity was the least important to them were those who had lost contact with the feminist network. One woman, who had formerly identified as a lesbian and had later married a man, reported that her resulting loss of membership in the lesbian community made it difficult to remain a feminist activist at the same level. Three other women who had moved to conservative parts of the country similarly found it difficult to remain active feminists because of the loss of a feminist network.

Because the lesbian feminist movement remained vibrant and large in the 1980s and 1990s and built a social movement community and political culture, lesbians often were able to maintain their commitment more easily than heterosexual women. The lesbian feminist community has aided lesbians in maintaining a feminist collective identity and has provided support and opportunities for practicing political principles in daily life and mobilizing collective action. As a result, fewer of the lesbians than the heterosexual women I interviewed moved into mainstream careers or lifestyles, and more lesbians have continued to participate in organized collective efforts for social change. The four women I interviewed who have remained fulltime radical feminist activists are all lesbians. Even for lesbians, however, the highly politicized activist community of the 1970s no longer exists.

The loss of community that accompanied the decline of organized feminism in the early 1980s left all participants feeling a sense of loss, alienation, and nostalgia, and deprived them of the networks and culture that supported their collective identity and translated it into mobilization. Male participants in the civil rights and student movements of the 1960s described similar feelings of dislocation.[56] Both in terms of the friendships they developed and the sense of shared political mission in life, participants felt that their experience in the women's movement of the 1970s in Columbus differed sharply from the communities of the 1990s. One woman expressed her nostalgia for the friendships she formed in the 1970s.

> I have never had the friendships, the significance, the meaning, everything that you could want in relationships, since then. . . . We saw ourselves as family. And I have never had that kind of family since, and I don't think I ever will.

Another woman compared the ease of making friends in a social movement culture with the difficulty she faces now.

> I find it very difficult to keep friends these days, because I don't run into anybody naturally. Like I used to just every day go into work [at WAC], you'd see all these people. You'd make plans to do things; it was just part of the flow. Now it's like you never see anybody, and you've got to call somebody up and make plans, it's this big effort.

The close-knit nature of women's movement culture fostered conflict, but it was nevertheless an important source of strength and continuing commitment for members, as this participant in WAC commented:

> We lived and worked together, literally. . . . It was just too much. You couldn't get away from anybody. And yet, the closeness of it was just not replicable.

Even in the absence of that "closeness," longtime feminists continued to rely on their connections to one another in the 1980s.

The clearest examples of how networks establish group boundaries come from separatist movements or those with separatist elements, such as utopian communes of the 1800s or the black nationalist movement of the 1960s.[57] In such cases, movements create "a world apart" from the dominant culture in which participants can redefine their group. Feminists of the 1960s and 1970s have not created such a world apart in the present. Rather, they have dispersed, holding jobs where they may be one of only a few feminists. Yet friendship ties, political cooperation, and a sense of shared past bind them together.

THE SURVIVAL OF FEMINIST COMMITMENT

The antifeminist backlash affected how longtime feminists understand themselves and their group. Changes in the external environment have not *determined* changes in feminist collective identity. They have, however, provided the context and events that feminists try to understand and interpret. Despite the hostility and opposition they encounter, the women's movement of the 1960s and 1970s forever marked participants' understanding of the world and their own place in it. Of course, not every participant in the women's movement has retained her radical feminist identity and beliefs to the same degree. A few women repudiate their earlier beliefs, and others vary in how much their outlooks have changed over the years.

Regardless of how women think of themselves and what they believe is true about the world, their daily lives have changed greatly. It is the conflict between this generation's enduring radical feminism and their limited opportunities for action in a constricting economy and hostile political climate that shaped feminist actions in the 1980s and early 1990s. This loss of political community, for most women, made it more difficult to continue externally oriented activism. Faced with the loss of the community that had sustained their activism, they turned to their jobs and their families, attempting to continue living their lives in a political way.

4 :: KEEPING THE FAITH:

WORKING FOR

SOCIAL CHANGE

> I think my essential orientation [is] to believe that there's something fundamentally wrong with our entire social structure and our entire society, so in that sense I'm still a radical feminist. But in terms of the way that I operate, and the sort of job that I have, and what I aspire to, there's no way you can be inside an institution and be a radical feminist. I'm a liberal feminist, in terms of what I do.

SO SAID A WOMAN in her late thirties who joined WAC in the late 1970s, was very active in that group, in the Association of Women Students, and in Central Ohio Lesbians, and came to believe that radical social transformation was necessary. But fifteen years later she worked in higher education, confessed to shaving her legs in order to gain credibility on her job, and noted that she occasionally felt uncomfortable with her feminist students' militance. Another woman, a few years older, also joined WAC in the late 1970s, where she served briefly as house manager and was a staunch defender of "woman-only space" against criticisms from the mixed-sex Left. By 1990 she worked for the state government and argued that the incremental changes she promoted in state programs were important. A third woman had been a faculty member at OSU active in the fight to establish the Center for Women's Studies; over the years, she gained tenure and promotion and was a respected voice in university administration. Yet another woman, one of the first organizers of WL in Columbus, spent many years marginally employed and making political art, but now works full time for a mainstream corporation.

These stories, like those of most of the women I interviewed, could be read to show the transitory nature of political commitment or the deep-rooted desire of individuals for economic security and social respectability as they age. They could be interpreted as pointing to the decline of the feminist challenge, or at least to activists' abandonment of the strong commitment of their youth. Yet such interpretations tell a partial and misleading tale. All of the women described above, and most of the others I talked to, continue to act on their political beliefs in their occupations and in their daily lives. Working for social change remains central to their actions and guides many of their choices. The venues of feminist activism have shifted, but veterans of the women's movement—and thus the movement as a whole—continue to have an impact on a broad range of social institutions, despite the fact that activists' ideals sometimes conflict with the actions that are possible in their present environment.

Participation in social movements can take a variety of forms. Most studies have defined social movement participation as involvement in collective action organized around a movement's goals and constituency, oriented toward changing social and political institutions.[1] Yet such activity is only one type of work for social change. The participants who were central to the women's movement of the 1970s have not all remained immersed in feminist organizations in the 1980s and 1990s. Because they nevertheless continue to challenge male domination in a variety of ways, it is apparent that we need a broader definition of social movement participation. Patricia Hill Collins provides the basis for such a reconceptualization.[2] She proposes in her work on black feminism that resistance to domination can occur at three levels: individual consciousness, culture, and social structure.

When a movement is at its peak, as radical feminism was during the 1970s, the struggle takes place simultaneously at all three levels. But even social movements that survive over many decades, like the women's movement, are not able to maintain a constant level of social-structural resistance. Direct confrontation with the dominant social system is costly in material resources and labor, and is often neither effective nor feasible when political powers are hostile or economic conditions are tight. The 1980s were a time when the women's movement was relatively quiescent at the social-structural level. Women's movement organizations did mount some important challenges in the political arena, but much of the movement's activity was located in the realms of culture and consciousness. Following Hill Collins, I will distinguish between two broad categories of social movement actions: the social-structural confrontations that students of social movements have discussed under the rubric "strategies and tactics," and politicized actions in everyday life that aim to transform individuals' consciousness and create alternative cultures.[3]

Collective actions aimed primarily at structural transformation in the traditional political or economic arenas generally have been organized by formal women's movement organizations, but sometimes have been organized by informal or ad hoc groups. During the 1980s and 1990s, the level of social-structural confrontation by the women's movement decreased. At the same time, the actions of all the micro-cohorts who led the earlier radical feminist movement changed. Some feminists who led the movement in the 1960s and 1970s have played key roles in contemporary women's movement organizations, but most have not. They continue to act on a commitment to feminism in a variety of ways, but their participation takes different forms than it did twenty years ago.

The women I talked to are less intensely involved in collective feminist activities such as women's movement organizations and are more likely to act individually through their work and daily lives. Of the 34 women I talked to, only 7 had no involvement in women's movement organizations at the time of the interview. Of the remaining 27 women, 13 had their only contact with the organized women's movement through their employment or through making donations to feminist organizations, and 14 continued to participate on a volunteer basis in feminist organizations in the late 1980s and early 1990s. However, even these 14 participate in substantially different ways now than during the movement's heyday.

Whereas in the 1970s virtually all of the women I interviewed were leaders or core members of feminist organizations and spent much of their time at work and leisure on feminist activities, their participation now is much more limited. Four of the women I interviewed are still leaders or core members in women's movement organizations. The others participate in feminist activity in a more sporadic and peripheral way: by attending (but not organizing) demonstrations; serving on the boards of feminist organizations such as Planned Parenthood and battered women's shelters; attending occasional women's studies conferences; joining women's caucuses in their professional associations; contributing money to women's organizations; and attending occasional meetings of NOW or the National Abortion Rights Action League. Clearly, the women I interviewed are still participating in the women's movement. Yet their participation is limited compared with their own activities in the 1970s and with the actions of newcomers who are now the movement's core activists.

Even as movement veterans withdrew from organized feminism, they continued to weave their politics into their daily lives, challenging undesirable assumptions and prescriptions about women and their position both directly and symbolically. Feminists from this political generation challenge dominant definitions of women in their workplaces through jobs oriented toward social change and in the way they structure their relationships, spend their leisure time, dress and behave, and raise children. It is not surprising, given the continuing centrality of feminism to veterans' sense of self and understanding of the world, that this collective identity would remain influential in their daily lives. To be "a feminist" implies living one's life in particular ways, whether those are certain behaviors, appearances, habits, or styles of expression. These are important both in public settings where people not part of the group are present and in private settings with other group members.[4] Incorporating feminist principles into everyday life enables women to transform the larger culture, create alternative cultures, and reshape their individual consciousness and lives. This politicization of everyday life, which relies as heavily on symbolic challenges as on direct confrontation, is often termed "identity politics." Of course, actions aimed at symbolically redefining womanhood have an indirect effect on social policies regarding women, while changes in women's legal status affect popular understandings of what it means to be a woman. "Identity politics," as we shall see, is about far more than individual identities.

EMPLOYMENT AND POLITICS

A feminist artist explained, "The difference between then and now is that then I did stuff mostly as a volunteer and now I do it professionally." Like her, most former leaders in the radical women's movement now act on their feminist convictions and effect social change through their jobs. During the 1970s, most of the women I talked to had been employed at least briefly by women's movement organizations; only 5 of the 34 had not.[5] They were employed as researchers, organizers, and educators for Women Against Rape and the Community Action Strategies to Stop Rape (CASSR) project; as house managers or development coordinators for WAC; as instructors, researchers, and administrators in the Center for Women's Studies at Ohio State; and in various other organizations. The CASSR grant and some smaller grants enabled WAC to hire paid workers and a house manager. In addition, CASSR received funding for employees through the CETA job training program, which existed in the late 1970s and paid the wages of formerly unemployed workers hired by certain social service agencies. Instead of simply hiring CETA workers sent by the employment agency, CASSR used the program to hire members who had been unemployed for the requisite number of weeks.

For nearly one-third of the interviewees (11 women), employment in women's movement organizations or women's studies represents virtually their entire employment history. But the remaining 23 had to make the transition from employment in the women's movement to other ways of earning a living. For most, this occurred around 1980. As they graduated from college or began looking for on-going employment throughout the 1970s, and as the women's movement changed and declined, they looked for jobs that would allow them to continue working toward social change.

As they searched for jobs, feminist veterans did not follow societal prescriptions about women's work. Instead, they worked in nontraditional occupations or ones that would allow them to pursue social change through their paid work. The occupational makeup of the women I interviewed is markedly different from that of women overall. All are employed outside the home, as compared with 43.3 percent of the general population of women in their age cohort.[6] They are considerably more likely than the general population of women to be employed in traditionally male occupations. Whereas 70 percent of white women college graduates in the population are employed in managerial or professional occupations, 94 percent of the interviewees' occupations fall into this category. The longtime feminists are underrepresented in female-dominated occupations. Twenty-four percent of all white women with college degrees are employed in technical, sales, and administrative occupations, which includes traditionally female-dominated retail and office jobs; yet only one woman I talked to (3 percent) holds a job in this category.[7] Because the women's movement has aimed to foster independence among women and to discourage economic dependence on men, it is not surprising that participants are self-supporting and employed outside the home; because the movement has challenged the exclusion of women from traditionally male occupations, it is not surprising that many movement veterans have sought employment outside women's traditional sphere.

Veterans of the women's movement not only chose nontraditional occupations for women; they also sought to merge their political and professional lives by finding work that contributed to social change. As former core activists, they were accustomed to organizing their lives—including how they earned their money—around the women's movement. Consequently, although they have chosen a range of occupations, 19 of the 34 are in jobs that are explicitly feminist. Of the remaining 15, 3 work in explicitly political jobs where feminist concerns are relevant, but not at center stage. Others chose their occupations for reasons growing from their involvement in the women's movement, and many of the others incorporate their politics into their work implicitly. Six of the 34 are now faculty members in colleges or universities. Four are currently feminist therapists, and another 4 are practicing lawyers. Three are employed in governmental agencies, two of whom deal primarily with women's issues. Of the remaining women, 2 are working for social change organizations associated with movements other than the women's movement; 2 earn their living as feminist artists; and 1 is a women's martial arts and self-defense instructor. The remaining 12 are in jobs that are not explicitly related to the women's movement.

Academic feminists are the largest group in the sample. Of the 6 faculty members, 2 are in English, 2 in sociology, 1 in Latin American studies, and 1 in economics. All either currently have joint appointments with Women's Studies departments or had such appointments in the past and continue to focus on feminist issues within their disciplines. These women see both teaching and research as related to feminist goals. Teaching provides an opportunity to expose students to a feminist analysis and challenge students' preconceptions about women's status. "I know that I influence people strongly, and I'm sure it's for the better," said an English professor who teaches courses in women's literature. "And I make feminists out of people who were wishy-washy to begin with." An economics professor described the process of feminist consciousness raising that her students go through in her classes. Explaining that most students enter her course believing that structural barriers to women's achievement in the business world have been eradicated, she described their response to course material on topics such as women in business and comparable worth:

> Sometimes they really begin to think about the issues. [In] the course on women and the economy, at the beginning of the semester, they're like, "Oh my god, this is the weirdest thing I've ever heard!" By the end of the semester a lot of them have really begun to think about it.

Feminist faculty also select research topics based in part on political interests and concerns. Faculty members' research topics include the economic prospects of teenage mothers, the writings of Toni Morrison, feminist literary criticism, women and ethnicity, and lesbian feminism. One woman helped to found a press that publishes work by and about women of color. In addition to teaching and research, feminists in academia, as in other professions, serve on committees dealing with issues like affirmative action and cultural diversity in the curriculum.

The growth of women's studies and of feminist studies in other disciplines including sociology, history, anthropology, economics, political science, English, literature, film studies, and social work is a direct response to the women's movement. Many of the activists who pushed for the formation of Women's Studies at OSU as students or as junior faculty members have remained in the academy and built careers around feminist studies. Along with veterans of the civil rights, student, and New Left movements of the 1960s, feminists have transformed higher education, calling attention to the political implications of all research and teaching and legitimizing the study of previously neglected groups such as women and people of color. One English professor described the changes in her discipline:

> English has just totally broken open as a result of poststructuralist theory. Feminism is much more possible to do here—in fact it's almost required. . . . English and literary studies are just overwhelmed by feminism, and . . . all the men are doing it too.

Similar trends exist, to varying degrees, in other disciplines as well. Academic feminists have formed professional associations that link like-minded scholars and have some influence on larger disciplines, including the National Women's Studies Association and caucuses within the American Sociological Association, the American Historical Association, and other disciplinary associations. Feminists are not a majority in the academy, however, nor are they in most positions of power. Even as they achieved reforms in the curriculum and incorporated politics into their own teaching and research, a backlash against multicultural curricula and "tenured radicals" grew outside the academy.[8] Despite this growing criticism, academia has seen substantial changes because of the women's movement, making it a relatively hospitable place for feminists.

The legal profession has also been popular among feminist veterans, again because it seemed to offer a chance to combine work for social change with paid employment. A typical respondent explained that her decision to go to law school was politically motivated and that she stated in her law school application "that what I wanted to do with my law degree was to further women's rights and minorities' [rights] and affirmative action." Another woman related similar reasons for selecting law as a profession, commenting that she "saw the law as a profession that allowed the nonconformist, the do-gooder, the progressive person to carve out a niche for him or herself without being punished."

The four practicing lawyers I interviewed have worked on cases dealing with a variety of feminist issues including civil rights, employment discrimination, pornography, violence against women, lesbian and gay rights, and abortion rights. For example, one woman represented battered women and worked to get domestic violence protection orders extended to gay men and lesbians whose partners beat them. However, as in other professions, some feminist lawyers faced conflicts between politics and professional survival. One lawyer related the difficulty of balancing her political convictions with her need to earn a living.

> I went into law school with that idealism of helping women, and certainly a great civil rights bent, until I realized the realities of working with women and civil rights issues. That sometimes the people who need it the most can afford it the least, and I certainly couldn't afford to pro bono my way through life. I had to make a living and I had to pay my overhead. It was a hard lesson to learn that law was a business, and that cut severely into a lot of the idealism that I brought going into law school.

Despite such conflicts, the lawyers were among the most politically active in the sample and felt more engaged with politics than many of the others. Like feminist scholars, lawyers have formed professional associations to address their concerns. For example, one respondent helped to found the Ohio Human Rights Bar Association, which educates lawyers about law relating to AIDS and gay and lesbian rights. One woman I interviewed has been elected judge and has been quite successful because of, not despite, her progressive political connections.

Like the law and academia, psychology is another profession that offers therapists the autonomy to shape their practices in accordance with feminist concerns. Four of the women I talked to earn their livings as therapists or counselors, including three in private practice and one elementary school guidance counselor. In consciousness-raising groups and by reading and developing feminist theory during the 1960s and 1970s, they learned to link women's personal difficulties with political domination and misogyny; now, in their practice as therapists, they see themselves as combatting patriarchy at the individual level. One woman described her work as "more on a micro level," and another commented that she spent her time encouraging women to be more self-confident in the face of a society that denies women self-esteem. Feminist therapists' specialties focus on women's issues, including women and AIDS, eating disorders, sexual abuse, career counseling for professional women, and relationship counseling for lesbian couples. The psychologist who specializes in eating disorders explained the link with feminism:

> I very much believe that in helping women recover from eating disorders I'm making a contribution to the women's movement. . . . It feels like it ties together a great deal of my earlier years. So many of the things that I did [in the women's movement] got me ready to be a specialist in eating disorders.

The woman who works as an elementary school guidance counselor, although she has less autonomy than those in private practice, deals with students' difficulties by drawing, in part, on a feminist understanding of their lives. For example, she described one girl who stopped doing her homework or paying attention in class. When questioned, the girl explained that an older male relative told her that "he would never marry a girl who was smarter than he was" and that she had decided "she wasn't going to be smart." The counselor's response drew on feminist analysis and emphasized gender equality.

> I told her all this stuff. Talked to her about partners in marriage, and why would a guy want to be with somebody who was a burden—just the general feminist perspective.

The girl's mother also prevailed on the relative to retract his statement, and the girl apparently returned to her studies. Such successes are both small-scale and monumental; the nature of their work both allows feminist therapists to have a direct impact on people's lives and restricts them to combatting sexism in small increments, individual by individual.

Outside the more autonomous professions, feminists sought work in a variety of other institutions. Despite the relative inaccessibility of the federal government to feminists in the 1980s, some state and local governmental agencies remained more hospitable. A number of feminists took jobs in state and local government, working in agencies that administered programs of benefit to women. In Australia, where feminists have made greater inroads into the government, the term "femocrat" is popularly used to describe such feminists within governmental bureaucracies.[9] Three women I interviewed found jobs as femocrats. One headed the state Women's Information Center, which coordinated and distributed information about women's issues and resources, responding to questions from individuals and groups on topics ranging from credit and employment discrimination to sexual harassment. Another administered a program providing services to elders, mostly women, within the state Department of Aging, and the third directed a state program of crime victim compensation.

All of these government employees organized their work and

the programs they directed around feminist goals and principles. For example, one woman explained that, despite her frustration with the time-consuming nature of collective process in the women's movement, it had taught her "how to run a meeting, how to have a discussion, how to have an argument, how to be direct." In her current government job, she tries to incorporate collective process in how she administers her program, with mixed results.

> It's really been fascinating to me to see how . . . the women are just fine with what's happening, but the men are very impatient, and much more [saying] sort of, "We've got to get to the end, let's get to the end and make decisions."

One woman explained that she attempted to restructure how health services are delivered to older people in order to "[put] a lot of management control in the hands of the folks at the local level." Another saw her work with crime victim compensation as a way of empowering poor people, minorities, and women, who are often victims of crime.

In some states, and during some administrations, feminists were seen as an asset in state agencies, and were hired in part for their social movement experience. For example, one woman explained why she was recently hired:

> Most of [the people that work there] are pretty white, middle-class, and unaware of class or race differences or of poverty. [They hired me] to make inroads into their way of thinking. . . . The program had its roots in the feminist movement. [The man who hired me] could see the roots of the program in what I had done in the feminist movement that allowed the program to exist.

In many cases, though, working within the governmental system proved frustrating and limiting. A woman who heads a small state agency recounted her difficulties:

You can get really frustrated when you see how the state's money is spent on things. When you know you can document you're actually helping people here, and you're sort of this little stepsister agency. I mean, everything we have is hand-me-down.

Another woman complained that when a Democratic governor was replaced with a Republican, and her program was dismantled, she lost all the gains her agency had built up over eight years. Yet she persisted in her commitment to working within "the system." She explained that when she finished graduate school in the early 1980s and chose to become a government employee:

I took my values and I infiltrated state government at the highest level I possibly could and began trying to make things happen. . . . I sort of perceive myself as a double agent. . . . I have to maintain my credibility as a good bureaucrat, a good decision-maker, a good manager, and yet always question authority, always question people's values, always remember my radical roots.

The choice to work inside rather than outside political institutions was not easy. Activists who spent their formative political years in the radical women's movement arguing that the existing system needed to be replaced, not reformed, changed their views about what strategies were effective in achieving social change and became more willing to compromise when they took government jobs. The woman quoted above explained her conflicts with radical activists who had "unrealistic expectations" about what the state administration would do:

I would try to say to them, "You have to understand about the legislature . . . you have to understand how protocol operates in state government. . . . " Those kinds of basic rules were things that many of us couldn't get some of our radical friends to understand. I understood where they were coming from because had I been in their position ten years earlier, I would have said the same thing: "I don't need to deal with the legislature. . . . Let's go march in the streets!" Well, marching in the streets still has its place, but there are other means to an end. And there's a lot more of us now who are in the system who can help make things happen.

Feminists in state and local government, although they remain a largely marginal minority, are one of the channels through which the aims of the women's movement are addressed.[10]

In addition to working in jobs directly related to the women's movement and feminist goals, some veterans of the radical women's movement have found employment in organizations that grew out of other progressive social movements. One woman, for example, worked with her state Health and Social Services Committee to recruit Indian families to adopt Indian children and tried to "heal some of the wounds between the state and the county and the tribes." Another woman, trained as a lawyer, listed a variety of social causes that she has pursued through her jobs.

> I've done nothing but social change work, primarily centered on civil rights sorts of things . . . . But it has not necessarily been women's rights work. I've worked on voting rights in Mississippi, I've worked on disabled people's rights to get to the polls without having to vote by absentee ballot, I've worked on consumer rights a lot in regard to the breakup of AT&T.

Feminists in these positions see their work as related to the women's movement, as the woman quoted above explained:

> I do view the work that I've been doing as part of the worldview of citizen empowerment. . . . So I do see it in a larger context. But it's also something that, when I'm looking at it in the larger context, is not something I'd pick to work on. . . . So it does have a relationship [to feminism], but [it's] very attenuated.

However, as her comments indicate, this woman has chosen her job not because it addresses the social issues that she sees as most important, but because it represents a way of earning a living that has some connection to her political view of the world. Another white woman saw her employment in an organization oriented toward African American rights as having both advantages and disadvantages over her previous employment in a women's movement organization.

> I can believe in what I'm doing, and I can stand behind the issue, but it's not my issue. And so I can leave it at the office when I come home, and it gives me more balance in my life. . . . But I do miss working around people who are like-minded, where we think politically the same, and I miss being in an atmosphere where I don't have to hide being a lesbian . . . and being around more women.

With the shrinking social movement sector and scarce funding for nonprofit social service agencies, most feminists have not been able to work in women's movement organizations during the 1980s and 1990s. When possible, they have worked instead in organizations that have grown from other social movements.

Twelve women held jobs that were neither explicitly feminist nor related to other social change goals; another was a feminist artist who worked at other jobs to support herself. Another woman was unemployed. It would be incorrect, however, to assume that their participation in the women's movement had not, for the most part, affected their work lives; regardless of their jobs, most veterans of the women's movement bring their politics to work with them. For example, an arts administrator brings exhibits by women artists dealing with feminist themes to the gallery. "I have a lot of power to say what pictures get in books," commented another woman, who works in a textbook publishing company. "To make sure that they're good images of women, and make sure that minorities and women are in-cluded." A third woman, who works as a printer, explained that she confronts sexual harassment in her workplace: "One of the roles that I play at work is there's no sexual harassment in this perimeter around me and the women who talk to me." Another woman took similar action in a job in higher education administration. She described the conflicts with her boss that developed as a result:

> One of the fights I had with a former boss was over the way he treated secretaries. They are human beings and he was treating them like machines. I'm sure he treated his wife the same way. . . . I am not afraid to speak out. I have been to City Council meetings. The Red Door Tavern [in Columbus] had a businessmen-only room for lunch, and we took them to the Civil Rights Commission. . . . When you've done those kinds of things, you are not afraid to tell somebody, "You are treating your secretary badly and this has got to stop. This is why, and this is what I expect from you."

Confronting one's boss is not generally a positive career move, however. The woman quoted above eventually left her job because she wanted a less hostile working environment.

Creating or selecting feminist-friendly working environments was important to many women's movement veterans. Some women were vehement that they would not work in mainstream corporations that they view as oppressive. A woman who is a freelance editor, for example, explained that she eliminated some kinds of work from consideration based on her politics:

> I think that I would never have been able to enter into a career or job that involved some really obnoxious corporation that was making bombs, or that was doing political underdealings or something. . . . I just never could follow a corporate kind of life, and I think that was a conscious choice that my feminist values made concrete for me.

The same woman went on to explain that she chose, instead, a job that gave her the flexibility she needed to participate in social movement activities.

I love the opportunity to go out in the middle of the day and attend a demonstration, or go out and do errands for somebody who has AIDS or something like that.

Instead of avoiding traditional corporations, others helped construct alternative forms for their workplaces. For example, one woman works in a small nonfeminist publishing company that nevertheless has been profoundly influenced by the structure of the women's movement.

Our workplace is structured very differently than the companies that have been started by men. We have our office in a home, we work our own hours, and our office is structured to accommodate children and pets.

Not everyone is employed in such settings; some of the women I interviewed work in traditional corporate environments. But even these women talk with co-workers about women's issues and see themselves as making some contribution to social change through their jobs.

Whether their jobs deal with social change or not, many women's movement veterans gained important skills as activists that they now put to use in their work lives. In some cases, these skills provided women entry into professions that would otherwise have been closed to them. One woman who worked as house manager and development coordinator for WAC and now works as an administrator in a nonprofit organization explained that her experiences in the women's movement were essential to her success in her current job.

I wouldn't be where I'm at right now with what I do for a living if I hadn't come to the Women's Action Collective. I learned how to speak in a group—that's not something I'd ever done before. . . . I learned a lot about a nonprofit organization. I know social service nonprofit organizations—I know how they function inside and out.

Another woman pointed out that collective structure, in which sharing skills and rotating jobs were emphasized, ensured that she learned a variety of useful skills:

> Organizing, writing, speaking in public . . . how to chair a meeting, putting together an agenda. . . . Because we rotated everything, you had to learn all that stuff. And you were encouraged so much . . . part of the whole thing was to encourage women to grow. There was a real big emphasis on that. Take on new things, do stuff you hadn't done before.

A respondent who now works for a public interest organization that does lobbying and education listed some additional skills she gained through her work with Women Against Rape and the Community Action Strategies to Stop Rape project, including planning programs and fundraising events, grant writing, dealing with volunteers and the media, facilitating and planning meetings, and speaking in public. She gave a specific example of how she applies these skills in her current job.

> I'm in the process now of trying to put together a grant proposal for a major study that I'd like this organization to sponsor and do. And I would have no idea how a study of this magnitude would be done, let alone how to write a grant proposal for it, had I not done the work I did at Women Against Rape.

Participants gained self-confidence from feminism and came to attribute their difficulties to structural causes rather than personal failings, and these qualities made a difference in their professional lives as well. For example, one woman commented that she went to law school in part because the women's movement gave her "a sense of I could do anything I wanted *because* I was a woman, not in spite of the fact." Another woman, now a professor, explained how attributing her problems to the gender system lessens her doubt in her own abilities as a researcher.

> I have this chronic self-doubt about whether I'm really a good [scholar], because it sort of taps into all of my math anxi-

ety. . . . What the women's movement has given me is this understanding of where that's coming from, which has made it possible for me to go on.

In addition to these sorts of general skills, women also built careers around feminist issues or gained specific experiences in the women's movement related to their future careers. For example, one lawyer wrote her first amicus brief for an antipornography ordinance. Another lawyer got the opportunity to write a brief for a major abortion decision because of her involvement in the women's movement. A woman who is now a professor wrote her first published article about a campaign against sexual harassment in which she was involved.

Not everyone's work is organized around feminist change to the same degree, of course. Those in more autonomous occupations, particularly the professions, are able, by and large, to focus more directly on their feminist interests. Government workers report greater frustration with the compromises they make and obstacles they encounter at work, but remain optimistic about their impact. Women who work in some nonfeminist settings are able to structure their work tasks and the organizations where they work to be consistent with feminist principles; in other settings, women are less able to do so.

Yet the overall pattern is that feminists continue to work for social change in their jobs either directly or indirectly. The ways they are able to promote feminist goals at work often differ sharply from their actions in the women's movement of the 1970s. In particular, working within institutionalized structures—inside the system—marks a substantial change for many women who now work in universities, government, or business. One academic typified a general ambivalence when she discussed her feelings about pursuing a career as a college administrator.

> I will always be a feminist. And I certainly realize that you can't be a radical feminist and be a president of a college, but I will always bring that with me. I will always be an instrument

through which things can change. . . . Not in the way I would have anticipated twelve or fourteen years ago, because I never thought I would be so much a part of the establishment. . . . Sometimes I feel compromised, but I'm really clear on who I am. It's not swallowed me up. And I think the point at which I feel like I had to compromise too much I would walk away from it. I know if you're on the outside, there are ways that you don't have power and influence, compared to if you're on the inside. And so now I'm comfortable being on the inside, even though that has its own set of problems or drawbacks.

Being "on the inside" does indeed have both benefits and drawbacks. It ensures that the effects of the women's movement extend beyond visible political gains to the mainstream institutions in which feminists are employed. For individuals, mainstream employment, unlike work in most women's movement organizations, provides a measure of financial security while still allowing feminists to work for social change. Few options remain for paid employment in women's movement organizations. Economic conditions have worsened, and few activists are willing—or can afford—to live on the minimal salaries they received in the 1970s. Yet because the feminist collective identity has been enduring, feminists from the 1960s and 1970s political generation bring a commitment to improving women's chances and lives to whatever jobs they hold. The feminist challenge reverberates outside the workplace as well, reshaping veterans' personal lives and interpersonal interactions as well as their professional activities.

EVERYDAY RESISTANCE

"The personal is political," an insight that grew from women's realization of common experiences and obstacles as they discussed their lives in consciousness-raising groups, guided much of the theory and practice of the radical women's movement. If women's difficulties as mothers, in relationships with men, at work, and in their views of themselves are rooted in structural causes—a social system that privileges men and relegates women to second-class citizenship—they have political solutions. For radical feminists in the late 1960s, the solutions to women's individual difficulties lay in changing the structural conditions that created them by collectively confronting the political system. Gradually, throughout the 1970s, radical feminists also sought to restructure their lives in the present in order to challenge and contravene the rules and limits placed on women. In what Wini Breines has called "prefigurative politics," feminists attempted to build organizations and treat each other in ways that were consistent with egalitarian ideals and foreshadowed a feminist future.[11] In addition, individual behavior came under feminist scrutiny. At least initially, this was not because feminists yearned for rigid control over each others' behavior; it was, rather, because of the feminist analysis of the personal as political. As women came to believe deeply that every area of life had political causes and ramifications, many naturally rethought the way they lived and sought to challenge patriarchy through their actions in daily life as well as through more conventional means of protest.

Although the politicization of personal lives during the 1970s and early 1980s was sometimes prescriptive and hostile to deviation, many veterans of the women's movement continue to believe that how they live their daily lives is an important mode of resistance. Much of the earlier rigidity about "proper" feminist behavior has softened, but being feminist has remained central to individuals' "personal" lives as they seek to redefine what it means to be a woman and construct new models of personal relationships. This continuity is largely a result of how integral politics were to life in radical women's movement organizations. A former member of WAC explained that discussions and debates about the organization's policies and structure taught her to incorporate political concerns into every aspect of her life, saying, "Not everybody examines what they do for internal political consistency and integrity, and yet those of us who went through the Action Collective process in this town really learned to do that." As a result, feminist principles are thoroughly integrated into women's sense of self and therefore into their daily practices. "I think it has permeated who and what I am," another former activist said about radical feminism. "And I think that there is rarely anything that I would do, either personally or politically, that wouldn't somehow bear the trappings of what I learned at that time."

Although many veterans of the women's movement were frustrated that they could not often participate in more organized social movement activities, they nevertheless believed that their everyday actions are important. One typical woman explained, "Personal stuff is just as political, and the way you deal with people that you run into every day can [cause] as much change as being in groups or marching. It all ties together, and there's room for all of it." Many women said that they put feminism into practice in their daily lives and argued that this was an even more profound source of change than protest. "If we don't live our lives in accordance with our values," said a former leader of W A C, "then we're not really providing a model for change. And I think change has to take place on a fundamental level in order for it to be very effective or to take hold."

Whereas during the peak years of the radical women's movement most of activists' daily interactions were with like-minded feminists, many move in quite different circles now. Co-workers, neighbors, even friends, may hold assumptions about women's lives and liberation that diverge sharply from basic feminist tenets. The seasoned feminists I talked to interact with people in everyday life in a way designed subtly to raise the consciousness of those around them by challenging assumptions about what women are like and can do. One woman who works as a school counselor explained that she attempts to influence her co-workers: "I haven't been politically active for years, but wherever I am I'm always trying to raise people's consciousness with some information I have or a feminist perspective." For example, she described her discussions with women teachers at her school about a forthcoming shift to site-based management, in which decisions about how each school is run are made by a group of parents, teachers, and the principal from that school rather than by centralized administration. Explaining that most of the administrators in the school system are male while most teachers are female, she saw site-based management as a way of returning power to women, and tried to communicate that to co-workers.

Another nonprofit administrator who works in an environment that she described as containing a lot of homophobia and sexism took some opportunities to discuss issues as they arose.

> When I'm around people and they say something offensive that's really blatant, then I always speak up and let them know how I feel about it. I don't do it every time a man calls me "honey" or every time a man says "girl" instead of "woman." . . . It's more that in the course of someone getting to know me, they will know what my attitudes are about things. And if they say something that expresses an attitude that I think is off the wall, I try to respond to them not by telling them that they're wrong but by saying, "Well, there's another way to look at this."

She believed that her workplace has become less homophobic in part because of her efforts.

Feminists' lives do take different shapes because of their politics, and this sets an example for people they encounter. A movement veteran who now works in state government, and whose husband works at home caring for their children and the house, explained that their nontraditional family sets an example in her community.

> When we're both at meetings . . . I'll indicate that I work for the Department of Justice, and my husband will say, "I'm ———. I'm her babysitter, and I cook too." . . . And in a way that's

branching out farther than your typical middle-class family that does that, because . . . of the kinds of groups we find ourselves in, Indian culture and also Black culture. And that example [is] being set and recognized humorously.

In a very different setting, a woman who holds a well-paying management job believes that she has an impact on her co-workers because she is an example of a nontraditional woman— she is successful and focused on her career, outspoken, and independent—and because she talks openly about her years as a feminist activist.

> [People] meet you and you are different from who they know, and it makes a difference. I suspect that on some level, that's the main way we've always made change. It is a litle sad that at this time that's about the only way we have. But I think we need to remember that that is, longterm, the most powerful way we have. We've said we want all these things, we've said we've made all these changes within ourselves, for ourselves. We're just gonna go live them.

Indeed, the women I talked to were emphatic that their everyday actions helped bring about social change, even if they were not part of collective feminist action. One longtime activist expressed the typical belief that the way she lives her life makes a profound political statement.

> I feel now that the way that change happens most profoundly is in the way people treat each other, just on a day-to-day basis. And the way that people are most changed is by their contact with another person that they know on a personal basis, not by a demonstration. And so if I live my life in a way that puts forward certain attitudes, and people get to know me and know that about me, then I like to think that that is how I make change.

Discussions—"informal consciousness raising"—are an important way that the women's movement has diffused into the larger society; however, they represent only one way that feminists make change in their daily lives.

Another form of everyday resistance is found in movement veterans' presentation of self. Women's appearance has been a focus of feminist contention since the 1850s, when feminists advocated dress reform and briefly substituted bloomers and shortened skirts for their usual long skirts.[12] With the resurgence of the women's movement in the 1960s, restrictive norms of feminine appearance and demeanor again came under attack. The radical women's movement criticized norms of feminine appearance that prescribed makeup, constricting clothing, shaved legs, or high heels as requiring women to conform to an unnatural and unattainable ideal of beauty, and often prescribed new ways for women to dress and appear.[13] In addition, activists viewed the expectation that women defer to men in conversation, decision making, and manner as perpetuating female subordination; instead, women were urged to speak their minds, disagree when necessary, and stand up for themselves in word, posture, and deed. A woman who entered WAC in the mid-1970s explained that the women's movement made a lasting difference in her demeanor.

> When I first got in the movement, it scared me thinking of all the things I'd have to give up. I'd have to quit deferring to men. I didn't know how not to defer to men. And as it turned out, that was the easiest thing to give up. That was the most liberating thing. And I think I still appall men left and right at every opportunity. Not even being rude or even necessarily confrontative unless it's called for, but just not deferring.

She believes that her behavior "appalls men" simply because she does not subtly and symbolically provide them with the customary message that they are better than she is. Another woman pointed out that her demeanor is perhaps more confrontational as a result of the women's movement, saying, "It's really been an inherent part of the way I present myself on the job and to other people in general, and it gives me an edge that some people don't want to deal with. . . . I don't tolerate people behaving or speaking in a sexist or racist way around me." Her unwillingness to tolerate sexism or defer to men, she believed, made her job search more difficult; another respondent agreed, saying that she had acquired a reputation as "aggressive" that made finding employment hard. Yet neither was willing to adopt a more deferential manner.

Along with an assertive demeanor, many participants in the 1970s women's movement adopted new norms of appearance, including wearing no makeup, not shaving their legs and underarms, and wearing gender-neutral and nonrestrictive clothing such as jeans, turtlenecks, and flannel shirts. As a singer at a 1979 women's music festival reportedly put it, "If the package ain't too pretty, it's because I'm not for sale."[14] A former member and paid worker in WAC commented about standards of appearance there:

> It's my perception now that we were very judgmental and very narrow-minded, even though I think the premises of what we were saying about women's oppression and why women do those things was well-founded. . . . At that point in my life, I found that very freeing, because I didn't have to dress up.

Like her, most women I interviewed still believe that societal expectations for women's appearance are unrealistic and oppressive, but the degree to which they have continued to challenge those expectations through their own appearance varies greatly. Many have moderated their looks either to meet the demands of professional jobs or because they no longer feel bound by the strictures of the 1970s feminist community. One businesswoman summed up the change in her appearance this way:

> Planning for the conference [in 1980] someone referred to ——— who had been invited to speak, and thought that perhaps we could get someone better, [because] after all, my god, she still wears lipstick! What you have to appreciate is that that was an

accepted criticism at that time. There's a tube in my purse now—don't tell anyone! [*Laughs*] . . . I can't do it that way anymore.

Many women I talked to were no longer interested in conforming to a rigid standard of appearance and were critical of that trend in feminist organizations of the previous decade. In fact, norms of appearance within the feminist community have changed sharply in the 1980s and 1990s. A lesbian activist described the shifts in presentation of self and lifestyle within the lesbian feminist community.

[In the 1970s] it was leftover hippie, the way people dressed. The lesbians that I knew, nobody would ever be caught dead wearing any makeup. Nobody shaved their legs. And everybody was so serious, everything revolved around political discussions. Nobody would have been caught dead owning a nice car, and I don't think anybody owned a house then. . . . Nobody owned a dress. . . . But now, a lot of people shave their legs, they own houses, they have nice cars. They wear makeup and they dress up fashionably, or whatever they consider to be fashionable. And they're not as judgmental about other people doing those things.

As feminists became increasingly willing to interact and work with nonfeminists in the 1980s, markers of group boundaries such as appearance became less critical, making it possible for women to dress in a variety of ways. At the same time, in an increasingly hostile culture, conspicuous aspects of appearance that branded one a feminist were more costly.

One such conspicuous attribute was unshaven legs. Radical feminists viewed (and many still view) the expectation that adult women's legs be hairless as a means of forcing women to conform to a male-defined standard of beauty and a feminine role that emphasized childlike dependence. For many movement participants, not shaving one's legs was a symbolic way of rejecting the standards of a male-dominated culture. Visible and socially unacceptable, growing the hair on one's legs was an act that made passing as a "proper" woman difficult if not impossible. As a result, when some women decided to shave their legs again in the 1980s, the act acquired great symbolic significance. Many women "confessed" in their interviews that they now shaved their legs; some of these realized that many of their cohort did so, but others felt that they had betrayed their feminist principles because of personal weakness or inability to withstand societal disapproval. One former member of WAC, Central Ohio Lesbians, and the Association of Women Students, now a professor who shaves her legs, described what she saw as a relatively rapid shift in feminist appearance.

> It really blew my mind that all of a sudden, everybody's shaving their legs, all these people who were very hairy and very proud of it. Suddenly something changed. And I think that's something in the external culture that we're responding to, and maybe backing off a little bit on being so insistently, visibly different. I finally decided that [shaving] was not the most important thing in the world, even if I don't like the way it feels.

Many women explained that they had changed their appearance not because their political beliefs had changed or because they wanted to, but because they felt they had no choice. "I shave my legs, I sometimes wear makeup," said an administrator in a nonprofit organization. "I don't do those things so much because I want to do them, or because it makes me feel better about myself. I do them because I feel that I have to do them to get by, to keep my job." Another administrator also made a conscious decision to change her presentation of self for pragmatic reasons.

> I have finally decided that I can get more accomplished if I look a little bit more traditional. So now, most days of the week I have on a dress or a skirt. And that's sort of astonishing. I shave my legs. I never will shave my armpits, but that's like the last bastion of hairiness or something. But when I first went to [my current job] I had not shaved my legs, probably for fourteen years.

The women I interviewed who felt pressure to shave their legs, wear skirts, and generally appear more feminine were those in middle-class professional or managerial jobs. Those who were in working-class occupations, were unemployed, or were self-supporting (as artists or feminist therapists, for example) did not feel the same strictures. Standards of appearance, of course, are class-specific. Some are also race-specific; shaving one's legs remains more compulsory in white than African American communities. Feminist veterans who are white and middle-class thus assimilate into a model of femininity specific to their race and class position.

Some women in working-class occupations and the self-employed continue to wear the "radical feminist uniform" of jeans, flannel shirts or T-shirts, sneakers, and no makeup even to work. A few others in professional jobs also refused to compromise past a certain point. Said one government employee, "I don't shave my legs, and I'm not in the closet or anything, either." Only a few women, regardless of occupation or class, ever wear high heels, heavy makeup, or elaborate hair styles: Even when they conform to expectations of feminine behavior, they do not go to extremes, and they conform primarily for pragmatic reasons. Although they view their appearances as radically changed, they appear far less traditionally feminine than most of their women co-workers. In the early 1990s, when micro-miniskirts, heavy makeup, and lace-encrusted bustiers were fashionable, this political generation's appearance continued to set them apart.

The women's movement of the 1960s and 1970s placed great emphasis on eliminating power differentials and minimizing dominance in relationships, and this remains very important to the women I interviewed. As a result, they have attempted to construct personal relationships that are as egalitarian as possible. One woman commented, "I certainly don't want an oppressive personal relationship, and I think I certainly have a good sense of what those dynamics are if they appear in a personal relationship." Such efforts to build in the present relationships and lifestyles that reflect feminist goals for the future are a good example of prefigurative politics.[15] For many movement veterans, avoiding hierarchy in intimate relationships meant forming relationships with women rather than men. Lesbian feminist theory popularized by the mid-1970s suggested that heterosexuality was inherently oppressive to women and equated relationships with men to "sleeping with the enemy."[16] Although many segments of lesbian feminism in the 1980s and 1990s retreated from this position, some publications and community events continued to reflect the assertion that lesbian relationships were more egalitarian than heterosexual relationships.[17]

Of the 34 women I interviewed, 20 identified as lesbians at the time of the interview, 9 as heterosexual, and 4 as bisexual; information was unavailable for 1. Many lesbians came out in the context of feminist activism. One woman described her coming out as one of the most significant consequences of participating in the women's movement.

> One big change that will be very lasting is that I came out. I don't know that I would have done that otherwise. . . . And it wasn't something that came to me without being involved with the women's movement. It came as part of it. I don't know if I would have come to [lesbianism] another way on my own or not. It was definitely not something that I'd thought of the first twenty-five years.

It is difficult to know how many of the lesbians would have come out regardless of the women's movement, but the women's movement facilitated coming out by encouraging self-reflection in consciousness-raising groups, decreasing the stigma of lesbianism, and providing a supportive community in which to build a lesbian identity.[18] Lesbians I interviewed believed that being intimately involved with women rather than men made their relationships less prone to power imbalances. Reflecting on what she saw as the advantages of being a lesbian, one activist stated:

> One thing that is a hard, painful realization is that no matter what kind of changes I make in my life, I can't get away from patriarchy. But that's one thing about being lovers with a woman is that those kinds of issues are external issues. They're never internal. Any fights we have about power and dominance are not based on sex roles. They're based on who feels stronger about whatever it is we're arguing about. And we're both very nurturing, and we're also both very dominating, and so we're a nice combination.

Another woman who identified as heterosexual throughout the 1970s and early 1980s, when she was at her most politically active, came out as lesbian later. She described coming out as making her personal and political lives mesh with each other better.

> When I was having relationships with men, they just did not fit into what was happening in the rest of my life. . . . It wasn't like I was having bad experiences with men, but it was just a whole lot easier putting my life together [when I came out].

Lesbians did report some changes in their relationship patterns. Radical feminist theory of the 1970s not only critiqued marriage, but also viewed monogamy as based on a model of possession and dependence that denied partners autonomy. As a result, many radical feminists—lesbian and heterosexual—experimented with nonmonogamous relationships during the decade. But by the 1980s, most of this had died down. "My social life is relatively stable and sort of unexciting," said a professional woman who lives with another woman in a house they own. "There was this whole big fad of nonmonogamy, heavy multiple relationships, open relationships. I feel pretty married right now." Half the lesbians I interviewed are in a committed relationship with another woman.

Very few of the women in the sample, however, are married to men. Only 7 of the 34 (21 percent) were married at the time of the interview, compared with over 90 percent of white women in their age bracket.[19] Two of the married women identify as bisexual, while the other 5 consider themselves heterosexual. Even among the 13 heterosexual and bisexual women in the sample, only 54 percent are married, well below the percentage for the the general population.

Feminist critiques of monogamy and of marriage as an institution of male dominance doubtless have made some movement veterans less willing to marry. "I felt like I was selling out to a community . . . to marry," explained a woman who did eventually marry the father of her son. "It was the hardest thing for me to introduce him as my husband." Women who did marry or lived with male lovers sought to maintain egalitarian relationships and avoid traditional gender roles. One woman described her husband as "somebody who allows me to be the kind of person I am without a problem. . . . [He] had to be a man with a lot of the feminine qualities that I found important to me as a woman." Regardless of whether women identified as lesbian, heterosexual, or bisexual, to have a blatantly unequal relationship was unthinkable.

Similarly unthinkable was to raise children to conform to gender stereotypes. Eight of the women I interviewed have children. One, a lesbian, chose to have a child through artificial insemination, and the other seven conceived children through heterosexual intercourse, although two later became lesbians. It is important to note that the 24 percent of women I interviewed who have children is much lower than the 81.6 percent of white women in their age group who have ever had children.[20] In part, the large proportion of lesbians, combined with the fact that lesbians' having children by artificial insemination has become a widespread phenomenon only since the late 1980s, accounts for this.[21] However, three of the seven mothers are lesbians. Even among the 13 heterosexual or bisexual women, only four have children, still a much lower proportion than in the general population. The feminist critique of traditional marriage and motherhood must account for part of this difference, combined with the emphasis on independence and developing careers. Both marriage and motherhood were viewed as fundamentally patriarchal institutions that reflected a sexist legal system and cultural values, and so rejecting traditional femininity and challenging women's oppression meant avoiding marriage and motherhood for some women.[22] Although this has changed somewhat in the intervening decades, as increasing numbers of lesbians and unmarried heterosexual women choose to have children, the change came too late to alter earlier feminists' child-bearing choices.[23] Many participants spent their twenties and early thirties—peak child-bearing years—as fulltime activists.

For women who do have children, raising those children in a feminist way is an important form of resistance. The mothers I talked to consciously attempted to raise their children in a gender-neutral way, setting examples as strong women and teaching daughters that they could do anything they wanted to do. One married heterosexual woman explained that she had tried to raise her son "unisex." In her household, her husband

> does all the cooking. We share the housework, so [my son] sees [that]. . . . He sees that women can do things, and he knows what I'm capable of. . . . And [my daughter] does the same thing. She sees that there are no roles, that nothing is really defined. So she sees both of us really equally involved in child raising.

At the same time, she acknowledged, her son and daughter had some gender-typed preferences, despite her best efforts: "[My daughter] doesn't like trucks, you see, although we gave her a lot, like we gave [my son] a lot of dolls. He had no interest in them. She likes her dolls." The dilemma for her, as for some of the other mothers I interviewed, is that her own influence over her children is balanced by their exposure to peers and popular culture. At core, though, she wants to impart a basic sense of empowerment to both her children, stating, "In all my dealings, I know I can do what I want . . . . And I hope that I can give that to [my daughter], and I want [my son] to know that too." Another woman who is raising daughters commented in a similar vein that "with our daughters, we're trying very hard to give them their culture and the strength of women that they can do anything."

Feminist mothers are helped in this task not only by husbands or co-parents but also by a network of feminist friends and fellow activists. One heterosexual woman described her childcare system when she was in school: "I'd have to have somebody from the [women's] organization meet me to take my kid to the library, and then after that class I'd collect the kid again. . . . If I've needed to take the kids with me, they've gone." A single lesbian mother who raised her daughter with the assistance of many friends thought that

> because she was one of the few kids who was being raised by feminists in the group, she just has a wonderful set of role models. . . . And as a result I think she's turned out to be a really unique kid. I mean, yeah, I was a single mother. But she was raised by all these other single women at the same time.

Feminist mothering is clearly an influential way of making social change. By raising both daughters and sons with self-confidence and respect for women, and by redefining what it means to be a mother, feminists directly affect women's position in society.[24]

Finally, the way that movement veterans spend their leisure time is shaped by their feminist interests and commitments. An extensive feminist community has developed since the 1970s that provides an alternative culture for members of this political generation. Feminist presses and bookstores provide reading material; women's musicians, recording companies, and festivals enable women to listen to feminist music; independent film-makers increasingly make it possible to view feminist movies. For example, one former member of Women Against Rape does not see herself as very active in the current women's movement. Yet, she explained, "What I choose to read, what I watch on TV, the things that I do, the movies that I go see, all that kind of stuff is colored by being a woman and being woman-identified." Another woman, a busy lawyer, described the impact of feminism on her free time as making her "more likely to pick up a book in a bookstore if it's from a women's press. . . . When I make a choice in my daily life, I choose women's culture when I can."

Holding feminist beliefs also makes much of mainstream culture offensive. A third woman's feminist commitments make it impossible for her to participate in much of popular culture.

> I don't make the same kinds of entertainment choices that other people make, because I'm a feminist. There are some things I don't want to see in the movies, and I don't care how popular it is, because I'm a feminist. And in a way it seems trivial, but it doesn't exactly immerse you in mainstream culture.

It is not surprising that some of the most enduring feminist institutions have been bookstores and music production companies. In Columbus, Fan the Flames Feminist Bookstore still serves as a gathering place for feminist activists of all ages. Movement veterans are both pulled toward feminist culture and pushed away from mainstream culture. Feminist collective identity is deep-rooted and enduring enough that it affects every aspect of former activists' lives.

SUSTAINING THE WOMEN'S MOVEMENT

In their jobs and in everyday life, feminists still contest dominant notions of femininity and women's place. "It will be nice to have a movement again," said one movement veteran long-

ingly, "but being a feminist doesn't depend on having a movement. And I think that I live my life in a feminist way." As a
result, her work and personal life remain sharply different from
those of other women her age. In the absence of a highly mobilized women's movement, feminists whose collective identities
were forged in earlier years continued to find ways to work for
social change, to "live their lives in a feminist way."

Yet, if longtime feminists remained committed to social
change and continued to act on that commitment, why did
they, by and large, cease being activists "in the street" and begin weaving their politics into daily life? As I have suggested all
along, the answers to these questions are complex. As many of
the women I interviewed told me, organizing protest is exhausting and often thankless work. A model of "activist" that required all-encompassing commitment and the sacrifice of other
pursuits lost its appeal as women aged and sought greater material and emotional security and more balanced lives. Sustaining
a high level of participation over more than a decade clearly is
difficult.

It was made more difficult by the increasingly hostile climate
in which radical feminists found themselves by the 1980s.
Grant money and other financial support dried up around 1980;
at the same time, the need for feminist mobilization was greater
than ever, as the Religious Right gained ground and the federal
government openly opposed the women's movement. The prospects for radical feminist progress at the federal level were dim;
and the large national feminist organizations were forced into a
defensive posture through most of the 1980s. Local radical feminist organizations were sometimes able to survive in diminished
form, but were not able to expand and had to focus more narrowly on service provision rather than social transformation.
When Ohio elected a progressive Democratic governor, Richard
Celeste, in 1984, even radical feminists were reluctant to maintain an antagonistic stance toward state government. Instead,
they cooperated with the state administration while distancing

themselves from largely futile action at the federal level. The federal action that did occur mostly involved reactive attempts to stave off antifeminist attacks or issues that were defined more broadly than women's issues, such as military intervention abroad.

In order to recognize veterans' overall continuity of political commitments and actions despite these changes, it is necessary to conceptualize social movement participation broadly to include such actions in professional and employment settings and daily life as well as the collective actions of women's movement organizations. Doing so also allows us to evaluate the impact of the women's movement more fully. As feminists diffuse into mainstream institutions, the women's movement reshapes those institutions from the inside as well as from the outside. There is, of course, considerable debate about whether such actions constitute a social movement. We could view feminists' employment in government, business, or universities as evidence for the cooptation of the women's movement rather than for its continuity. We could view the politics of daily life as depoliticized "lifestyle" changes that leave structural inequality unchallenged.

These points are not without merit. But I want to suggest instead that the women's movement takes multiple forms in the present, and the political threads that still run through veterans' lives are meaningful even if they look different than they did twenty years ago. If the criteria for defining a social movement require that it have an impact on the external environment, feminists in the institutions clearly have some impact, even if it is reformist. If the standard is whether participants see themselves as making change—the movement's collective identity—then longtime feminists still compose a social movement. If the criterion is the extent to which the movement sustains organizations and a community, the radical women's movement, again, fits.

This is not to say that the women's movement and the lives

of participants have not changed. For individuals, life is very different now. Instead of being fundamentally collective actors, they are left to act as individuals most of the time. Instead of demanding revolutionary change, they find themselves working for small increments, although arguably even revolutionary movements often adopt incremental goals for strategic purposes. As committed feminists incorporated politics into their daily lives, they built a testament to the importance of their vision. This vision sustained individual women, and it also enabled activists to nurture each others' commitment. The political world, rich in culture and social ties, that veterans of the radical women's movement constructed during the movement's peak in the 1970s did not vanish in the 1980s. Instead, the ties that linked activists stretched as the network became more diffuse. The actions of individuals took new forms as activists sought to accommodate both their radical politics and the new context in which they worked.

For the movement as a whole, connections with the mainstream have increased even as a separate and radical feminist community and culture have grown. Further, as opponents mobilized not only against the women's movement, but against peace, civil rights, liberal religion, and a spectrum of progressive movements, activists in the radical women's movement increasingly made common cause with activists in other struggles. Some veterans of the women's movement entered other social movements, and women's movement organizations addressed new issues, reformulating the connections between women's issues and other causes, the relation between political and cultural change, and the connections between "internalized oppression" and structural inequality. Many of the most important changes in the women's movement, and a good measure of its continuing impact, grow from its ties to other social movements. It is to these links that I turn next.

5 :: UNITED WE STAND:

THE IMPACT OF THE

WOMEN'S MOVEMENT ON

OTHER SOCIAL MOVEMENTS

FOR A SUPPOSEDLY conservative, apathetic decade, the 1980s witnessed a lot of upheaval in Columbus and around the country. Environmentalists protested against toxic waste in their communities; peace activists mobilized in huge numbers for a freeze on nuclear weapons. Protests erupted over U.S. intervention in El Salvador, Nicaragua, Grenada, Panama, and Iraq, and religious activists offered sanctuary to illegal political refugees in their churches. Antiapartheid protests prompted South African disinvestment by colleges, universities, and businesses. Gay men and lesbians organized—separately and together—more visibly and militantly than ever before, both on behalf of their own rights and in response to the AIDS epidemic. And movements coalesced around new issues—animal rights, spirituality, and a host of self-help movements that linked solving political problems to solving personal ones. Seemingly diverse, these movements shared stiff opposition and a sense of being besieged by the growing conservative momentum. They also shared an important debt to feminist organizing and analysis.

The prevailing story that the women's movement grew from

the civil rights and New Left movements casts feminism as influenced *by* other movements rather than as exerting an influence *on* them.[1] Yet the women's movement and individual feminists profoundly changed many of the social movements that flourished in the 1980s and 1990s. Feminism has been carried into other movements for social change by individual activists who have entered those movements, by feminist organizations that have addressed broader issues, and by the diffusion of feminist ideology, structure, culture, and tactics into the wider "progressive" social movement community.[2] The legacy of the radical women's movement, as a result, reverberates not only in feminists' actions at work and in their daily lives but also in the reformulation of what progressive social change entails.

These closer connections between feminism and other struggles grew from the same influences that changed longtime feminists' actions in the 1980s. Political opposition required activists from various movements of the Left to band together. As the Right linked feminism, gay rights, peace, and "godless" New Age spirituality, advocates of these various causes often became allies. At the same time, tightening resources and a smaller pool of committed activists from which to draw meant that organizations within each social movement had trouble maintaining operations. Increasingly they turned to each other, sharing space and relying on members of other organizations to publicize and attend their demonstrations. Thus, just as a relatively open environment encouraged the proliferation of multiple challenges in the late 1960s and early 1970s, the hostile context of the 1980s fostered greater cooperation and overlap among movements.

We cannot fully understand what happened to movement veterans and the radical feminist challenge in Columbus without considering the related movements that became integral to the feminist political scene in the 1980s. Examining the intersections of the women's movement with other challenges in Columbus gives us a detailed picture of how such alliances proceeded. The changes in Columbus took place in the context of similar changes at the national level and in other communities. In this chapter I describe interactions between the women's movement and other social movements in Columbus, as well as sketching out the broader national patterns.

CONNECTIONS AMONG MOVEMENTS

Social movements are not distinct and self-contained; rather, they grow from and give birth to other struggles, unite in coalition, and lock in conflict. Just as a movement's origins often lie in earlier movements, its significance rests in part on its "spillover" effects on subsequent ones.[3] But despite growing substantive documentation of mutual influence among social movements, theoretical literature on the topic is scarce. John McCarthy and Mayer Zald's classic formulation of resource mobilization theory highlighted competition among social movement organizations for resources and adherents, but turned little attention to cooperation among organizations or the ways that challenges shape each other.[4] Since then, others have examined interactions among separate organizations within one movement and coalitions among multi-issue organizations working toward a common goal such as abortion rights.[5] Yet the overlaps and shifting alliances among movements that address related but distinct issues or constituencies are more complex and subtle than simple coalition or competition.

The repercussions of one movement on others are informal and elusive. If we focus too narrowly on formal organizations, we overlook much of the complexity of relations among social movements. Once again, we can make use of Steven Buechler's notion of social movement community.[6] It is not just individual movements that organize in community form, but sets of social movements that share broad goals and perspectives and spotlight different issues. A broader definition of social movement community includes overlapping networks of individuals who are part of related social movements, participate in shifting co-alitions, attend common community events, provide support for overlapping organizations, and share a fundamental collective identity. A "progressive community" existed in an earlier (more male-dominated) incarnation during the 1960s, when the civil rights movement, the student movement, and opposition to the Vietnam War converged into a larger, multi-issue New Left in which the different causes influenced each other and shared or-ganizations, resources, and members.[7]

Thinking of related movements this way is nothing new to activists, who frequently refer to "the progressive community." Participants in the progressive social movement community share the view that sexism, racism, class inequality, and hetero-sexism are important social problems (although they may differ sharply on the relative importance of and connections among these different oppressions), and they support common goals. These goals include ending oppression based on gender, race, ethnicity, class, religion, or sexual orientation; environmental protection; peace and nuclear disarmament; increased AIDS funding; and an end to U.S. military intervention abroad. Ac-tivists from related social movements are drawn together by events such as demonstrations that address a "laundry list" of demands; concerts by artists, like Holly Near or Pete Seeger, who combine feminist, environmental, peace, antiracist, lesbian and gay, and other issues; and national and local publications that address issues from a range of social movements, such as *Mother Jones, The Progressive, In These Times, Out/Look* (now defunct), *Ms.,* and local "alternative" newspapers.[8] Of course, there are also formal organizational coalitions among various "progressive" groups, but many of the links are informal and based on the overlapping networks and participation in shared events that mark a social movement community.[9]

Social movements need not be contemporaneous to influence

each other. In fact, the effects of one movement on its successors are more widely recognized. The second wave women's movement, the gay and lesbian movement, and community activism of the 1980s grew out of the New Left and provide a picture of the emergence of a new social movement from an existing movement. The later movements drew on skills and analyses that participants gained in the New Left and raised additional grievances that the New Left did not address.[10] The connections between the women's movement and other social movements of the 1980s and 1990s, however, are not so clear-cut. The environmental movement, for example, did not emerge from the women's movement; activism around the issue surged in the late 1960s along with feminism. Rather, the women's movement has affected environmentalism by existing simultaneously, constructing and disseminating an ideology that links patriarchy to environmental exploitation, and cooperating on specific issues and campaigns. Although contemporary progressive movements owe their existence as much to the mixed-sex movements of the 1960s as to the women's movement, feminism has profoundly changed the spectrum of progressive social movements in the 1980s and 1990s.

The women's movement has influenced other movements in Columbus in three ways. First, women's movement *organizations* addressed broader issues and formed coalitions with other social movements, and explicitly feminist organizations emerged to address other issues, notably nuclear disarmament and the protection of the environment. Second, some *participants* in the radical women's movement turned to other causes in the 1980s and 1990s; they carried a feminist perspective into other movements. Third, the women's movement *community* and its writings, political actions, and cultural events overlap with the larger progressive social movement community. The innovations of the women's movement—ideology, tactics, organizational structure, and culture—have thus diffused into other movements even when feminist personnel have not. We can see similar intersections between feminism and other movements at the national level.[11]

Many contemporary challenges have grown from both the mixed-sex New Left and the women's movement. These movements organize around issues that were first articulated by the New Left, but now encompass feminist-influenced ideology, organizational structures, tactics, and strategies; they include the environmental, peace and antinuclear, anti-intervention, socialist, antiracist, labor, and antiapartheid movements. Feminism has also been a primary influence on several social movements that raise new issues that the movements of the 1960s did not address; these are the gay and lesbian, AIDS, New Age spirituality, and recovery and self-help movements. Of course, many —although not all—of these movements overlap. Individuals with multiple organizational memberships, protests that address shared issues, and a general outlook that opposes the actions of the current U.S. government connect movements to each other.[12]

The women's movement had an impact on four broad clusters of social movements: (1) the progressive coalition, including the movements that grew out of the New Left, (2) the lesbian and gay and AIDS movements, (3) spiritual movements, and (4) recovery and self-help movements.

FORGING A FEMINIST PROGRESSIVE COALITION

Women's liberation grew out of the civil rights and New Left movements in response to sexism within those male-dominated struggles.[13] Although women's movement organizations and individual feminists retained some ties to other Left organizations, such connections were not prominent after the early 1970s, with the exception of socialist feminist women's unions in some cities. Columbus had no visible socialist feminist organizing. Although WAC members and others who considered themselves radical feminists pursued many of the same goals as socialist feminists did elsewhere, they did so without much connection to the mixed-sex Left. In essence, most segments of the women's movement and many individual feminists had split off from male-dominated progressive movements by the early 1970s. Yet feminist activists did not abandon their roots; they retained and expanded a perspective that linked women's liberation to ending racism, war, and environmental destruction. At the same time, the men and women who remained in the shrinking New Left could not help being affected by feminism. Both the critique of sexism within the New Left and feminist innovations in ideology, political culture, organizational structure, strategies, and tactics affected mixed-sex Left organizations throughout the 1970s.[14]

Beginning in the late 1970s, the New Right grew more vocal and successful around the country in its struggle against feminism and other movements for social change. Conservatives opposed abortion and the ERA, lobbied for school prayer, opposed busing for school integration, and supported U.S. military actions in Central America. Far-right groups like the Ku Klux Klan also stepped up their organizing in Ohio, as they did nationwide.[15] Ronald Reagan's election to the presidency, many activists felt, was the final straw that galvanized them into more vigorous opposition. In response to the conservative backlash, feminists and other Left activists formed coalitions that began to bridge the gap between women's movement and mixed-sex progressive organizations.[16] In Columbus, feminist organizing in response to a right-wing backlash began in 1978 when WAC members discussed and approved resolutions opposing the Ku Klux Klan and Nazi Party and formed a discussion group on white supremacy that covered topics such as the conservative backlash and coalitions with groups on the left. Notably, unlike other WAC activities, the discussion group was initially

open to men, although it later became women-only.[17] By 1980,
WAC had formed coalitions with other groups to oppose the
federal Family Protection Act and to fight state regulation of
alternative health practitioners, and had transferred its account
out of a bank that had investments in South Africa.[18]

In the early 1980s, coalitions between WAC and other social movements grew, and WAC itself addressed a range of issues that included militarism, U.S. intervention in El Salvador,
apartheid, racism, and the destruction of the environment. Organizers defined such activities as an outgrowth of feminist beliefs. For example, in 1981 after a concert by the feminist musi-
cian Holly Near, WAC co-sponsored a vigil "in solidarity with
the revolution in El Salvador" and sponsored an antinuclear rally
called "A Feminist Celebration for Life." The antinuclear rally,
which drew only 18 participants, linked militarism to patriarchy, saying in a promotional flier, "The dogged expansion and
promotion of nuclear dependency . . . exposes the madness of
the patriarchy." A letter to WAC members announcing the
rally for El Salvador explained that the issue was relevant to
WAC because of the women's movement's political clout and
because women shared interests with other oppressed groups:

> [A]fter almost twenty years of organizing and growth, the cur-
> rent women's movement in the U.S. is a very powerful progres-
> sive force. We have seen that on a national level we can effect
> progressive change if we mobilize our forces. On an international
> level it is equally important that we wield our power in the
> interests of other oppressed groups. We are all well aware of how
> racism and sexism affect us in this country, and we have an
> obligation not to export our forms of oppression or to support
> injustice globally.[19]

New organizations grew from coalitions between the women's
movement and other progressive movements. In 1981 WAC
joined one such group, the June 21st Coalition, which sponsored a rally against President Reagan. Labeling Reagan "the
ultimate patriarch," a letter published in the WAC newsletter

argued that feminists belonged in the coalition because of the connections between feminist ideals and opposition to imperialism, budget cuts in human services, and the nuclear arms race.

> Obviously, Reagan is overtly anti-feminist. . . . We must be clear, however, that the broader policies of the Reagan administration are also inimical to feminist goals and ideals. . . . Feminists must take a stand against these policies for they are repugnant to our ideals of equality, self-determination, and the right of all people to have food, health care, education, and to live free from terror, violence, and oppression. We as feminists must oppose the budget which Reagan proposes. . . . We must oppose these barbaric attacks on the human rights of minorities and of lower income people in this country. Finally, it is clear that Reagan, the ultimate patriarch, is aggressively pursuing the nuclear arms race, which is the ultimate expression of the patriarchal desire to dominate, violate, rape, and kill. . . . Cuts in human services, government-endorsed racism, imperialist foreign policy, and militarism: these are all FEMINIST issues.[20]

WAC continued to work in coalitions after the June 21st rally, organizing protests such as a Hiroshima Day Die-In and participating in the Columbus chapter of the Federation for Progress, a national organization that aimed to bring together organizations concerned with a range of issues, including "employment, housing, health care, disarmament, confronting racist, sexist and homophobic practices, classism, poverty, education, foreign policy, energy conservation and ecologically sound resources, military spending and the draft." A WAC member who was part of the Federation for Progress described it at the time as "a concrete opportunity to plan a radical feminist United States."[21] She saw its broad focus as integral to radical feminism and was confident that a radical feminist agenda would be central to the mixed-sex effort. Although the organization was short-lived, it served to bring together feminists and other progressive activists in Columbus.

In the later 1980s and early 1990s, the women I interviewed

continued to participate in mixed-sex organizations that addressed broad social change issues. The majority regularly donated money to a variety of organizations working for social change, both in response to direct-mail fundraising appeals and through personal contact with local groups. One woman explained that her social movement participation was limited to making financial contributions.

> My involvement is peripheral. I do it the way a middle-class person with extra money does it. I contribute to half a dozen or so organizations. And when they send me stuff in the mail and I can stand to open one more piece of junk mail, I do the questionnaire and send it back. And I sign the petitions and write the letters and whatnot, and that's about it.

Making donations was important, explained another woman, because it reflected on what kind of a person she was.

> [Feminist author] Letty Pogrebin once said that instead of worrying about what your underwear looked like if you were caught in an automobile accident, you should look at the last check you wrote. I'm very conscious of that as an index of what you'd want to be known for. Every month I try to give twenty-five dollars to something. It's usually either antiwar stuff, [or] environmental, like Sierra Club, Greenpeace. Lately the Southern Poverty Law Center Klanwatch program gets a lot of my money. Very occasionally, a political candidate. Amnesty International. Stuff like that.

Many feminists did not limit themselves to financial contributions, but participated more actively. Some did so by joining mixed-sex organizations. The groups that the women I interviewed were part of included the *Columbus Free Press* (an alternative newspaper), the New Jewish Agenda (a progressive Jewish group that addresses a variety of issues), and the National Lawyers' Guild. Women also joined groups that opposed U.S. intervention in Central America and Iraq; taught conflict resolution, peace education, and radical economic education to unions and environmental and peace groups; and opposed racist violence and gay-bashing. Others worked with a socialist organization, a home for retarded adults, and organizations promoting recycling and opposing the dumping of toxic waste. Some produced peace and antinuclear cultural events, including concerts by the Latin American musical group Sabia and the Wallflower Order dance troupe.

I spoke with these longtime activists during the U.S. intervention and war with Iraq (between August 1990 and March 1991), and almost all were involved in opposition to the war, in ways ranging from talking to co-workers about why they thought the war was wrong, to signing an advertisement in the *New York Times* by faculty opposed to the war, to attending and organizing antiwar demonstrations. At one large antiwar demonstration in Columbus, I observed at least four of the women I had interviewed. Considering that 79 percent of the American public supported the war, this level of opposition among feminist veterans is striking.[22]

Participating in progressive organizations brought women at least some of the rewards they had received in the women's movement of the 1970s. One former member of Women Against Rape described the sense of community and the satisfaction of working for a common cause that she experienced in the National Lawyers' Guild, a group of lawyers concerned with social reform, in the early 1980s.

> It was just a wonderful time, because it brought back all the feelings that I had when we were doing Women Against Rape and the Rape Crisis Center. . . . It was some of the same people who came up through similar organizations, [although] not just WAR. People would come up through the Community Union, which was civil rights and community organizing, Tenants' Union, Open Door Clinic.

Within mixed-sex organizations, feminists built on lessons they learned in the women's movement. For example, a woman who now focuses on Native American issues explained that one of the reasons she speaks in schools about Indian culture is that the women's movement taught her the importance of one-to-one contact for promoting social change, that "you have to speak to people to get them to understand."

In addition to working in mixed-sex organizations and coalitions, feminists formed women's organizations to address issues such as peace, nuclear power, imperialism, racism, unions and workers' issues, and the environment. Nationally, organizations like the Women's International League for Peace and Freedom, the union women's organization 9 to 5, the Seneca Falls Women's Peace Camp, and Women's Action for Nuclear Disarmament mobilized feminists into a variety of visible actions. These organizations developed and disseminated influential feminist perspectives on issues of peace and social justice. By defining "patriarchy" to include domination of women, militarism, and exploitation of the natural world, they fused feminist and New Left insights.

Within the peace movement, feminists have been visible in a variety of activities nationwide.[23] Women's peace encampments formed and were sustained for an extended period at military bases in Seneca Falls in New York and Puget Sound in Seattle; there were also many other smaller and shorter-lived women's peace camps.[24] Feminists organized affinity groups or caucuses within larger mixed-sex peace organizations, particularly those focusing on direct action, like the Clamshell Alliance, Abalone Alliance, and Livermore Action Group.[25] Participants in some peace camps continued to function as affinity groups after the encampment itself ended and engaged in periodic demonstrations, street theater, and other actions.[26] In addition, feminists organized women's peace demonstrations, most notably the Women's Pentagon Actions in 1980 and 1981. The Women's Pentagon Actions, like feminist collectives, emphasized lack of hierarchy, full participation by all attenders, and speaking from personal experience. For example, in 1981 participants attended a one-day preparation session for the demonstration on the following day, in order to allow the women in attendance to create the Action jointly with organizers. Women spoke from their personal experiences by painting mock tombstones with the names of women they knew who were victims of patriarchal violence or militarism.[27] In ideology and rhetoric, the women's peace movement repeatedly linked militarism to male dominance. For example, an anthology of feminist antinuclear writings is entitled *Exposing Nuclear Phallacies*.[28] Columbus activists who attended the Women's Pentagon Actions reported back to local activists, and the women's peace perspective was influential in participants' thinking about links between feminism and peace.

The environmental movement of the 1980s and early 1990s has been closely tied to the peace and antinuclear movements. The women's movement—especially the emerging perspective of "ecofeminism"—has contributed to this close linking of the environmental cause with questions of peace, nuclear weapons and energy, racism, imperialism, and animal rights. Ecofeminism is associated with an "earth-based" spiritual approach that emphasizes treating all humans, animals, and the earth with respect; from this perspective, all forms of domination are connected, since patriarchal violence is directed not only against women, but also against animals, the earth, people of color, and Third World countries.[29]

Ecofeminism reflected the links feminists drew between patriarchy and militarism and strongly influenced organizational structure and tactics. Barbara Epstein shows that direct-action groups in the antinuclear movement drew on feminism and anarchism to shape a utopian perspective and structure that emphasized consensus decision making and egalitarianism. The ethic and actions of these "anarcha-feminist" groups were highly influential in the larger antinuclear, peace, and environmental movements. In short, Epstein suggests that the "cultural revolution" pursued by the direct action movement grew from the feminist revolution.[30]

Many Columbus activists subscribed to a feminist perspective that linked multiple forms of domination, although most did not label that perspective "ecofeminism." "There's greater issues, like war and the destruction of the planet, and they're all tied together," commented one woman. "I don't think they're separate. I think that as long as people don't value human life, the life of the other, then of course how can they value anything except greed and anger and stupidity?" Feminists' participation in other social movements reflected their broad perspective on domination. For example, a woman who had worked in the antirape movement during the 1970s continued to oppose violence against women and also worked to combat racist violence, saying, "I see it as the same as pornography, and see it as the same as my antirape work." Another woman gave workshops on sexual harassment in which she discussed a continuum of violence against women and linked it to war and the delusion that violence can solve problems.

Although feminism has profoundly changed social movements in the progressive coalition, points of difference between feminists and nonfeminists remain. Particularly fierce conflicts raged in Columbus over separatism during the early 1980s. In 1982 WAC sponsored a series of women-only dances, at the Northend Community Center, which housed many of the mixed-sex Left organizations in Columbus. Men's exclusion from these events led to complaints of "reverse discrimination" by male activists, and the Community Center allowed the dances to continue only after protracted argument.[31] Shortly afterward the Northend Community Center burned down (in an unrelated fire), and WAC offered space in its house to the Columbus Tenants' Union, a mixed-sex organization that had previously been housed in the Community Center. WAC members hotly debated having men in the house, and the collective members who originally approved the presence of the Tenants' Union were roundly criticized.[32]

In short, the transition from independent feminist organizing to working in coalition with male-dominated or mixed-sex groups was not smooth. Yet as feminists and others continued to work together, the lessons of the women's movement gradually altered the larger social movement context. Feminist organizations worked independently, in coalition with mixed-sex progressive groups, and as affinity groups or caucuses within mixed-sex groups, and individual feminists also entered other social movements. The women's movement has, in a way, come full circle, returning to reshape the social movements that sparked it twenty-five years earlier.

LESBIAN AND GAY ORGANIZING
AND THE RESPONSE TO THE AIDS EPIDEMIC

The lesbian and gay movement and the AIDS movement have been two of the largest and most vital social movements in Columbus and in the United States as a whole during the late 1980s and early 1990s.[33] Although each has an independent existence, the two movements overlap considerably. Lesbians were central to the Stonewall Riot in New York City in 1969, often considered the birth of the gay liberation movement, in which lesbian and gay bar patrons violently resisted a police raid on the Stonewall Tavern.[34] Nevertheless, the organizations that were sparked by the events at Stonewall were usually, although not exclusively, dominated by males, and early organizations such as the Gay Liberation Front and the Gay Activists' Alliance focused on issues like police entrapment, which lesbians did not see as relevant.[35] During the 1970s and early 1980s, the movement grew, established such national organizations as the National Gay Task Force, and gained notable successes, including the removal of homosexuality from the American Psychiatric

Association's classification of diseases and the election of a few openly gay and lesbian politicians.[36]

A specific concern with lesbian freedom arose nationwide in the early 1970s as lesbians in both the women's movement and the gay liberation movement protested against their exclusion from those struggles' agendas and began to organize on their own behalf.[37] Women's movement organizations addressed the issue of lesbian rights and formed some limited coalitions with gay male groups during the 1970s, but lesbian feminism remained largely separate from the male-dominated gay liberation movement throughout the 1970s and early 1980s. In Columbus, the two major lesbian feminist organizations, Lesbian Peer Support and Central Ohio Lesbians, worked in limited coalitions with mixed-sex organizations such as Ohio State University's Gay Liberation Front and the Gay Alliance during the 1970s.[38] Central Ohio Lesbians sponsored the first gay and lesbian pride march in Columbus at the Statehouse on Labor Day in 1976 and drew in gay male groups.

When Central Ohio Lesbians folded in 1977, its activities were taken up by both feminist organizations and mixed gay male and lesbian groups. For example, the Women's Music Union took over publishing the *Columbus Women's Community Calendar* (which was soon adopted by the Office of Women's Services at OSU). Yet an emerging organization called the Central Ohio Gay Coalition planned to begin publishing a gay community newspaper, and Central Ohio Lesbians encouraged former members to join this new mixed-sex group.[39] Although the Central Ohio Gay Coalition did not survive, it and Central Ohio Lesbians were precursors to the Stonewall Union, a mixed-sex gay and lesbian organization that continues to be the core of the gay and lesbian movement in Columbus. By the mid-1980s the male and female movements had moved closer together at the national level as well, as lesbians assumed positions in previously male-dominated organizations like the National Gay Task

Force, which changed its name to the National Lesbian and Gay Task Force.[40]

In the 1980s and 1990s, both feminist individuals and women's movement organizations in Columbus focused further attention on lesbian and gay rights. Many veterans of the radical women's movement—along with lesbians who were new to activism—began to work with mixed-sex gay and lesbian organizations in the late 1980s. Of the 34 women I interviewed, 12 lesbians and 1 heterosexual woman participated in the gay and lesbian movement. Their activities included serving on the board of the Stonewall Union, organizing a legal association that educates lawyers about AIDS law and gay and lesbian rights, participating in gay and lesbian groups within churches or professional associations, and attending demonstrations and meetings of groups including the Stonewall Union and Queer Nation. One college instructor who actively incorporates advocacy of gay and lesbian rights into her teaching explained that the issue was central to her:

> My primary issue now is how to have healthy recognition that a gay and lesbian lifestyle is a legitimate focus. . . . That's probably more direct and more related to my own set of things than other kinds of issues like childcare or abortion or broader quote "women's issues." But they're still all related.

The overlap between feminist and lesbian and gay organizations in Columbus was substantial by the early 1990s as they worked together on specific campaigns. Women Against Rape worked with the Stonewall Union to write a grant proposal for a project combating violence against gay men and lesbians and helped implement the program once the grant was approved. The Stonewall Union presented an award to Fan the Flames Feminist Bookstore at its annual dinner in 1988, in recognition of the bookstore's contributions to the gay and lesbian community.

One of the factors that sparked the entry of lesbian feminists into the mixed-gender gay and lesbian movement was the AIDS epidemic and the increasing homophobia that accompanied it.[41] As AIDS and publicity about it spread in the mid-1980s, both lesbians and gay men mobilized in response, forming service organizations as well as activist groups like the AIDS Coalition to Unleash Power (ACT UP). Lesbians have been a mainstay of AIDS activist and service organizations in Columbus and nationally since the beginning of the epidemic.[42] Many of the lesbians in AIDS organizations are younger or more recent activists, but longtime feminists also work on the issue. Five of the women I interviewed, four of whom are lesbians, have done so. The lesbian AIDS activists are also active in the lesbian and gay movement, underscoring the extensive overlap between the two movements. They have served as buddies to people with AIDS, attended demonstrations and meetings, and worked with the Columbus AIDS Task Force on organizing art auctions, producing public service announcements, working at AIDS testing sites, and publishing newsletters. One woman who has worked with an AIDS buddy program explained what prompted her commitment:

> For the first time I identified that this is happening to my tribe. These are my people and I need to stand with them now, because this is important. All these other silly things they were fighting for over the years were not important enough. But this is important. Nobody deserves to die alone, and no one deserves to be told that "It's your own fault that you're sick; we don't care that you're suffering."

What is at stake for her is more than which issue is most important; it is her sense of herself, her "tribe," her people. To work on AIDS means to identify herself in a fundamental way with gay men, emphasizing the commonality of sexual orientation rather than the difference of gender.

Because of these dilemmas of collective identity, some of the women I interviewed felt ambivalent about expending large amounts of energy fighting AIDS rather than working on women's issues. One typical respondent commented about her work as an AIDS buddy: "It feels pretty strange to be working and identifying with gay people instead of with lesbians or with feminist women." Her ambivalence is mirrored in the national women's movement and in the feminist press. For example, the feminist newspaper *Off Our Backs* published a commentary arguing that because women, especially lesbians, were at a low risk for contracting HIV, they should not panic about the necessity for safe sex. A few months later, the paper published a rejoinder from the women's caucus of ACT UP, New York, who argued that lesbians do engage in activities that can transmit HIV and that women should view the spread of AIDS as a political issue rather than a strictly medical one. To separate lesbians from so-called high risk groups, the authors argued, divides white, middle-class lesbians from women of color and poor women who are disproportionately affected by AIDS, and "pit[s] groups of women against each other."[43] This debate—repeated in varying forms in many publications and conversations—reflects differences over whether to redefine the lesbian feminist identity that has been shaped by white, middle-class women broadly enough to include women of color, poor women, and women who use intravenous drugs or have sex with men. In essence, the dilemma stems from working with gay men after a decade of separation from them.

The AIDS movement gave rise to new gay and lesbian groups as predominantly younger activists, politicized in ACT UP, formed mixed-gender organizations such as Queer Nation. Both ACT UP and Queer Nation are loosely organized local groups with no formal national affiliation, and both have brought direct-action tactics back into the movement. For example, ACT UP members blockaded the San Francisco Bay Bridge and demonstrated during a Catholic mass to protest against the lack of federal funds and drug testing for AIDS.

Queer Nation chapters organized "visibilities" around the country that aimed to make the heterosexual public aware of gay and lesbian existence through public displays of affection or other means of visibly claiming a queer identity. In Columbus, Queer Nation activists held "Kiss-Ins" in public settings such as local shopping malls and the Columbus Zoo. At these events, members held hands, kissed each other, and wore buttons and stickers with slogans such as "Visibly Queer" and "Dykes Take Over the World."[44]

On one hand, new lesbian and gay groups seek to encompass lesbians and gay men from various racial and ethnic groups and classes, as well as bisexuals, transsexuals or "transgenderists," and those who participate in sexual practices defined as deviant, such as sadomasochism. These groups have constructed a collective identity that embraces diversity, as exemplified in the Queer Nation slogan "Queer = Difference, Nation = Sameness."[45] On the other hand, many Queer Nation groups remained male-dominated, and in some cities conflicts over both sexism and racism tore chapters apart.[46] In Columbus, Queer Nation members were mostly young women associated with OSU. This was typical of the Columbus pattern of lesbians' centrality to mixed-gender organizations, dating back to the 1970s, when the visibility of Lesbian Peer Support and Central Ohio Lesbians was key to organizing efforts.

In the 1980s, the influence of the women's movement was apparent in women's visibility as leaders both in professionalized groups such as the Stonewall Union and the Columbus AIDS Task Force and in militant organizations such as ACT UP and Queer Nation. In 1992 the executive directors of both the Columbus AIDS Task Force and the Stonewall Union were women. The Stonewall Union mandates that 50 percent of board members must be women, in part because its first president came directly out of the women's movement and recruited committed feminists to serve on the first elected board of directors.

The women's movement has also shaped how gay and lesbian

activists define their issues and grievances, prompting mixed-sex organizations to expand their healthcare agenda from AIDS (an issue that affects more gay men than lesbians) to include support for increased funding for breast cancer, abortion rights, disability rights, and universal access to health care. Further, the gay and lesbian movement has begun to address racism within movement organizations, a development that Urvashi Vaid, former Executive Director of the National Gay and Lesbian Task Force, believed grew from lesbian feminist attempts to reckon with racism.[47] Feminist antirape organizations in Columbus and nationwide have been instrumental in the growing move against gay-bashing, helping gay and lesbian groups to conduct self-defense training and to set up crisis hotlines for survivors of attacks. Gay men, sometimes reluctantly, have begun to participate in debates that have permeated lesbian feminist communities over issues like sadomasochism and sexual power and have become increasingly willing to discuss subtle dynamics of gender inequality within the gay and lesbian movement. For example, one member reported that male activists in the Columbus chapter of Queer Nation have discussed sexism as a problem that affects them. Within the Stonewall Union, active feminists on the board confront male members who monopolize conversation and debate. One lesbian activist even reported that a young gay man told her he had begun to identify publicly with the label "lesbian feminist."

Although lesbians and feminists have transformed the gay liberation movement into a mixed-sex movement that addresses lesbian feminist issues, the transformation is far from complete. Conflicts between lesbian feminists and gay men over questions of sexism and organizational structure remain. One woman I interviewed who is active in the Columbus AIDS Task Force explained that, although she works with gay men and feels a sense of connection to many of them, she finds their sexism troubling. She believes that sexism among gay men is increasing rather than decreasing in the 1990s.

I still think that they [gay men] have a lot of blind spots, and it's in their interest to accept male privilege, so they do. At least they used to be a little guilty about it in the seventies, but now it's like [they say], "Yeah, we're rich. What of it? What's it to ya, babe?" [*Laughs*] Gay men don't have much better consciousness than straight men. They never have, and I can't say whether they're getting better or not. I guess I'm more tolerant of them now than I used to be.

Another point of continuing frustration for many feminist veterans who now participate in professionalized gay and lesbian organizations is those groups' formal structure, hierarchy, and lack of grassroots involvement. A woman who served on the board of the Stonewall Union pointed out that its structure differed greatly from feminist structure.

Their structure is so different than in the women's movement. I was barely a member of the group, and they called me and asked me to be on the board, and said, "All you have to do is go to four meetings [a year]."

The changes in structure that occurred in the post–New Left movements as a result of feminist critiques have not taken hold in the professionalized wing of the gay and lesbian movement.

Although changes in organizational structure have made more headway in Queer Nation, sexism is not, of course, limited to professionalized gay and lesbian organizations. A participant in Queer Nation in New York wrote that, as a result of male dominance in the group, she eventually came to believe that "the map of the new queer nation would have a male face and . . . mine and those of my many-colored sisters would simply be background material. . . . [I]t is nearly impossible to cross the million-year-old canyons that make men, men, and women, women."[48] Although Queer Nation differs from chapter to chapter, and in Columbus is largely female, groups made up of younger activists are not necessarily more hospitable to feminists than are professionalized organizations.

Yet despite such conflicts, lesbian feminists, gay male activists, and those working on AIDS issues have formed a sometimes uneasy working alliance that is prompting changes on all sides. Just as feminism reshapes the lesbian and gay movement, participation in struggles over AIDS and lesbian and gay freedom alters the women's movement. The debates and conflicts that arise—over collective identity, ideology, organizational structure—point to long-lasting splits in the women's movement around the question of separatism and raise new questions about the extent to which other movements have really adopted a feminist perspective.

THE RESURGENCE OF FEMINIST SPIRITUALITY

A variety of religious and spiritual movements emerged nationally during the 1980s, and Columbus was no exception to this trend. The Religious Right grew during this period, but a religious Left also gained strength within mainline denominations. In addition, a "neo-pagan" movement flourished, including Wiccan groups and others that draw on a variety of nature religions.[49] The number of participants in neo-pagan movements nationally has been estimated at two hundred thousand.[50] Eastern religions, particularly various forms of Buddhist practice and Yoga, also grew in the United States. Outside organized religions, a spiritual revitalization often referred to as the "New Age" movement popularized a range of practices, including spiritual healing, channeling messages from spirits, interest in the magical properties of crystals, belief in reincarnation, and an overall interest in spiritual growth and philosophy.[51]

Much of this spiritual revival has taken a specifically feminist slant. Feminist caucuses and critiques of sexist language, male conceptions of the deity, and women's exclusion from leadership have proliferated within traditional Judeo-Christian religions.[52]

Outside such institutions, feminists are constructing what they term a "postpatriarchal" spirituality that builds on a holistic spiritual tradition, emphasizes the "intrinsic unity of all forms of being," and includes "women's spirituality, Goddess spirituality, Wicca, Native American spirituality, Taoism, Buddhism, Sufism, and yoga."[53] Feminist spiritual groups include Wiccan covens, women's spiritual affinity groups within antinuclear organizations, and a loosely knit network of individuals and groups that conduct rituals on solstices, equinoxes, and other occasions and that are linked by national and local publications, conferences, and festivals.[54] In Columbus, a number of feminist covens are active alongside feminist groups within traditional religions.[55]

Few core radical feminist activists in Columbus considered themselves religious or spiritually active during the 1970s, but many became interested in spirituality during the past decade, although others remained uninterested or disdainful. Five of the women I interviewed have become involved with Wicca or other forms of neo-pagan spirituality, ranging from one woman who was ordained as a Wiccan priestess to others who attend women's spiritual circles observing the solstices and full moons. Others reported miscellaneous activities including participating in a meditation group, attending a class in psychic awareness, organizing a spiritual healing workshop, and simply adopting a general focus on the transcendent qualities of the natural world. Three women are practicing Buddhists. In addition, some have brought their feminism into other established religions. For example, two are active in women's groups in the Methodist Church, and one is part of a feminist theology group in the Unitarian Universalist Church. One woman who has adopted a feminist spiritual outlook explained that it represented an important change for her:

> Sometimes I make the mistake of thinking that there are no more "ah-ha" experiences, that now I've got it all down. The

final issue of spirituality was like one more "ah-ha . . . " I did not realize the extent to which even I, radical feminist that I was, did not finally put aside a Christian frame of reference.

Feminist organizations in Columbus did occasionally address issues of spirituality during the 1970s, but it was often a source of controversy in those days. Recall the disagreement within WAC over changing the newsletter's title to "Womoon Rising" and the accompanying question of "goddess worship."[56] One former member of WAC who joined the organization in the early 1970s and remained uninterested in spirituality expressed bafflement about its popularity.

> I think a lot of my friends are just weird, the stuff they're into. It's all interesting to me, but I can't get into it. All the goddess worship, all the stuff with crystals. I can understand it on a certain level, but on another level it doesn't have any meaning to me.

Some feminists decried the emphasis on spirituality as detracting from what they saw as more political direct confrontation of social institutions.[57] Yet the women's movement and individual feminists have had an impact both on the larger New Age movement and on traditional religions. One woman who has become active in the Methodist Church explained that she was able to do so because her church has made changes inspired by the women's movement.

> I've gone back to the church after twenty years of rejecting Christianity. . . . I've discovered a church that has made substantive changes over the past twenty years. I found that the church now supports women's issues from the pulpit and supports gay issues from the pulpit. And the church I belong to is in fact a very liberal church that does work with AIDS.

Another woman who is a practicing Buddhist sees the ideas of New Age spirituality as important to social change and as essentially consistent with feminism.

I think that the interest in Eastern religions and the interest in New Age spirituality, all of these things are coming together in the same direction. What is it that they all have in common, that they all teach? Personal responsibility. . . . I think that's a spiritual idea of great power.

In addition to an emphasis on personal responsibility, even the popular New Age movement conceptualizes deities or the divine as not exclusively male and suggests that the everyday experiences of women can be spiritually meaningful.[58] The "new paganism" includes goddesses as well as gods and draws on Native American teachings with respect for the experiences of both women and men.[59] A burgeoning "men's movement" incorporates spiritual traditions from Native American and Jungian sources to redefine masculinity.[60]

Many feminists criticize both the men's movement and the New Age movement for viewing gender differences as innate and for sometimes celebrating masculinity at the expense of women. Others are disturbed by New Age cultural imperialism, or the appropriation of Native American religions.[61] These are valid critiques. At the same time, the New Age movement could not exist in its current form without the changes wrought by the women's movement. As with the lesbian and gay movement, feminist veterans are both central to the burgeoning spiritual movement and ambivalent about its impact on the women's movement. But for better or worse, "New Age" spirituality has profoundly altered the face of feminism.

THE IMPACT OF FEMINISM ON THE RECOVERY AND SELF-HELP MOVEMENTS

Another source of ambivalence and debate among women's movement veterans is one of the most active and visible social phenomena of the 1980s and early 1990s: the movements around psychological self-help and recovery from addictions. Groups using the 12-step technique developed by Alcoholics Anonymous (AA) multiplied, not only for individuals recovering from addictions to alcohol and other substances, but also for individuals who define themselves as adult children of alcoholics, co-dependent, incest survivors, batterers, sex addicts, compulsive shoppers, overeaters, and others. Along with these groups, a body of popular self-help literature outlines countless ways to improve oneself, be more effective, or increase happiness.[62] Women are much of the constituency of 12-step groups and the target audience of most self-help books.[63]

Within the feminist and lesbian communities, large numbers of women have "gotten into recovery" and attend 12-step meetings.[64] A organized concern with substance abuse arose in the Columbus women's movement in April 1980, when Lesbian Peer Support, OSU Women's Studies, WAC, and the Women's Music Union co-sponsored a workshop on alcohol and substance abuse among lesbians.[65] The first on-going women's recovery group in Columbus was the Lesbian Association on Substance Abuse, which joined WAC in March 1981 and was defunct by the following year.[66] It explicitly linked substance abuse to the societal oppression of lesbians, writing:

> Being a lesbian in this community for many women means facing alienation, isolation, and oppression. The result can be tremendous stress. One out of three lesbians are finding a personal solution in numbing themselves with alcohol and/or drugs. . . . As lesbians we need to support each other to make our lives healthy and chemical-free. We also must confront the societal oppression that isolates and debilitates us and is the root of higher rates of substance abuse in our community.[67]

In 1982, feminists and other women who were attending Alcoholics Anonymous meetings formed Women's Outreach for Women, a center that provides space, organization, and networking for a variety of 12-step programs. The center quickly grew to encompass what one organizer estimated as "hundreds of lesbians coming through and getting sober." One participant described the rapid growth of the recovery movement.

> I got into recovery because everybody I drank with got into recovery. . . . I remember us sitting in the bar one night, drinking, looking around us, and there were all these people in there who we knew weren't drinking anymore, who were going to these meetings. We were talking about how it was like the invasion of the body snatchers. And then within a month, I think, both of us had started getting into recovery.

As a result of the recovery movement, many feminist cultural events do not serve alcohol, and most communities have support systems for women who are part of 12-step programs. For example, the Michigan Womyn's Music Festival, a yearly week-long event that draws between five thousand and ten thousand women, has a "Sober Support Tent" with round-the-clock 12-step meetings and provides "chemical-free" seating and camping areas where alcohol, cigarettes, and drugs are prohibited. The Ohio Lesbian Festival, a one-day event, also provides an area for sober support in which women conduct 12-step meetings or talk with others who are part of 12-step programs.

Despite the visibility of sobriety in the feminist community, only 4 of the 34 women I interviewed identified themselves as "in recovery," whereas many others expressed opposition to the women's movement's current focus on recovery and self-help.[68] Nevertheless, those who have entered 12-step programs have been very influential there. One woman who was a co-founder of Women's Outreach for Women explained that experienced lesbian feminist activists who were new to recovery were instrumental in establishing the organization.

> These straight women [who had been in recovery longer] had talked about their dream of having a women's center for like a year and a half. But they had none of the organizing background that all of us had. And so nothing was happening, they just kept

talking about it. Well, we got wind of this, and like about six of us went to this meeting, and then within a month after that, there was a center.

The new women's 12-step groups were a significant change from previous male-dominated groups. One co-founder of Women's Outreach for Women described how difficult mixed-sex A A meetings were for feminists:

> If you were kind of a woman-identified woman, straight or gay, A A is kind of a problem. Especially back then when the meet-ings were mostly men. . . . If a woman made a comment at a meeting about not liking the [sexist] language, the guys would just say, "Oh, that's heresy. We don't need to worry about how this is written." It was kind of oppressive.

Such problems at mixed-sex meetings have become less com-mon with the growth of women's 12-step groups and, indeed, a feminist recovery movement. Many self-help books written by feminists, such as Ann Wilson Schaef's books on addiction and Laura Bass and Laura Davis's guide for incest survivors, have been widely read by both feminists and nonfeminists, and femi-nist 12-step groups are part of a larger 12-step network.[69] In 1991 two Columbus feminists opened a store called "Carpe Diem" (now defunct) that sold a variety of recovery-related items, such as books, T-shirts, and artwork, and catered to cus-tomers both male and female, feminist and not.[70] Self-help movements that are not based on the 12-step program have also grown out of and been affected by feminism. The postpartum depression self-help movement, for example, gained momentum from the earlier women's health movement and models its sup-port groups on feminist consciousness-raising groups.[71] The feminist emphasis on the value of personal experience as a tool for understanding the world and the notion of the personal as political are central tenets of the recovery and self-help move-ments.

Feminists' turn toward self-help and personal growth has

transformed the women's movement as well as the recovery movement. One woman who has been part of Women's Outreach for Women since its inception explained that she sees recovery from addictions and hurtful childhood experiences as providing explanations and solutions for social problems that are more pivotal to social change than those addressed by the women's movement.

> We are getting more conscious of the extent to which there is child abuse, and sexual abuse, that kind of stuff. I think the real fundamental answers to our problems are there, somehow. Really getting in there at the real personal level of how people deal with one another in the family and in organizations. I think recovery has a lot to do with . . . our potential for correcting some of the problems that we've created.

Participants in Women's Outreach for Women believed that recovery was important to the success of the women's movement because addictions prevented activists from contributing fully to efforts for social change, as this member explained:

> I thought we could show that [Women's Outreach for Women] could sort of be a channel for women getting themselves together, and then having energy to put into things. I believed that women who were in recovery would stand a chance of being a lot more positive and constructive in the way that they were able to contribute to things.

In some ways, this belief was a natural outgrowth of an increasing emphasis in feminist circles on "internalized oppression," or the ways that women's experiences in a sexist society made them distrust and criticize other women, think poorly of themselves, and limit their own aspirations.[72]

Nevertheless, many experienced feminist activists disapproved of the growing attendance at 12-step meetings while political change organizations languished for lack of participation. These women viewed recovery as an apolitical distraction from organizing for social change. One woman who had not entered recovery viewed the popularity of 12-step organizations as a fad and questioned the notion that feminist recovery organizations were nonsexist.

It became in [for women] to say they were an alcoholic and then not to do that [drink] anymore, and start the [recovery] groups. I think that AA didn't quite do it for a lot of them, because of their politics, so they tried to restructure and do things differently. But I don't think they really did do anything differently. [*Laughs*]

Another woman, disappointed at the form taken by emerging 12-step groups for women, complained that

from a feminist value structure with a feminist perspective, all they did was imitate AA. They went and said the Lord's Prayer, for God's sake. I would say to my friends, "What are you doing? You come over here and talk about radical feminism and then you go over there and say the Lord's Prayer? Doesn't that cause a little dissidence in your mind?" [They would say], "No, no, God is whoever you want it to be . . . "

Writers in feminist and lesbian/gay publications criticized the self-help movement as apolitical and even antifeminist for its focus on personal growth rather than social change, lack of concern with structural causes of individual difficulties, acceptance of hierarchy, and connections to traditional Christianity.[73] One woman who began attending 12-step meetings in the early 1980s confirmed that her political involvement has become less confrontational, but she saw this as a positive change:

I would rather try to feel empowering and empowered, constructive, as opposed to trying to attack the patriarchy. A group of us [in my workplace] are filing a complaint with Affirmative Action. . . . And I really hate to do it. I just really wish that there were some other way. I wish that we could engage with these men who run this program, in a way that would somehow not have this confrontation over this.

Although she saw the avoidance of confrontation as a necessary strategy for individual recovery, activists who were not involved in the recovery movement believed this was a dangerous turn for the women's movement. One of the women who worked to keep WAC alive in its final years believed that the popularity of Women's Outreach for Women was part of what made it hard for WAC to survive:

> I think a lot of women who would have joined the Women's Action Collective in earlier years went to join WOW and sort of conveniently became addicted to something so that they could have a social gathering place.

With the rapid growth of the recovery movement, feminists who did not join 12-step programs found themselves excluded from a growing and vital segment of the women's movement community. One such woman explained how this made her more marginal in the feminist community:

> Everybody went through this phase where they were concerned about co-dependency, any kind of substance abuse or chemical dependence, or being an adult child of an alcoholic. And I guess I feel fortunate enough not to have to deal with any of that. But I also feel left out, because I didn't get to go to any of those meetings and have any of those wonderful—whatever it is they do. They formed this community that I'm not part of any- more. . . . At first, we were all [saying], "What's happening here? Everybody's going off to these meetings, it's so apolitical." And then, all of a sudden, that was it. That's all that was hap- pening.

Like the move toward feminist spirituality and the lesbian and gay movement, recovery and self-help reshaped the women's movement as they were transformed by it. Participants hotly debate the effects of recovery on political organizing in the women's movement. Proponents argue that drinking was exces- sive in the feminist community of the 1970s and that a sober group of activists can be much more effective than addicted women. Others view the focus on addiction and co-dependency as a way of taking the political wind out of the movement's sails, diverting women away from collective action into personal solutions for problems of dependence and passivity (relabeled "co-dependency") that actually have structural roots in female socialization.[74] More broadly, this debate reflects fundamental questions about feminists' participation in other causes: How are women's collective problems linked to individual experiences and to other issues? Is the women's movement spreading its influence by linking to other movements, or is it spreading itself too thin?

TRANSFORMING PROGRESSIVE POLITICS

The women's movement has affected other movements both directly, through feminist individuals and organizational coalitions, and indirectly, as a feminist critique of sexism gained credence and activists from different movements met through overlapping community and cultural events.[75] The "progressive social movement community" shares many members and organizers, ideological perspectives, opponents, and a political culture that resists the dominant culture.

The movements that make up this community do not share everything, however. Substantial disagreements remain, particularly between more separatist elements of the women's movement and mixed-sex organizations, between lesbian, gay, and AIDS groups and those that grow from the heterosexual-dominated Left, and between groups that emphasize personal transformation and those that focus on collective action to confront social structures. In the first case, the conflicts arise from feminists' belief that feminist activists should make women's issues their first priority and their impression that male activists remain domineering, and from male progressives' resentment of their exclusion from women-only events or spaces.

In the second case, the conflict centers around whether lesbian and gay oppression is a central political problem or, as some heterosexual Leftists maintain, a more peripheral question of "lifestyle." Part of the job of forging a coalition between lesbian and gay groups and the Left has been accomplished by the women's movement. Coalitions between the two camps increased in the late 1980s and early 1990s as gay and lesbian organizations addressed issues such as inequalities of race and class, and Left organizations began to include the oppression of gays and lesbians as one of their concerns. Feminist personnel with overlapping group memberships built part of this bridge by bringing a concern with heterosexism into Left organizations and incorporating a commitment to broad social transformation into lesbian and gay groups.

The final conflict, over individual versus structural courses of action, is at core about whether and how culture and identity—the politics of daily life—are political. Are spirituality and self-help crucial to social change, or are they diversions from confronting the power structure? How important is combatting "internalized oppression" along with oppression from external institutions? If we take seriously the idea that inequality is maintained by cultural hegemony and that domination and subordination are reproduced at the micro as well as the macro level, we must also take seriously actions that aim to challenge the effects of oppression on individuals in their daily lives.[76] The self-help and spiritual movements certainly are not inevitably revolutionary; they often leave structural inequality unchallenged, and they can be regressive. But they are not inherently apolitical or conservative simply because they address internalized forms of oppression.

These remain heated debates that have the potential—often realized—to polarize activists. But it is important not to underestimate the power of a shared enemy for producing coalitions. Lesbians, gay men, longtime peace activists, and even proponents of New Age spirituality are faced with a unified counter-movement. By mounting broad opposition to the range of movements for social change that developed in the 1960s and 1970s, the New Right has drawn together a progressive coalition to resist a conservative backlash.

We can see the connections between the women's movement and other social movements of the 1980s and 1990s as another result of tightening political opportunities, the hostile cultural climate, and widespread social movement demobilization. As the women's movement moved into a period of relative quiescence, other social movements absorbed feminist activists and helped to preserve and disseminate feminist ideology, culture, and innovations in strategy, tactics, and organizational structure. At the same time, the political climate became more hostile to other movements for social change as well as to the women's movement. Feminist individuals and organizations have helped other social movements survive by constructing new organizations and innovative actions. Simply, in the low point of a cycle of protest, activists and organizations from different social movements overlap in order to stay alive and maximize their impact. By attending each others' rallies, signing each others' petitions, and donating money to each others' causes, members of overlapping movements in a broad social movement community help each other survive a hostile period.

In so doing, social movements transform each other. The women's movement influenced many progressive and personal transformative social movements of the 1980s and 1990s. As the civil rights movement was in a sense the genesis of an era of struggle, the women's movement, in turn, sparked the next phase of organizing. Yet transformations went both ways. When the women's movement addressed both broad progressive issues and personal growth beginning in the late 1970s, it too changed. As new and longtime feminists began to focus on recovery from addictions or spirituality, racism and other inequalities within the women's movement, the struggles of gay men and people with AIDS, and broad issues such as nuclear disarmament, others questioned whether these were productive directions for the women's movement. Does the new blending of feminist organizing with other social movements signal the spreading influence of the women's movement, or a new era of women's invisibility? The Columbus case suggests that women's concerns have not been lost in other movements even when they have been more broadly defined.

The growing overlap between the women's movement and other social movements strongly affected longtime feminists. Some supported the changes while others opposed them, but all faced a new environment as activists. The same hostile climate that led veterans of the 1960s and 1970s movement to pursue social change in their work and daily lives also led some feminists and women's movement organizations to make common cause with other movements. The political generation that led the women's movement in the 1960s and 1970s was influential in other movements by the 1980s, to be sure. But younger activists also spurred some of the changes, and generational differences produced some of the conflicts over what constituted *political* actions and what were legitimate feminist issues.

Such debates and changes in the definition of feminism were not confined to points of overlap with other movements; the radical feminist movement itself changed during the 1980s. Changes within the radical feminist challenge were partly an effect of the influence of other social movements, but were also a response to the hostile political and social climate. In addition, differences between longtime feminists—all four of the microcohorts that made up the heyday political generation—and newcomers to the movement led to conflicts and reshaped radical feminism's directions.

6 :: FEMINISTS IN THE "POSTFEMINIST" AGE: THE WOMEN'S MOVEMENT IN THE 1980S

THROUGHOUT MY CONVERSATIONS with longtime feminists, "the Eighties" loomed as a grim symbol of antifeminism. Yet even as veterans left women's movement organizations in the 1980s, they sustained a feminist challenge in their work and daily lives and within other social movements. In short, women who joined the movement in the 1960s or 1970s remained active feminists, but, as we have seen, most were no longer core participants in the organized women's movement. What, then, became of the organized women's movement in the 1980s? Women's movement organizations and feminist culture survived through the decade, staffed by some longtime activists along with many new recruits. Survival does not necessarily entail stasis, however, and in fact the women's movement changed significantly during the 1980s. It faced setbacks and won victories; stuck with some goals and strategies, abandoned others, and defined new ones; and emerged at the end of the decade changed in structure, strategy, and collective identity. "Feminist" came to mean something quite different by 1990 than it had meant in the 1970s.

Both the survival and the transformation of the women's

movement grow from the intersection between the persistence of feminist *individuals* and the endurance of women's movement *organizations and culture*. This chapter and the following one analyze the changing course of the women's movement in the 1980s and early 1990s and consider the part played in these changes by the political generation who organized the movement in the 1970s. Shifts in the women's movement, I suggest, did not result primarily from changes in the perspective or actions of longtime radical feminists. Instead, they grew from the entrance of a new political generation whose collective identity was forged both by the women's movement's strength in the 1970s and the virulent opposition it faced in the 1980s. Just as we can understand the shifting course of the movement during the 1970s by tracing the entrance and influence of successive micro-cohorts of participants, we can view its development in the 1980s and early 1990s in light of the influence of a new political generation.

The four micro-cohorts of the radical feminist heyday congealed into one political generation during the 1980s when their commonalities with each other and their differences from newcomers to the movement outweighed their differences from each other. After the movement's decline, the simple experience of immersion in a more flourishing movement distinguished the earlier political generation from new entrants who had never been part of a growing, thriving, grassroots radical women's movement. Members of the four micro-cohorts still differed in their perceptions of the 1970s women's movement, but, as we have seen, they did not differ significantly in how they responded to the hostile context of the 1980s by weaving their politics into work and daily life. They also did not differ significantly in their orientation toward the organized women's movement in the 1980s.

SOCIAL MOVEMENT CYCLES AND
THE 1980S WOMEN'S MOVEMENT

The notion has gained credence that social movements—especially those based in persistent social cleavages such as gender, race, or class—survive over decades or even centuries, going through cycles of growing and shrinking levels of mobilization. In contrast to approaches that see each wave of protest as emerging anew, a cycle approach emphasizes links between the organizations and activists that make up successive waves of protest. In this vein, new evidence points to links between the woman suffrage movement and women's liberation, the Old Left and the New Left, and the Old Left and the radical women's movement.[1]

Central to the idea that challenges survive over the long haul is an examination of the ways that they endure the lean periods. Movement organizations can sustain their challenge by adopting what Verta Taylor terms "abeyance structures," organizational forms that can survive when protest is not feasible, sustaining a core of activists and the ideas, institutions, and resources of the movement through a hostile period. In the case of the women's rights movement of the 1940s and 1950s, the National Woman's Party's tightly knit structure and homogeneous membership allowed it to endure.[2] Similarly, the early civil rights movement rested on what Aldon Morris calls "movement halfway houses," small organizations such as the Highlander Folk School that maintained the rudiments of challenge during the 1930s, 1940s, and early 1950s when there was little externally oriented activism around African American freedom, and that trained a subsequent generation of activists.[3] Relatively small and limited organizations can be influential through their contacts with the emerging organizations of a later wave of mobilization. By passing on their knowledge, resources, and point of view to their successors, movements in abeyance effectively create continuity between one surge of mobilization and the next.

It is not only organizations that see movements through lean times. The people who staff those organizations are also important, as are others who internalized the movement's goals and identity during more prosperous years—the political generation of activists who energized the preceding wave of protest. The remnants of mass collective action that survive in quiescent periods, whether organizations or individuals, can accomplish only limited gains without a mass movement and more favorable political opportunities to back them up. But they are important to the overall survival and success of a social movement because they preserve its legacy for a later political generation of activists.[4]

Lasting social movements are not staffed by only one political generation. Multiple micro-cohorts of activists work side by side during a movement's peak. After the peak, activists who joined the movement during its heyday (one political generation) coexist with a smaller number who have come to the movement more recently (a second political generation). Each of these political generations forms a relatively stable collective identity based on members' initial transformative experiences in the women's movement. Because the experience of entering the women's movement during its peak is quite unlike that of entering during a downturn, it is not surprising that activists in different political generations have constructed different feminist identities.

The women's movement entered a tough period of retrenchment and opposition in the 1980s. Nevertheless, the 1980s women's movement was not "in abeyance" in the same sense as the post–World War II women's movement, largely because new recruits continued to enter, albeit in smaller numbers. On one hand, the 1980s contained massive opposition and setbacks for feminism that drove longtime activists out of social movement organizations and into more individual forms of agitation. "Feminism" became a dirty word in many circles, and polls showed that many of those who agreed with feminist goals did not consider themselves feminists. But open hostility from the Presidential administrations of Ronald Reagan and George Bush galvanized previously inactive women into action even as it rolled back gains on abortion, pay equity, educational funding, sexual harassment, and other central feminist goals. New recruits continued to enter the movement, and feminist organizations and culture remained dynamic and vital; this was not the case in earlier "abeyance periods."[5]

In some ways, the women's movement actually grew more visible and accepted during the 1980s. National organizations such as NOW, the National Abortion Rights Action League, and the Women's Equity Action League gained more secure financial footing and built political contacts on Capitol Hill and within the Democratic Party. At the state level, growing numbers of feminists were elected to state legislatures and local office. Women's studies programs, long a movement goal in most college towns, grew in number; the program at OSU, like many, achieved a measure of intellectual credibility and financial security. Feminist perspectives on rape and sexual harassment—as widespread social problems for which victims are not to blame—received widespread attention and credibility. Some local organizations secured government and grant funding and settled into providing services to women.[6] Simultaneously, the alternative feminist culture that grew during the 1970s alongside feminist protest remained vibrant, and national cultural events and institutions, such as women's music festivals, lesbian travel agencies, and countless publications, increased in size and number. In short, despite opposition, the women's movement firmly established many gains and organizations.

Yet at the same time, most forms of grassroots mobilization declined. Despite substantial donations and "paper membership" in national organizations such as NOW and the National Abortion Rights Action League, grassroots participation in local chapters dropped. Most autonomous local women's movement organizations—whether radical, socialist, or liberal feminist—

also fell apart by the early 1980s. In Columbus, as we have seen, only Women Against Rape and Fan the Flames Feminist Bookstore survived among the many organizations of the 1970s. The women's movement community and lesbian feminist culture, couched in political terms, provided the most vital activities at the grassroots. In other words, both nationally and locally, lesbian feminist cultural institutions and institutionalized social movement organizations staffed by paid professionals predominated.

In addition to taking new organizational forms, the women's movement as a whole emphasized different goals than it did in the 1970s. The changing definition of what constitute "feminist issues" was a result of underlying shifts in collective identity as well as activists' response to external threats and opportunities. Many concerns that feminists raised in the previous decade, such as violence against women, employment discrimination, child care, lesbian rights, and reproductive rights, remained central to the 1980s agenda, but additional issues gained prominence as connections between the women's movement and other social movements grew. There was more attention than ever to differences among women and to racism, classism, and the issues of disabled women and other groups within the "women's community." Self-help groups, including 12-step recovery programs, support groups, peer counseling groups, and feminist therapies became a large sector of the women's movement in the 1980s and 1990s.[7] Feminist spirituality flourished. These trends show both an increasing focus on personal growth and transformation—the elimination of "internalized oppression"—as a means of social change, and a greater recognition of variation in the experiences and structural positions of women.

In short, feminist collective identity, or how participants understood what it meant to be a feminist, changed in the 1980s along with women's movement organizations and culture. But changes in the identity and activities of the organized movement and in those of longtime feminists do not always coincide.

Most women I interviewed are not centrally active in professionalized liberal feminist organizations, institutionalized radical
feminist service organizations, or lesbian feminist culture, and
most view themselves as different from incoming activists. I
turn next to a discussion of the place of veterans of the 1970s
movement in changing women's movement organizations and
culture during the 1980s.

WOMEN'S MOVEMENT ORGANIZATIONS

Twin trends characterized the course of women's movement organizations in the 1980s. On one hand, national organizations
founded in the 1960s and 1970s took center stage as most local
and radical groups folded. Prime among these were NOW, the
National Abortion Rights Action League (NARAL), and the
Women's Equity Action League. All relied heavily on paid
national leadership, direct mail fundraising, and tactics that
required little grassroots participation, such as lobbying and
funding candidates for elective office.[8] On the other hand, organizations that survived from the "radical" wing of the movement—mostly those that received grant funding or had other
sources of income—established formal, often bureaucratic structures, focused on service provision, and often allied closely with
the state. These included shelters for battered women, rape
crisis centers, job-training programs for displaced homemakers
or women entering traditionally male occupations, and the like.[9]

Distinctions between "liberal" and "radical" wings of the
movement grew blurrier than ever as "liberal" organizations addressed formerly taboo issues such as lesbianism and adopted
some of the innovations of collective structure, such as modified
consensus decision making and consciousness-raising groups,
and as "radical" groups became institutionalized social service
providers.[10] Veterans of the 1970s movement faced unpleasant
dilemmas: whether to participate in organizations that they

viewed as insufficiently radical in analysis or structure but that addressed issues with which they were concerned, and how to respond to the institutionalization of radical feminist organizations.

The Dominance of Professionalized Organizations

The fight for the ratification of the ERA in the early 1980s produced a groundswell of support for women's movement organizations that operated in the political arena. NOW, the Women's Equity Action League, and the National Women's Political Caucus grew in size, visibility, and influence as feminists from all segments of the movement, including radical grassroots organizations, joined together to urge the amendment's ratification.[11] Columbus was no exception to this pattern. Members of NOW, the Ohio ERA Task Force, Columbus–OSU Women's Liberation, WAC, and unaffiliated feminists had worked together to achieve Ohio's ratification of the ERA in 1974. As the 1982 deadline for ratification approached, many feminists who considered themselves radicals again pitched in alongside NOW to press for national passage of the amendment, although many remained convinced that the ERA should not be the key item on the feminist agenda.

After the ERA's defeat in 1982, the organizations that had spearheaded the ratification campaign at both national and state levels changed in membership, structure, and direction. NOW had expanded into a mass movement organization during the ERA drive. When the ERA failed, membership in NOW dropped at both national and chapter levels, leaving at the national level a professionally structured movement organization that lobbied for legislation, supported candidates for elected office, and operated as a pressure group within the Democratic Party.[12] Some local NOW chapters retained active membership, but many did not.[13] Columbus NOW held regular meetings throughout the 1980s, organized press conferences, issued posi-

tion statements, lobbied state and local officials on relevant legislation, organized or participated in occasional protests, and
worked to elect women to public office. But a woman who was
active in Columbus NOW during that period reported that by
the mid-1980s it was not unusual for meetings to attract only
two or three people, despite the fact that, on paper, chapter
membership did not drop below two hundred fifty or so.

Although Columbus NOW survived while WAC did not,
veterans of WAC and other radical feminist organizations were
reluctant to become involved with local NOW chapters wherever they lived. A former member of WAC who now lives in
Washington, D.C., gave a typical explanation for her unwillingness to join NOW or similar organizations.

> There's a lot of national women's groups located here, but
> they're mostly liberal groups and I'm not interested in working
> with a liberal group. Even NARAL tends to make what I con-
> sider to be the wrong arguments in favor of abortion, and I don't
> feel like I could work with a privacy mindset rather than a
> women's autonomy mindset.

The distinction between liberal and radical feminism remained
important to her perceptions of women's movement organizing;
similarly, most radical movement veterans deemed NOW,
along with NARAL, too liberal.

A few women who had moved to less hospitable cities reported that they had tried joining local NOW chapters—
briefly. "There were some interesting national changes in
NOW that impressed me that NOW had finally, twenty years
later, gotten off its ass and was dealing with some real issues,"
explained a veteran of WL who briefly joined the NOW chapter in her small town. "[But] the NOW issues that I was interested in were still quite shocking to the women in [my chap-
ter]. The local organization was dealing with some employment
issue, and they were afraid to take a stand. And I thought, I
don't need this shit." Another former participant in WL and

WAC has searched for an organization to get involved with in the southern city where she currently lives. NOW, she said, was not what she was looking for.

> The NOW chapter is a very stodgy, conservative organization. It's very into Robert's Rules of Order. It might as well be the Kiwanis Club. . . . There is a Commission for the Status of Women in the County that issues reports, and I don't see that they go further than that. There is just something missing.

Participation in NOW is significant because the organization is the largest and most visible feminist group, not only on the national stage but also in many local communities. Despite their frustration with NOW, many veterans were quick to say that they believe its efforts are far better than nothing; some make donations to NOW and are members "on paper." In a hostile period, say many, NOW is clearly on their side. But despite its endurance, movement veterans who were not part of NOW in the 1970s were not, by and large, active in it in the 1980s.

NOW was not the only mainstream feminist organization that frustrated radical movement veterans in the 1980s. Many women I interviewed also disapproved of the way that many groups framed the central issue of abortion. Abortion rights became a central focus of feminist organizing again in the late 1980s in response to antiabortion Supreme Court appointments, judicial and legislative limits on abortion rights, and the bombing of abortion clinics. Abortion rights activities drew large numbers of participants, including many younger women and men. A national demonstration organized by NOW and abortion rights groups in Washington, D.C., in April 1989 drew between three and six hundred thousand participants, and NARAL's membership grew from two hundred thousand in 1989 to four hundred thousand in 1990.[14]

Women who were radical feminists in the 1970s agree that abortion rights are critical to the feminist agenda. In interviews they expressed great distress at recent restrictions on women's ability to choose abortion and agreed that it was important for feminists to protest against these restrictions. Yet many were lukewarm about the women's movement's recent emphasis on abortion. The exclusive focus on the issue troubled many radical feminists, who saw single-issue politics as limited and divisive, as this longtime activist on the issue of reproductive rights explained:

> [In the 1970s] we were always careful to include sterilization. We tried to keep the focus on reproductive rights, not just abortion. Not to make it single-issue. I guess that's why I never joined NARAL in those days, 'cause I thought the focus was pretty narrow and somewhat conservative. . . . But I'm a member now. It seems like these days, we all need to stick together as much as we can.

Although she did not agree with the emphasis on abortion and omission of women's other reproductive rights, this woman was willing to work with NARAL because she felt that the strength of attacks on reproductive choice and the shrinking women's movement mandated it. Others were less willing to focus on abortion, and not just because the single-issue vision troubled them. One lesbian discussed her unwillingness to become actively involved in the abortion rights movement.

> My feeling as an older lesbian is that I don't want to lead the abortion movement. I mean, it is not my problem. . . . Young heterosexual women of childbearing age need to lead this one. And if they're too lazy to lead it, or if they're not smart enough to lead it, then they deserve to lose it.

Most women I interviewed, including this speaker, did participate in pro-choice demonstrations and felt angered and demoralized by attacks on abortion rights; yet almost all emphasized the need to place those rights in a broader context than they believed the 1980s movement did.

Many longtime radical feminists felt alienated from the general vision of feminism put forth by professionalized organizations in the 1980s. For example, one former WAC member contrasted mainstream feminist ideas about women's problems at work with her radical feminist perspective.

> I've always had a great deal of difficulty with the reform movement of the feminist movement. And the one thing that happened recently that just drove me up the wall was that whole mommy track idea. I heard these women trying to argue that, "Yes, I can work sixty hours a week and still be a mother." And that's not true! Nobody, man or woman, can work sixty hours a week and be a good parent, and the point isn't for us to turn into men. The point is to change everything.

Feminist theorists have argued that the demands posed by so-called liberal or moderate feminists in fact constitute a sweeping challenge to the existing social system; if women were really equal to men in employment, politics, and the family, the resulting social transformation would be too extensive to be considered reformist.[15] And NOW includes radical demands in its platforms, such as lesbian rights and economic self-determination for poor women. In many ways the distinction between liberal and radical wings of the women's movement no longer holds true. Yet the women I interviewed see professionalized women's movement organizations as built on a reformist political perspective that seeks to modify, rather than transform, the oppressive system. Although they sometimes work with such groups for pragmatic reasons, in general they see themselves as a different kind of feminist.

Part of their aversion stems from questions of strategy rather than disagreement over goals. Although NOW has adopted many of the positions that radical feminists put forth in the 1970s and the ideological gap between NOW and radical feminist organizations is relatively small, differences of strategies and tactics divide liberal and radical organizations.[16] The issue

of working within "the system" or outside it—a source of fric-
tion throughout the 1960s and 1970s—remains a point of contention. The professionalized women's movement of the 1980s
established itself as a player within dominant institutions, including the political establishment and academia. Veterans of
earlier radical groups expressed numerous doubts about this
strategy, despite the fact that as individuals they often worked
within mainstream institutions to make change through their
jobs. A current member of Columbus NOW who joined the
women's movement in the early 1980s described the organization as "still pretty committed to working in the mainstream to
achieve change" and noted that local membership has remained
mostly heterosexual, which she saw as evidence that the group
was mainstream. Further, the growing security of women's
studies programs made them more "mainstream" than ever. One
founder of the Center for Women's Studies at Ohio State explained her qualms:

> I worry about women's studies getting too middle-of-the-road.
> The reason we started women's studies programs was to trans-
> form everything that was going on in the university for young
> women. And if they're just going to teach traditional kinds of
> stuff and throw the word "woman" in now and then, and pub-
> lish esoteric papers that are virtually meaningless—well, it
> brings up the old question: Can you transform [the system] at
> the point that you're still living within [it]? And to me the
> answer is no.

Activists who sacrificed financial security and respectability to
found now-entrenched women's studies programs or antirape organizations were often mistrustful of feminists working in established institutions who seemed to use the women's movement to
advance their own careers. "When we were incredibly poor and
struggling," proclaimed one founder of Women Against Rape,
"the only women who came to work for us were women who
wanted to do the work. But once there was a respected product,

money to be made, then we started attracting another crowd of women."

On one hand, it is unremarkable that women who spurned mainstream feminist organizations in the 1970s, except for occasional strategic coalitions, continued to do so in the 1980s, despite the predominance of such organizations in the women's movement. The dilemma for radical feminist veterans is larger than whether or not to participate in NOW or a similar group. It stems from the fact that, for most, their *own* present activism is more within "the system" than outside it. As feminists have brought their politics into mainstream employment, they have lost much of their outsider status. The conflict is difficult to resolve, and many women felt ambivalent about the frequent contradictions between their political convictions and their work roles. It is difficult and dissonant for radical feminists who scorned the mainstream, cooptation, and compromise to live in a world where "feminism" has too often come to mean political power-brokering and where their own political victories occur in professional arenas rather than in the streets.

Radical Feminist Service Provision

It was not only organizations associated with the liberal wing of the women's movement, such as NOW and NARAL, that became institutionalized and professionalized in the 1980s. The organizations that radical feminists founded in the 1970s also adopted professionalized structures and gained acceptance in institutional arenas. What Janet Boles calls the women's policy network grew, linking local women's service and advocacy groups with state and local bureaucracies.[17] The seeds of these developments were sown in the mid-1970s when radical feminists first sought—and often received—funding from government agencies or foundations for social change projects like rape crisis hotlines, self-defense classes for women, and shelters for battered women. When communities were brimming with feminist action organizations, public protest, consciousness-raising groups, publications, and general ferment, the provision of services to women existed in the context of the larger movement. The same individuals were usually involved in multiple forms of activism: teaching self-defense classes, organizing demonstrations against sexist advertising, writing pamphlets about the feminist perspective on violence against women, and staffing the rape crisis hotline. But by the early 1980s, service organizations were the main survivors, and were forced to look beyond the shrinking women's movement for support, funds, labor, and influence.

Women Against Rape typifies this process. Many of the longtime feminists I interviewed founded the group in 1974 as part of WAC. Although it operated on a shoestring for its first year or two, organizers actively pursued grant funding. Women Against Rape, as noted above, received a nearly half-million dollar grant from the National Institute of Mental Health from 1976 to 1980; it won other sizable grants from foundations in the 1970s and used these grants to research rape prevention, develop feminist theory about violence against women, and support self defense classes and rape crisis services. Clearly Women Against Rape never operated entirely outside "the system." Yet it existed as part of WAC, and members engaged in a range of protest and organizing activities, of which service provision was only one part. Women Against Rape and staff on the Community Action Strategies to Stop Rape project saw their work as central to radical feminist social transformation.

In contrast, Women Against Rape was relatively underfunded during the 1980s. It had difficulty getting more than small grants after 1980 and survived on contracts with various organizations to provide training on dealing with rape survivors, fees for speakers and self-defense classes, and a door-to-door canvass. Yet the women I interviewed—none of whom were still active in the group—perceived it as more mainstream and less explicitly feminist than it was fifteen years ago. For example, one woman indicated her view that it was no longer a radical feminist organization.

> WAR has certainly continued, but it's become much more of a service organization than a radical feminist theory group or something like that. I suppose they still mouth a lot of the principles, like a feminist perspective on rape. But that's not really what they are about. I mean, they are the rape crisis center, for the most part. . . . I think it's a very different group now than it was. And I think there are probably a lot of young people.

The degree to which Women Against Rape actually became more "mainstream" is debatable. According to a staff member, the organization retained a collective structure, and although in practice staff members made many day-to-day decisions without referring to the collective, that happened in the past as well. Almost all labor was provided by paid staff members—but Women Against Rape and Community Action Strategies to Stop Rape staff were paid in the mid-1970s as well; in fact, the organization's founders believed strongly that feminist work was important and therefore worthy of some pay, no matter how small. In its training and publications, Women Against Rape continued to link sexual assault to the larger question of patriarchy, and members believed that all forms of oppression must be eliminated and the social structure transformed.

In practice, Women Against Rape worked closely with the police and with Community Mental Health Centers by the end of the 1980s, whereas in the past such alliances were shaky and involved mutual suspicion at best. Yet the organization still did not accept funding from the United Way or from business, which earlier members had strongly opposed, believing that their radical feminist politics would be compromised by the strings attached to such grants. The United Way, for example, requires a more hierarchical organizational structure than feminists wanted, and it would, they believed, restrict their political advocacy. By the late 1980s, current members of Women Against Rape were no longer unanimous in rejecting United Way funding; they discussed the possibility, and some members argued that such a change would benefit the organization, although others remained adamantly opposed. A member spoke in 1991 of the group's activities primarily in terms of providing services—both crisis intervention and rape prevention —rather than agitating for social change. Yet she also noted broader political concerns.

> We are a political entity, and we take an activist stance. It's not just about having self-defense classes, but being in the paper, calling up when they have a story that is just totally stereotypical. . . . It's not just about rape or sexual assault, but the condition of women in general. We consider ourselves a radical feminist organization.

The dilemmas Women Against Rape faced after the mid-1980s—weighing crisis intervention against rape prevention, balancing service provision and the need to survive financially with longterm feminist goals, retaining collective principles while functioning from day to day—were not all that different from those it faced all along.[18]

The larger changes in Women Against Rape during the 1980s were not decreasing radicalism but a reflection of changes in the women's movement overall. The organization allied more closely with the mixed-sex gay and lesbian movement than in its early days, despite the fact that, according to one member, its membership in the late 1980s was only about half lesbian or bisexual. It worked in close coalition with the Stonewall Union, a gay and lesbian organization, providing assistance on a project to combat violence against gays and lesbians, advertising in Stonewall publications, and making referrals. In addition, Women Against Rape expressed concern for increasing racial and cultural diversity among members, staff, and those who use its services and attempted to build coalitions with other social movement organizations that address the needs of people of color, such as the Urban League. In sum, the view that Women Against Rape "sold out" and was no longer radical is too simplistic, although it changed in some ways and, because it was no longer embedded in as active a women's movement, saw itself as more a social service agency than in the past.

Other feminist groups founded in Columbus in the 1970s—both radical and liberal—have spawned organizations that are unambiguously within the political and social service mainstream. For example, the Women's Research and Policy Development Center, founded by moderate campus and community activists in 1974, was short-lived but gave rise to two organizations. One is the Women's Information Center, an agency of the state government directed by a movement veteran that collects and dispenses information on a range of issues relevant to women and sex discrimination.[19] The second organization to grow from the council, according to a participant, is the Foster Care Network, which works with foster parents. An abortive effort to form a women's center in the mid-1970s gave rise to the Center for New Directions, which assists displaced homemakers, and feminist organizing within the Young Women's Christian Association led that organization to address feminist issues as well. Finally, the Child Assault Prevention Project grew out of Women Against Rape in the late 1970s. Successful in gaining contracts to provide assault prevention training in schools, the project has since become the National Assault Prevention Center, a national organization independent of Women Against Rape that conducts assault prevention classes for children, publishes and dispenses educational materials, and networks with other agencies.[20] Although all of these organizations are quite different from their "mother" organizations, they continue to work for feminist change within established institutions.

Movement veterans, regardless of their micro-cohort, dropped out or were forced out of the organizations they had founded, by and large, by the early 1980s and were not part of the increasing institutionalization of radical feminist groups as they achieved a measure of legitimacy. Rather, those who continued to organize collective action founded new groups in order to pursue activities similar to those they focused on in the 1970s. Many returned to more loosely structured small groups like the rap groups out of which the radical women's movement emerged. A number of longtime feminists, mostly founders and joiners, formed reading groups in the late 1980s and early 1990s, in an effort to invigorate their own radical feminist commitment and to encourage other women to do the same. A typical former member of Women Against Rape remarked that she had initiated a feminist theory and reading group "because of this fear that everything that we know is going to waste, disappearing."

The growth and survival of radical feminism is a central goal for the women who have remained active in the women's movement. One woman who was frustrated by many of her contacts with mainstream feminist organizations commented on her desire to revive radical feminism:

> I don't think there is a radical feminist movement out there. I think there are little cells of radical feminists gathered together to do things, and there's radical feminists in women's studies, and there's radical feminists sort of scattered here and there, but there's not really a radical feminist movement. . . . Movement rejuvenation sorts of goals tend to be at the center of my list right now. Both how do I rejuvenate myself to be able to work with other women, if I'm finding them disappointing to work with, and what kinds of activities should radical feminists be involved in that would really rejuvenate the radical feminist movement.

Feminists attempted to rejuvenate radical feminism by running sexual harassment workshops, having reading groups, working within existing feminist organizations, and founding new ones. One veteran of the Columbus movement founded the Feminist

Institute, a national organization that serves as a clearinghouse for a variety of projects and literature, in the early 1980s. She explained that she hoped to bring radical feminists together:

> The radical branch of the women's movement never had a national place. It never had a way of people sort of tuning in, and I really want the Institute to be that. I want it to be a beacon to old radicals and young radicals.

Another woman conducts workshops on sexual harassment that are based on workshops she and others developed in Women Against Rape through the Community Action Strategies to Stop Rape grant. She commented that, in accordance with the principles of Women Against Rape, she spends half the workshop "placing sexual harassment in the patriarchal scheme of things and boring a lot of women," and does not charge for attendance. She uses principles shaped in the radical feminist movement of the 1970s as a guide to her actions, by continuing to connect violence against women to male dominance and by emphasizing the workshops' accessibility for women of all income levels.

In sum, neither the survival of local feminist groups nor the transformation of those groups into social service agencies is primarily due to the actions of the political generation that came of age during the feminist resurgence of the 1960s and 1970s. Veterans of the earlier movement entered more conventional and institutionalized occupations in the 1980s and 1990s, through which they have continued to work for feminist change. But they have done so individually, not as part of an organized women's movement. They have chosen to work for change through their employment in mainstream occupations rather than through women's movement organizations that operate within dominant institutions. Meanwhile, some organizations that this earlier generation of feminists founded have continued with a new political generation of women staffing them. The new generation's experiences, obstacles, and hopes combine with those of their predecessors to shape the direction of the surviving organizations.

WOMEN'S MOVEMENT CULTURE

As women's movement organizations were becoming institutionalized in the 1980s, an extensive feminist culture also grew. The existence of a women's movement community with its own cultural institutions and events was nothing new. The content of that culture and its position in the movement as a whole shifted in the 1980s, however, and as with organizational changes, veterans of the earlier radical feminist movement did not always change along with feminist culture. As we have seen, cultural events are not just apolitical entertainment, but are an expression of feminist collective identity that rejuvenates committed feminists, recruits new women, and contributes to social change in the wider world by challenging hegemonic definitions of women.[21] As such, they were an integral part of what sustained the movement in the 1980s.[22]

Rooted in the feminist collectives, consciousness-raising groups, musicians, artists, and bookstores of the 1970s, the women's movement community expanded throughout the 1980s and, like feminist organizations, became further institutionalized.[23] National cultural events proliferated, such as the Michigan Womyn's Music Festival, smaller yearly festivals in other regions, and a multitude of local events such as feminist concerts, lesbian writers' workshops, and conferences and gatherings for various groups, like women motorcyclists, practitioners of Diannic Wicca, survivors of incest, Jewish lesbian daughters of Holocaust survivors, women recovering from addictions, and others.[24] An elaborate infrastructure of women's newsletters and publications, feminist bookstores, festivals, traveling speakers,

and professional or business associations maintains the community.[25]

This "women's culture," although it includes feminists of diverse political persuasions, has been largely maintained by lesbians in the 1980s and 1990s. Many events are aimed specifically at lesbians, and often other events that address a general
audience are organized and attended primarily by lesbian feminists. Lesbians and lesbian politics, in other words, have become
more indispensable than ever to the women's movement. Further, while a "gay–straight split" may have been the central
manifestation of lesbian politics in the movement in some cities
during the early 1970s, that was no longer the case by the
1980s. Instead, there was widespread agreement in most wings
of the movement that lesbian issues were important to the feminist agenda. The tensions that remained between lesbian and
heterosexual women took a backseat. Some heterosexual feminists—although less so in Columbus than elsewhere—criticized
what they saw as the dominance of lesbians in the movement
and an overly close association in the public eye between lesbianism and feminism. But even the critics, by and large,
worked alongside lesbian activists on reproductive rights, electoral struggles, violence against women, or women's studies,
and agreed that lesbian issues were a legitimate concern for feminists. The labor of lesbian activists energizes much of feminist
organizing. In addition, lesbian feminist communities construct
and support a feminist collective identity that is not limited to
those communities or to lesbians, but is important to the survival of the women's movement as a whole.[26]

The lesbian feminist community of the 1980s built directly
on organizations and culture established by the 1970s radical
women's movement.[27] In Columbus, Fan the Flames Feminist
Bookstore, founded by WAC members in 1975, remained
healthy in 1995 and serves as a mainstay of the feminist community. The Women's Music Union, begun in 1976 to produce
feminist concerts, disbanded in 1990, but was central to the

local cultural scene through the late 1980s. Some members of the 1960s and 1970s political generation continued to organize feminist cultural and community-building events in the 1980s and saw such events as an attempt to continue the projects they had undertaken in previous decades. One woman who still organizes a yearly summer camp for feminists explained why she thinks cultural events are important to the women's movement:

> We have to give women a vision of what is possible. And we worked on it so hard with [Women Against Rape], to show women what society could look like, that I figured I needed to be doing something that would run experiments and show women what it could look like to be in a woman-oriented environment.

Her organization, the Feminist Institute, operates a number of projects that aim to give women such a vision, including the summmer camp, feminist walking tours of Washington, D.C., a videotape of "croning" celebrations of women's aging, and a project on "social relations for the future" that includes workshops on chosen kinship and a study of lesbian mothers and their children by donor insemination.

It would be inaccurate, therefore, to suggest that 1980s feminist culture was entirely organized by newcomers to the women's movement or that women from the earlier political generation opposed it. Their earlier organizing laid the groundwork for the cultural institutions of the 1980s, and at least some longtime radical feminists were instrumental in the women's movement community. More typical, however, is the woman who was part of WAC in the 1970s and explained that although she defines herself as part of the lesbian feminist community, she rarely participates in any community activities.

A new political generation of activists (made up, like the earlier political generation, of multiple micro-cohorts) gained influence and began redefining feminist culture in the early to mid-1980s. By the late 1980s, women's movement culture had

changed substantially, and earlier feminists from all micro-
cohorts did not look favorably on many of these changes. Disagreements over culture were mostly between lesbians of different political generations; in other words, they were not conflicts
between lesbians and heterosexual women over feminist culture,
but rather among lesbians over that culture's content. Some
longtime feminists simply felt left out in settings where they
were once comfortable, like this cofounder of Women Against
Rape.

> I'll go places and I'll think I should know people, and I don't
> know anybody. . . . It seems like there's a whole new crowd that
> I don't know. It's kind of interesting. I'm starting to feel like an
> old lady. I'll be forty this year, so it is getting to be a little bit
> that way.

Others felt suspicious of, disappointed in, or excluded from lesbian feminist culture for reasons stemming from its increasing
centrality to the movement or its content. Some women viewed
the focus on cultural events as apolitical or retreatist. One lesbian activist described what she saw as a depoliticizing of the
women's movement in Columbus around 1981.

> Somehow feminism in Columbus began to be framed around
> cultural feminism, as opposed to politicized feminism. So for a
> while, there were a lot of concerts . . . and it seemed like that
> was where everybody was. And then now, my current perception
> of what's happening is that we're very therapeutically based.
> Everybody is in some sort of a 12-step program. So now we're
> off in this personal development, recovery kind of phase. And I
> don't think there's much political work going on.

A WAC member recalled that although the feminists who led
the shift to what she called cultural feminism were both experienced activists and newcomers, there was much discussion
among experienced core activists about what was happening to
the movement in the early 1980s.

It seemed like the people who were getting involved didn't have the same need for a political base. It was like they were looking for something else. They were looking to be entertained, or they were looking to be part of a community. But not so much to change women's lives. . . . I remember lamenting all of this with . . . people who had been around and been involved.

An exclusive focus on alternative feminist institutions seemed retreatist to the women I interviewed, who were vehement that it was necessary to confront dominant institutions. "I remember hearing about this Wisconsin Women's Land Co-op," said one woman who remains an antiviolence activist. "That's like a far-flung kind of fantasy. That's escapism. It would be personally very satisfying to go work a self-sufficient farm of women enclosed in ourselves, but what good does that do anyone?"

The perception that women's movement culture and lesbian feminism celebrate femaleness within separatist communities but do not challenge male dominance in wider society was widespread among the women I interviewed. Although some still attend music festivals or other cultural events, they were critical of those events' lack of political focus. One lesbian who helped initiate Columbus–OSU WL in 1969 characterized the Michigan Womyn's Music Festival that way.

There's still some kind of a seed out there of rebellion against the patriarchy. But it seems like maybe they're not as political in some ways as we used to be. Like if you go to Michigan or whatever, everybody's just into having a good time.

Another woman who helped organize the Michigan Womyn's Music Festival during its first few years and no longer attends complained that the original purpose of women's music festivals, to provide a model of what a society based on women's values could be, has been abandoned in recent years.

The neatness about them in the beginning was it was just all these women coming together—they had no idea how they were gonna exist on the space. And it worked. We all helped each other out and did everything. And it just seemed like it changed into people getting into their power trips and being security guards, and all the other things.

Even one woman who saw good reasons for the existence of feminist cultural events saw them as helpful for other women, rather than for herself, commenting:

> We've laughed about . . . the women's music festivals as Brigadoons that flower for a few days and close down again until the next year. What does this mean, this phenomenon of the late seventies and eighties? Vast numbers of women come to these events and then go home again. And what are they doing the rest of the year? But those are the transforming experiences that women seem to need.

The culture's *content* in the 1980s sometimes disturbed long-time feminists as much as the increasing emphasis cultural events received. One important strand of feminist culture was essentialism, or the notion that gender differences are so deeply rooted as to be insurmountable and that "women's ways" are inherently preferable to men's. In the early 1980s in Columbus (and in the late 1970s in some major cities), both incoming activists and some members of the earlier political generation increasingly emphasized women's difference from men, spirituality, unity with the earth, and natural peacefulness, and focused on celebrating women's "energy" (giving rise to conflicts such as the debate over changing the name of the WAC newsletter to "Womoon Rising"). Celebrations of the female in local communities were inextricably linked to a body of popular and scholarly theoretical writing that discusses women's nature, constructs differences and boundaries between women and men, and sees "women's ways" as superior to the ways of male-dominated society. Such authors, including Nancy Chodorow, Mary Daly, Carol Gilligan, Marilyn Frye, Susan Cavin, Sonia Johnson, and Sarah Lucia Hoagland, have been widely read within the women's movement, both by members of the earlier political generation and by more recent recruits.[28] Some of these authors are often included in women's studies classes, where young women encounter them and are influenced by their perspectives.[29]

Yet feminists who were part of the movement in the 1970s expressed less than total agreement with such authors. One feminist professor explained her disagreement with the perspective of recent feminist writings:

> I also think there's been some bizarre trends in radical feminism. For example, I simply do not comprehend what Mary Daly's up to. . . . I don't see what she's contributing, and I don't see why all these women think she's the best thing since sliced bread. And within academic feminism, Nancy Chodorow and Carol Gilligan, Sara Ruddick. Some of that stuff is useful, but I think a lot of it is deflecting attention from really understanding the institutional foundations of power.

Despite WAC's commitment to "women-only space" and to sisterhood among women, most of its members did not view differences between women and men as innate. Further, their development of rigorous feminist theory, combined with an intense and often critical atmosphere in the collective, made them unwilling to affirm automatic solidarity with all other woman. These factors combined to make movement veterans suspicious of essentialist tendencies in the feminist culture of the 1980s. At the same time, however, many WAC veterans did romanticize women's connections with each other and disapproved of traits or behaviors they saw as "male-identified." Far from idealizing women, these radical feminists were often quite critical of each other and outsiders for displaying unacceptable behavior. Echoing these concerns, one woman who had been a WAC member since 1976 expressed dismay at the selection of poet

Amy Lowell as the focus of the last WAC-sponsored "Famous Feminist Day" in 1984.

> I thought the person that had been selected was not a feminist. It was some lesbian poet, and she was . . . real male-identified, and she sat around on the fence-post smoking cigarettes. I couldn't see anything that she'd ever done for other women. . . . It just felt like it was no longer the organization that I had been involved with. It was just some shell that somebody was dragging around.

Although the sponsor of Famous Feminist Day was the same organization that had claimed her loyalty for eight years, membership turnover had produced such changes in collective identity—definitions of who qualified as a feminist—that she could no longer recognize herself. The activists who entered the women's movement in the early to mid-1980s began to challenge the notion of women as gentle earth-mothers or victims of patriarchy, redefining the collective identity of feminist broadly enough to include historical figures like Amy Lowell. Clothing at feminist events in Columbus reflected these shifts visually, changing from gender-neutral, antifashion jeans and work shirts in the 1970s and early 1980s to more flamboyant dress, such as bright-colored baggy overalls and flowing gauze or ties, vests, and tuxedo shirts, in the mid-1980s.

A year or two later, the change in feminist identity had progressed even further. Dress at feminist events in Columbus in the late 1980s included such overtly gendered styles as miniskirts, silk shirts, leather, and black muscle shirts (sometimes all in one outfit). Similar shifts occurred around the country, although on a somewhat earlier timetable in major cities.[30] Popularized both by lesbian "sex radicals" and by pop icon Madonna, overtly sexual dress made a comeback among newer feminists and lesbians, who saw the strictures of "politically correct" dress, dictated by the rejection of traditional feminine appearance, as narrow and boring. A more flexible and flamboyant style, they argued, allowed them to celebrate their womanhood and define their own sexuality—for the pleasure of other women rather than for men. These new norms of appearance were foreign to earlier feminists, even the sustainer micro-cohort that had entered the movement only a few years earlier. "I notice they're all really young . . . ," commented a former WAC member about Women Against Rape members in the late 1980s, "and they all have Mohawk haircuts."

The disjuncture between political appearance in the 1970s (uncontrived, avoiding the trappings of femininity) and political appearance by the late 1980s (overtly sexual, adopting and redefining gender stereotypes) corresponded to an intense nationwide debate over the relationship of politics to sexuality. Beginning in New York City, San Francisco, and other metropolitan movement centers around 1980, the debate came to a head at a 1982 conference on sexuality at Barnard College.[31] What came to be called the "sex wars" pitted a so-called anti-sex or vanilla camp, which emphasized the often violent nature of heterosexual relations and idealized women's sexuality as inherently less violent and more gentle than men's, against a "pro-sex" camp, which argued that women should be able to pursue sexual pleasure in whatever forms they desired. The debate filtered into local communities, including Columbus, through the feminist press, women's studies, and the national network of women's music festivals. In Columbus, the conflict never reached fever pitch. But most longtime radical feminists took the former position, while entering activists were more open to the sex radical stance.

As a result of this disjuncture, the new political generation altered other aspects of feminist culture that the earlier generation of feminists took for granted. For example, a dance following a "Women Take Back the Night" march in 1991 featured recorded music by male artists, including songs with lyrics like

"I can't help myself" that earlier political generations would have seen as promoting rape. At another 1991 fundraiser for the same organization, a women's chorus (made up mostly of recent entrants to the movement, but including one or two longtime activists) sang the song "Fight Back" by the feminist songwriter Holly Near. The song, an anthem about fighting back against violence, had been popular in the late 1970s. A chorus member prefaced the song with the announcement, "This song was written during a period when the women's movement was filled with anger—at patriarchy and at women's treatment by patriarchy. Although we have moved through that stage of anger now, this song is an important reminder of the spirit of those times." At the same event, women in their early twenties —mostly African American—did "voguing," a contemporary dance style originating in urban gay dance bars and popularized by Madonna's music and videos, that involves striking and holding poses to music. Women in their forties clustered around watching them, some asking each other, "What are they doing?" This interaction, relatively insignificant in itself, symbolized the way that the public culture of the women's movement has changed as new women have entered it, whereas the norms, values, and expressions of the earlier political generation have remained largely, although not entirely, constant.[32]

Does this evidence show that what Alice Echols calls "cultural feminism" supplanted radical feminism in Columbus, albeit a few years later than in larger cities?[33] I believe the forces at work were more complicated. The increasing centrality of cultural events to the contemporary women's movement was largely a result of shrinking external opportunities for political confrontation; and longtime activists' discomfort with the new content of feminist culture grew partly from a generational disjuncture. The early cultural efforts of the women's movement were very explicitly political and grew from women's common experiences as activists in organizations that confronted the social structure directly. Few organizers of or participants in cultural events limited their activism to those events; they also participated in other feminist organizations and activities, which remained as vital as women's culture.

As time passed and a new political generation came into the women's movement, some women were recruited through the publicly visible women's culture.[34] Women whose first contact with the feminist movement was women's music concerts or festivals had initial transformative experiences that were quite different from those of the earlier generation of feminists. At the same time, participants still conceptualized cultural events as political. By the mid-1980s when the organized women's movement had waned, feminist cultural events were the largest remaining public activity of the movement. Further, the culture undeniably included essentialist elements: Celebration of "women's energy" in contrast to men's and appeals to a mythical matriarchal past are only the most obvious.

But neither the scope nor the essentialist tendencies of feminist culture precluded it from promoting externally oriented feminist mobilization. Participants in the "women's community" of the 1980s also engaged in political confrontation through the women's movement organizations I described earlier in the chapter. Their membership in an alternative feminist world sustained them as activists in a much more hostile arena. This was also true for veterans of the 1970s movement, who worked in mainstream settings and sustained each other through enduring friendship networks despite their feelings of exclusion from lesbian feminist culture. Newcomers to the movement drew on the information, connections, and vision they found in lesbian feminist culture to mount challenges to external structures of domination. Women's movement culture in the 1980s, as in the 1970s, served as a means of recruitment and support for activists, and was embedded in a larger movement context that linked it to both radical and liberal women's movement organizations.

POLITICAL GENERATIONS IN THE
CHANGING WOMEN'S MOVEMENT

During the 1980s, national and local women's movement organizations adopted professionalized structures and worked more
closely with mainstream institutions. Feminist culture took a
front seat at the grassroots, and its content promoted both idealized views of women and, later, overt celebrations of lesbian
sexuality in all its variety. These changes reflected the impact of
hostile external conditions that opened a narrow avenue of access
for professionalized movement organizations and closed off
routes for more radical influence, encouraging feminists to turn
their attention inward to building "women's community." In
other words, as the political context became less receptive to
feminist claims, the actions that were possible and effective were
more modest and limited than in the previous decade. Activists
either worked within dominant political institutions as part of
mainstream feminist organizations, or sought to build an alternative community that maintained the collective identity of
feminism and provided a home base from which activists could
mount protests. It is this community that has sustained the
cultural legacy of radical feminism, while the women's movement in the external political arena—also shaped by radical
feminist goals, ideology, and individuals—has adopted pragmatic, achievable goals and institutionalized tactics.

The changes in the women's movement also resulted from an
intergenerational struggle over the definition of the collective
identity "feminist." As we saw earlier, in the 1970s women's
movement, each incoming micro-cohort redefined the collective
identity associated with the women's movement to accommodate its own circumstances. These differences among the micro-
cohorts of the 1970s paled as radical feminists entered the sharply
different period of the 1980s, and their similarities bound them
together as a recognizable political generation. The circumstances of their lives differ greatly from those of women who

have come of age and entered the women's movement in the
1980s. As a result, their understandings of feminism also differ
sharply.

Veterans of the radical women's movement have retained their
commitment to radical feminism and continue to act on that
commitment. However, as the women's movement changed directions, most withdrew somewhat from organized feminism.
The major changes in women's movement organizations and
culture during the 1980s left feminist veterans feeling "left behind" by the women's movement, dissatisfied with the directions the movement has taken yet feeling unable or unwilling to
redirect the movement. Reluctant to work through mainstream
feminist organizations they had long dismissed, believing radical feminist service organizations had betrayed their political
roots, and disappointed in the centrality and content of lesbian
feminist culture, movement veterans continued to participate in
collective action in limited ways and often sought to rejuvenate
radical feminism as they knew it. But most of their activism
took a more individual form or centered on other social movements.

There are two possible views of the role of longtime feminists
in the movement's recent metamorphosis. One possibility is
that members of the political generation that led the resurgence
of the women's movement in the late 1960s and 1970s remained the leaders of the women's movement in the 1980s and
have changed their collective identity. In other words, former
radical feminists might have become sex radicals, "cultural feminists," or pro-choice activists. The evidence shows that this is
not the case. Feminists from the 1970s have retained their collective identity with only minor changes, despite the transformation of the women's movement as a whole.

The second and, I believe, more accurate view is that the
women's movement changed direction as new cohorts of activists entered and redefined feminist goals and collective identity
at the same time as many longtime activists became less in-

volved in women's movement organizations and community. Shifts in the women's movement reflect the contested collective identity "feminist." Incoming activists are seeking to alter the meaning of "feminist," while earlier cohorts retain their own definition of feminism and feel alienated, confused, or disapproving as the new movement promotes a changed collective identity.

In other words, as I began to suggest earlier, social movements change not just because participants change their collective identities, but because new cohorts of activists enter and redefine the collective identity associated with the movement. "Feminism" has been redefined by a new generation of activists in the women's movement to mean something different from what it meant to the political generation I interviewed for this study (and sometimes appalling to members of that generation). This new political generation of feminists is not simply a younger age group, but contains both young women and older women, including some who are the same age as or older than members of the earlier political generation.[35]

Individuals' commitment to feminist goals has endured over time, as have women's movement organizations. Yet we cannot equate individual and organizational survival, because social movement organizations are not necessarily staffed by the same individuals over time. If we hope to understand how movements survive and how they change, we must examine both individual and organizational levels. How one political generation "passes the torch" to the next provides important insights into social movement continuity. I turn next to a closer examination of intergenerational relations in the rapidly changing women's movement during the late 1980s and early 1990s.

7 :: THE NEXT WAVE

THE RADICAL WOMEN'S movement did not survive the 1980s unchanged, but it did survive. As the movement entered the 1990s, it began to grow again. Columbus and national organizations gained new members and mounted visible campaigns, and a new political generation of feminists came of age as activists. Where is the radical women's movement going in the 1990s and beyond? Part of the answer to this question is contained in the preceding chapters: Veterans of the 1960s and 1970s movement are still active and influential feminists shaping the direction and outcomes of the challenge. As we have seen, longtime feminists remained a political force even as their activism moved out of the streets and into their workplaces and daily lives. Another part of the future of feminism, however, depends both on the next political generation and on interaction across generational boundaries. The connections and conflicts between feminists politicized in the movement of the 1970s and women, often younger, who have come to the movement in the very different era of the late 1980s and 1990s are one of the central forces directing feminism's course. Ultimately, intergenerational connections and conflicts shape the extent to which the legacy of the second wave of feminism is transmitted to the activists and organizations that will mobilize the third wave.

To understand the future of the women's movement, we must examine the persistent collective identity and actions of long-time feminists (the subject of Chapters 3, 4, and 5) and the collective identity, actions, and intergenerational relations of newcomers, often younger women who have been labeled, misleadingly, a "postfeminist" generation. This generation came of political age during the 1980s and early 1990s and entered a more quiescent and unpopular women's movement. Their actions as activists were limited by scant available resources and narrow political opportunities. Their collective identity, not surprisingly, differed from that of longtime feminists who acquired a sense of the world and themselves in a different era. In addition, as veterans of the 1970s movement increasingly pursued change within mainstream institutions and daily life, they diverged further from the newcomers who have become core activists in contemporary women's movement organizations. Together, the two political generations of feminists carry the movement into the 1990s, but their differences are considerable.

Political generations matter to the longterm survival and transformation of social movements, but not in any simple way. Age is less important in shaping political outlook and actions than the time that one enters a movement and the experiences one has as an activist.[1] And even activists from the same era do not always see eye to eye, of course. Although collective identity is basically lasting, everyone changes over the years, not always in predictable ways. Class, sexual identity, race, ideology, and experiences, along with political generation, all shape commonalities and conflicts among activists. Changes in the external context also limit and direct how individuals and organizations evolve. Yet political generations are particularly useful for understanding how the women's movement has changed over time because relations across generations are an unavoidable feature of the long history of the women's movement.

A look at the next feminist political generation and interactions between recent and longtime activists helps to sketch out some of the forces shaping the women's movement's future. Predicting the future is always dicey, and sociologists do not have a particularly good track record. I do not pretend to know what form the women's movement will take over the next years; I can only speculate about the dynamics that shape its course. In doing so, I revisit some of the ground covered in the previous chapter, with particular attention to the relations between political generations. I intend this analysis to raise questions about the role of political generations in social movement continuity and change and to illustrate the forms that intergenerational conflicts and connections have taken in the early 1990s radical women's movement.

THE "POSTFEMINIST" GENERATION

As early as 1982, and at regular intervals after that, observers labeled women in their teens and twenties the "postfeminist" generation.[2] This meant, according to pundits and pollsters, that young women enjoyed the fruits of the women's movement—better access to employment, equal education, being taken more seriously—but believed the battle had already been won. Widely cited polls in the mid-1980s showed that strong majorities of young women supported feminist goals and ideas but were reluctant to call themselves feminists because the identity has acquired negative connotations of stridency, lesbianism, and man-hating. Far from being unappreciative of the efforts of earlier feminists, young women seemed to believe that the changes wrought by the women's movement of the 1970s were beneficial but that all the necessary changes already had been achieved.[3] This behavior is consistent with Alice Rossi's suggestion that the generation after a successful social movement enjoys the movement's achievements rather than seeking further gains; it is the third generation that takes the new status quo for granted and, expecting better, protests again.[4] As one young woman wrote in 1983, "The content of the old slogans is so obvious to us and to our male peers that we're free to move beyond political formulas: instead of polemicizing on the significance of being a woman painter, my roommate Rebecca cleans her brushes and gets to work."[5]

The "postfeminist" generation of the early 1980s, though, is now ten years older. As Gloria Steinem points out, discrimination at work, the difficulty of balancing employment and mothering, and inequalities in personal relationships become more apparent with age.[6] In fact, the supposedly apolitical generation that came of age in the early 1980s produced many outspoken feminist voices: Susan Faludi, author of *Backlash;* Naomi Wolf, who wrote *The Beauty Myth* and *Fire with Fire;* Natalie Kamen, postfeminist turned activist and author of *Feminist Fatale;* and other less famous, but equally feminist, women now in their late twenties and early thirties (including me).

Feminists who came of political age in the early 1980s are better viewed as one micro-cohort within the "postfeminist generation" because they are distinct from those who came of age later. In other words, the "postfeminist generation" is not a homogeneous, unified group. Just as the earlier political generation included several micro-cohorts, we can identify at least two micro-cohorts among more recent entrants to the women's movement. Women—and some men—who graduated from high school in the late 1980s and early 1990s make up a second micro-cohort, and are even farther from "postfeminism." Coming of age in the Reagan era, they also witnessed huge protests for the nuclear freeze, studied shop as well as home economics in school, and cut their political teeth on recycling drives. They not only supported feminist goals in opinion polls, but increasingly joined in collective action to achieve those goals. The prochoice movement pulled in significant numbers of these new activists, male and female, but other local feminist organizations grew too.[7] Not surprisingly, given the more activist context in which they came of age, this second micro-cohort was more amenable to a militant, "in-your-face" style of activism than was the first.

Young feminists in the 1980s and the 1990s (in both micro-cohorts) are, perhaps, a smaller proportion of their age group than their mothers were, but they are by no means nonexistent. As an active campus feminist in the early 1980s responded to older women who wondered why there are no young feminists, "The wondering gives me the sense of watching my own funeral—struck dumb—and unable to tell my mourners that I am still very much alive."[8] Nevertheless, they were "postfeminist" in one sense: Their understanding of what feminism entailed departed in important ways from that of their predecessors. As we have seen, they structured organizations, framed issues, and understood the world differently.

FEMINIST ORGANIZATIONS IN THE "POSTFEMINIST" ERA

A close look at the surviving women's movement organizations in Columbus in the late 1980s and early 1990s shows both that feminist organizing was alive and well and that newcomers played important roles.[9] The late 1980s and early 1990s were a time of flux for most of the organizations that survived or grew out of those founded in the 1970s. I described many of the changes of the 1980s earlier: Organizations became institutionalized, alliances with other social movements grew, and feminist culture shifted away from emphasizing the political implications of every action toward a more flexible, more overtly sexual, and less serious tone.

The most noticeable feature of the late 1980s and early 1990s was an influx of active members of all ages. While organizations barely hung on through most of the 1980s with dwindling numbers, mobilization swelled at the end of the decade. Fan the Flames Feminist Bookstore, for example, survived with only three active collective members (two of whom were paid staff) until 1993, when three new members who had been gradually increasing their volunteer commitment joined the collective. NOW's Columbus chapter went through a similar slow period in the early and mid-1980s, when paper membership dropped and attendance at meetings was sometimes only two or three women. In the late 1980s the chapter's active membership also increased. The Association of Women Students at OSU, which was staffed in the 1970s mostly by members of WAC who were also students, faltered along with WAC in the early 1980s. Incoming activists revived the group in the late 1980s. It grew, allied with the OSU Gay and Lesbian Alliance and a new lesbian group on campus, Women in Comfortable Shoes. These campus organizations became more visible as participants began to use direct-action tactics.

Those tactics mark another change of the late 1980s. Many young feminists came to the women's movement through lesbian organizing in the militant Queer Nation or ACT UP and were willing to use confrontational tactics. The Association of Women Students was the most visible proponent of this approach in Columbus, organizing, for example, a picket of a women's oil-wrestling match at a campus bar, spray-painting billboards, and a die-in on the campus to protest restriction of abortion rights. Often socialized to feminism in women's studies classes and lesbian separatist events, these young women defined themselves as radical or socialist feminists and selected tactics to match their ideology.[10]

At the same time that a militant edge of the movement was regaining prominence, many long-lived organizations shifted away from collective structure and evolved organizational forms that allowed greater efficiency in making decisions and gave individual members more leeway to act independently. This change was most striking in Fan the Flames Feminist Bookstore, but occurred in Women Against Rape and Ohio Women Martial Artists (a successor to Feminists in Self-Defense Training) as well. For many feminists in the 1970s, "feminist structure" or "feminist process" meant collective and consensus. The de-coupling of feminism and collective structure began during the movement's heyday as staffers in the federally funded Community Action Strategies to Stop Rape project made day-to-day decisions on their own; but they were roundly criticized by other WAC members for "power-tripping." Many veterans of the early movement later became disillusioned with collective structure, as we have seen. More recent recruits share this disillusionment, and many have restructured organizations as a result. One current member of Fan the Flames described the group's structure in the mid-1980s as a collective in which "we pretended we all had equal power . . . but we don't all have equal power." Now, she explained, although the group still discussed major decisions collectively, "some of us are going and doing what we want regardless [of the collective]." For example, bookstore members discussed whether men should be allowed to work as occasional volunteer staff in the store and came to no agreement on the question. One member went ahead and, on her own, trained a man to do so. The collective still had the power to decide whether or not he would work, but her actions would have been unthinkable under the earlier, more strictly collective process.[11] Similarly, one of the founders of Ohio Women Martial Artists commented that

> we started out very collectively, trying to run this club. You know, what colors does everyone want T-shirts in? When should we have class? Every decision involved a group meeting. And that doesn't work. For some things it works, but for this you just can't [do it]. We've come to a pretty comfortable level about some things that do require some input [from the group] and other things that decisions have to be made.

Both Fan the Flames and Ohio Women Martial Artists are businesses that provide a product or service for a fee as well as feminist organizations. As such, they have faced distinct dilemmas. A member of Fan the Flames explained that, after a number of years of losing money, they had to "start running it [the store] like a real business and not be embarrassed to make a profit." This posed some conflicts with feminist principles, she noted.

> None of us were from a business background. We don't know how to be ruthless capitalists. [*Laughs*] [We say,] "Oh, you can't pay for that book? Okay. We understand your socioeconomic conditions." We have to learn how to be both ethical and capitalist at the same time. We were so concerned about each other's feelings that we forgot the bottom line.

Yet Fan the Flames remains committed to the women's movement; it has not become simply a business that capitalizes on the feminist book-buying market. "We still maintain ourselves as a community resource center," said a collective member.

> We have one whole room for meeting space, fliers, fundraising appeals. We haven't lost that focus—it just doesn't look so "sixties" anymore. You know, we actually have a color scheme! It used to be just dust and beige. [*Laughs*]

Along the same lines, Ohio Women Martial Artists not only teaches martial arts and self-defense classes to women; members also do demonstrations at antiviolence marches and other events and speak to diverse audiences about self-defense.

Other organizations, also revitalized in the late 1980s, carry on very much in the tradition of their predecessors. Take Back the Night is the best example of this. Originating in antiviolence marches planned by members of WAC and OSU Women's Studies and Women's Services, Take Back the Night has evolved into an independent organization that plans a yearly march, raises money for Women Against Rape, and does public speaking about the problem of violence against women. Beginning in 1989, a new group of women, one or two who had been active for many years and others who were new to feminist activism, took over the moribund organization. Now one of the most visible public feminist events in the area, the march draws hundreds of women each year, with the triple goals of educating the public about violence against women, empowering women, and calling media attention to the problem. Take Back the Night remains committed to a women-only event, despite regular debates about the role of men. A 1992 flier explained their position in terms familiar to 1970s feminists:

> Through this event, designed and carried out by women in an environment free from fear, participants and viewers begin to dream of their freedom and take steps to ensure it. Ending isolation within a patriarchal society is a first step towards declaring our freedom from domination and abuse.[12]

Does all of this activity signal a feminist resurgence? Or do feminist organizations' partial rejection of collective structure and the cultural changes I described in Chapter 6 show that the women's movement has been coopted by the antifeminist backlash? Are we at the beginning of a "third wave" of feminist activism, the end of the second wave, or merely midway through a long, continuous cycle of protest? The answers to these questions hinge in part on relations among feminist generations. "Second wave" feminists who participated in the 1960s and 1970s movement are still relatively young—most in their forties and fifties. They remain very active feminists politically and personally, through their jobs, daily life, and collective action. As a new wave of activists comes into the women's movement, their relations with their predecessors will shape how much the next wave of activism builds on or diverges from feminist work of the 1970s. Such intergenerational relations are characterized by cooperation and connection as well as discontinuity and conflict, but the connections are fewer and weaker than both generations would like.

CONNECTIONS ACROSS GENERATIONS

Incoming feminists are not operating in a vacuum, of course. There are several means by which they encounter and learn from their predecessors. Some longtime activists are still part of women's movement organizations, but most women I interviewed experienced little intergenerational connection within women's movement organizations. Instead, as more veterans moved into mainstream occupations, contact in those institutionalized settings was more common. The success of the 1970s women's movement's in establishing feminist enclaves within mainstream institutions provided a reliable way of passing the movement's legacy to a new generation. Women's studies programs are one such gain. Women's studies classes expose students to feminist ideology and provide a way for incoming feminists to find and enter women's movement organizations and the feminist community.[13] Similarly, movement veterans who run government agencies or work in nonprofit organizations dealing with women's issues reported hiring young women as interns and "showing them the ropes" of feminist policy making.

Activist organizations established by veterans of the 1960s–1970s women's movement also foster connections with younger women. For example, the Feminist Institute, founded by an activist in the Columbus women's movement as a clearinghouse for radical feminist publications and projects, hires new women's studies graduates as staff. Less directly, Women Against Rape, like other institutionalized radical feminist organizations, is an important part of the legacy left by second wave activists for younger women. Many college women became activists by joining WAR as paid canvassers; although they had little direct contact with earlier activists, they learned the political ropes from training sessions and readings designed years earlier.

Relations between mothers and daughters form another connection between the generations. The three women I interviewed who had grown daughters felt that they passed on their political perspective on women's lives in many ways. In addition to trying to raise daughters without traditional gender roles and encourage them to be strong and confident, mothers talked about their activism with their daughters and served as feminist mentors. One woman explained that her college-aged daughter, now an activist for feminist causes herself, was very interested in her mother's activist history.

> I have gone to visit my daughter at [college] a couple of times, and stayed in the dormitory with her. She always makes a point of inviting her friends over. . . . It's sort of like they're asking questions about the old days. . . . I feel like Granny in the rocking chair. It's like, "Here's a relic of the early women's movement." [*Laughs*]

Relationships between mothers and daughters were not always straightforward, however. One woman, a professor who was involved in establishing women's studies, recounted her feminist daughter's less than favorable views of her mother's politics.

> My daughter lectures me on feminist ideology. . . . As I was washing the dishes in the kitchen, she came out to me and she says, "I have a question. Do you consider yourself a feminist?" Looking at me washing the dishes. And I said, "In theory, in theory." And she said, "That's what I thought you'd say." . . . She thinks that I'm a little too much in theory, and I ought to practice a little bit more than I do. . . . She's very political, period. Got definite ideas about not wearing fur, not eating meat, and things like that. . . . But I eat meat occasionally, stuff like that. She's pure, and so she lets me know that I'm impure, that I may have fallen and faltered by the wayside occasionally.

Their differences are not due to any simplistic "youthful rebellion." Just as the links between political generations grow from structural and social relations—enduring feminist organizations, family structures—so, too, are the differences grounded in the changing social structures and cultural contexts that organize the lives of women at different times. Despite the very real links forged between mothers and daughters or teachers and students, coming of political age in the 1990s entails such different experiences and assumptions from those of the 1960s and 1970s that, even as the younger generation learns from the older (and vice versa), the two also often diverge.

THE "GENERATION GAP"

None of these links can eliminate the gap between political generations, although they provide some bridges. Both new and experienced feminist activists reported feeling more discontinuity than connection with each other. Activists who led the radical feminist challenges of the 1970s believed that too few women had entered the movement after them and that it was still primarily up to women of their own political generation to maintain the women's movement. "What happens is that [the first] generation has to move on into doing something professional 'cause you have to eat," said an artist who has been part of the women's movement since 1970. "And there should be a new generation that comes along to do that, and there was no new generation." Like her, many veterans of the women's movement longed for others take over some of the work of social change. A longtime organizer who now works in state government complained that having to sustain the challenge for so many years without incoming feminists was exhausting.

> The women I have known who have been very active and made a significant contribution, I would classify as the walking wounded of the women's movement, because they have given up an awful lot. . . . And I'm getting old and tired and just wondering where are all the people coming along?

Many veterans of the radical women's movement bemoaned younger women's lack of commitment to a feminist struggle. Ironically, activists criticized their nonfeminist peers during the

1970s for the same lack of commitment. But their critique of young women is couched in generational terms; accurately or not, longtime feminists believe younger women are apolitical because of their generation. Some women I interviewed commented that it seems to them that young women think feminism is no longer necessary in the 1990s because the position of women has improved. "They just sort of assume that we're all liberated now," complained a college professor about her students. "They have a real hard time understanding that systematic social factors make it difficult for women to get ahead. They think it's all individual attributes." Further, veterans of the 1970s women's movement believe that younger women do not understand that feminist agitation in the 1960s and 1970s improved the position of women and by extension that women's efforts can have an impact on the world. A longtime activist's comments typify this position.

> It is discouraging and infuriating to me that young women not only are not feminists, but they act as though they don't understand what on earth we are talking about. They act as though we were just off the wall. They don't have any historical sense to understand that we changed their life.

Another respondent described how young women at the college where she works use programs and perspectives that exist because of the struggles of feminists without understanding their history or implications.

> They're all playing sports. Women didn't have any sports to play when I was their age. And there are a hell of a lot more women in economics classes now than there ever were when I was there, and the textbooks have been purged of some of their more obvious sexist content. . . . There are little support groups and stuff for women who are victims of incest and women who have eating disorders and that kind of stuff. So people are aware of it, but sort of on an individual counseling basis. And it's a counseling that's informed by feminism, but it's not one that tends to develop into any kind of activism.

Her hope, like that of many women I interviewed, is that younger women would feel empowered to be activists themselves if they realized the scope of feminist gains.

Yet women who were active in the women's movement of the 1960s and 1970s do not always agree with the political directions that newer feminist activists have taken; in fact, they sometimes see them as mistaken or even antifeminist. For example, one activist in the antirape movement worried despairingly that the growth of coalitions with men and "sex radicalism," or support for women's sexual expressiveness including sadomasochism and pornography, marked the death of radical lesbian feminism. Younger lesbians, she complained, were working in groups like Queer Nation, which she did not see as radical because they entailed working with men. Other longtime feminists, like this founder of an organization, worried that they would be squeezed out if women's movement organizations were taken over by younger feminists.

> One of the starters of the women's self-help group in California
> . . . found herself surrounded by what I would call young whippersnappers telling her that her time was over, that she should move on. Well, I don't want to be fifty-five and have someone in their twenties tell me that I've outlived my usefulness. I'll be willing to work with them, but I'm not willing to go through the agony of the eighties as far as starting this [organization]
> . . . only to have some young woman come about the time I'm retirement age and tell me that that was all very nice but it doesn't count anymore. Bullshit!

Her fears are not unfounded. Just as micro-cohort conflicts in the late 1970s pushed many founding members out of feminist organizations amidst accusations of power-tripping and elitism, conflicts between political generations occur in the 1990s too. It is painful for longtime feminists to see newer entrants to the movement dismissing their dearly held beliefs or changing organizations they struggled to form. Recent debates within the feminist community exacerbate many women's feelings that they and their beliefs are vulnerable to attack. In the "sex wars," in particular, lesbian practitioners of sadomasochism, along with heterosexual women and others, argued that women should have the right to act freely on any sexual desires, and accused those who thought otherwise of being antisex, "vanilla," or puritanical.[14] The sex wars crossed generational lines, and some "sex radicals" were veterans of the 1970s radical women's movement. But the criticism of "vanilla" lesbians stereotyped them as rigidly enforcing standards of politically correct appearance and sexuality that were established in the 1970s radical movement. The sex radicals, in effect, accused those who disagreed of being stuck in the 1970s.[15] For many longtime radical feminists, the increasing visibility of sex radicalism combined with the widespread criticism of those who viewed sex and appearance as political to increase their sense of isolation from contemporary lesbian and feminist culture.

A similar sense of isolation stems from the lack of links between movement veterans and the feminist organizations that have survived into the 1990s. Many women I interviewed commented that although some of the organizations they founded still exist, such as Women Against Rape and Fan the Flames bookstore, the women who lead those organizations now have little sense of the groups' past. One activist since the mid-1970s compared the sense of connection she had to founders of Women Against Rape with the disconnectedness of new feminists now.

> There was a demonstration here [in D.C.] and we were standing on the sidelines . . . and we saw the banner from WAR. We got real excited and ran out into the street. And there was nobody we knew there. And I got the feeling from them that they didn't care that we were old members, and want to know about us. It was like a divorce. It was really painful. But it made me remember once when we were [at] the community festival in Columbus. . . . This woman comes up and tells us that she was one of the original members of WAR [Women Against Rape].

And it was like, not like she was a goddess, but maybe a minor deity. And we begged her for stories. . . . It was a wonderful feeling of connectedness. And so when the women that we saw at that march really gave off this sense of not wanting to know us, it felt really unconnected. That's what really felt like the doldrums to me. Without our history, where are we?

Another woman, formerly a member of the WAC, saw the women who were presently running Women Against Rape as

very young, very naive. . . . They come to my door and they don't know the history of WAR. I invite them in and I say, "Do you understand what the organization is that you belong to?" I pull out my CASSR [Community Action Strategies to Stop Rape] book and I say, "Have you ever seen this before?" and [they say,] "No." I pull out [other publications] and they have never seen these before, and [they say,] "My, aren't these marvelous publications." Well, see the name WAR on the back, that's your organization, it's your business to know this.

This woman's frustration, like that of many former WAC and Women Against Rape members, comes from the fact that the women who have taken over the surviving groups seem unaware of the organizations' history and end up, as a result, reinventing the wheel.

But it is not only longtime activists who wish for more intergenerational connection. A current member of Women Against Rape, in her early twenties, noted that she has little contact with earlier members, and she finds this frustrating. She and other members believe—accurately—that many of the problems they encounter with collective structure, the programs they contemplate starting or changing, and the benefits and pitfalls of working with mainstream funding agencies are issues that the organization must have confronted before. Yet they have little sense of when and how similar issues arose in the past or of what the outcomes were. Although they occasionally make a random connection with an early member, usually through their door-to-door canvassing, they have no institutionalized means of learning the lessons of the past.

Despite younger feminists' belief that the older generation is not interested in helping them out, longtime feminists I interviewed remain willing to pass on the lessons they learned in the 1970s. One early member of WAC who was frustrated at younger feminists' lack of interest in those lessons commented:

> We've always had these ancient little old ladies who were involved in the National Woman's Party and stuff to call upon. . . . There are all these ancient feminists sitting around waiting to tell us what they learned. And there are going to be a lot of us left in my generation. So as soon as anybody's ready to come around and listen, we've got the experience and the stories to tell.

Many women felt great longing for more connection with new generations of feminists and for a resurgence of activism that would not require them to do all of the work. A former member of Women Against Rape who is still active in the antirape movement reflected on her hopes for movement continuity.

> One of my favorite fantasies is that when I'm in my eighties or nineties . . . feminism will be popular again, and that my role when everybody's out marching and working and stuff, will be to plop myself down in my wheelchair and have some younger woman push me through the march. . . . And all my hard work will be done, and I'll see younger women picking it up, knowing it's going to go on to the future and I don't have to worry about it anymore, and that I'll be valued for the fact that I survived.

Why, if both longtime and newer political generations are eager to connect with each other, are they so often unable to do so? It is largely because the experiences and structural positions of the two groups of women are so different. Movement veterans and newcomers have different structural locations partly as a result of life stage: The first political generation, whose members are establishing themselves in work and family, rarely over-laps with the second political generation, consisting largely of younger students who spend their time in their own social net-works.[16] As movement veterans found mainstream occupations, they distanced themselves from the daily operations of women's movement organizations. Sometimes they became less comfort-able with militant tactics, like the college administrator who said she sometimes found herself wanting to "put on the brakes" with her radical students. Other times they simply became un-familiar with the actions and dilemmas younger activists en-countered. In any case, the political generations' differences *now* contribute to their disjuncture along with the lasting conse-quences of their initial politicization.

Ironically, the women's movement's success has also widened the gap between political generations. Not only do recent re-cruits benefit from the gains of the 1970s women's movement, but they also have different problems and needs as a result of those gains. One current member of Women Against Rape, anx-ious for further connections with earlier members, commented that she nevertheless feels the need for the organization to con-tinue to change.

> I almost feel like we're stagnating in a way. This [what Women Against Rape does now] is really neat, but it's almost like a relic of the past. I feel like everything else is moving forward and we're standing still. . . . I want to see us developing stuff again. I feel like everything's gone back to, "Well, back in 1970-some-thing we did this. We were really hot then. We developed this literature, and we did this, and we did that." Well, that was years ago. So now what are we going to do?

Because many of the group's earlier advances gained widespread acceptance, it needs to evolve continually. As she and other re-cent entrants to the movement search for new directions that fit their experiences, they sometimes overlook or dismiss the beliefs and experiences of longtime feminists. And at the same time, longtime feminists sometimes wish that new recruits would merely follow in their footsteps and hate to see "their" movement change. The generational disjuncture stems from deep differences between the social locations of the two groups and the interactions through which they construct their collective identities.

PASSING THE TORCH

Newcomers to the women's movement are mobilizing for feminist goals in different ways from longtime activists, who sometimes see their successors' efforts as apolitical or misdirected. But the social and political climate has changed and, as a result, so have the perspectives and the opportunities of both longtime and incoming feminists. Veterans of the movement of the 1960s and 1970s adapted to the limited resources and political opportunities of the 1980s by turning their activism to their paid work and daily lives. Young women face their own dilemmas in a context that offers little opening for the mass feminist mobilization of twenty years ago. At the same time, the context is not universally negative to feminism. Many aspects of gender inequality have decreased, and with the election of Bill Clinton support for some women's issues briefly appeared forthcoming at the federal level. As young women respond to this new context, some conform to the postfeminist image by denying that feminist issues are relevant to their lives or by refusing to identify with or participate in the women's movement. But others who are activists respond by redefining the meaning of feminist, asking earlier feminists, "How does your rhetoric fit into my life now?"[17] In short, while longtime feminists' collective identity remained remarkably consistent, newcomers constructed a different model of themselves as feminists.

Change over time in the women's movement is due not only to changes in the external context, but also to how that context affected the collective identities each political generation constructed. As new political generations redefine feminism, they take the movement in new directions. The resulting discontinuity between activist generations has contributed to the decline of mass mobilization in the 1980s along with external changes. Because of conflict between political generations with differing collective identities, the lessons of the earlier generation are not fully transmitted to the newer generation, who then have to "reinvent the wheel." Of course, the earlier generation cannot hope to pass on its lessons unmodified to the newer generation, because the organizing context changes over time.[18] The strategies that worked well in 1975 will not necessarily be successful in 1995. Nevertheless, for a social movement to continue, there must be connections among activists of different ages and from various eras.

The significance of the radical feminist movement of the 1960s and 1970s, then, rests not only on its own actions but on how it passes its legacy to subsequent groups. We have seen that veterans of the 1960s and 1970s movement persisted in their own political commitments; they have not abandoned the women's movement. But as veterans found new arenas for political action, a new generation took the helm at many women's movement organizations. The women's movement's continuity and its transformation over time, therefore, rest on intergenerational dynamics. Social movements are never static, but are continually in transition as successive micro-cohorts of activists struggle over the definition of the movement. During the 1980s and early 1990s, two very different political generations struggled with each other and with the larger society over the future of radical feminism. In the end, though, both generations shared important goals: improving women's lives and ultimately freeing women of all races, classes, and sexual orientations from domination. These passionate commitments link the generations as part of a continuous feminist struggle.

CONCLUSION:

THE PERSISTENCE

AND TRANSFORMATION

OF SOCIAL MOVEMENTS

WHEN RADICAL FEMINISM emerged from the New Left in the late 1960s, it brought with it the notion that politics and culture were inextricably linked.[1] To change the world meant both to change social structures and to change the ways that people lived, interacted, and thought about themselves and others. Among feminists, the development of consciousness raising took the connection between daily life and social change one step further. The notion that "the personal is political" meant both that "personal" problems had political roots, and that making feminist revolution entailed constructing new communities and identities. From the very beginning, cultural activities like women's bands, the writing of nonsexist literature, and feminist film making went hand in hand with more conventional political activism.

As the radical women's movement grew, other social movements of the 1960s receded. By the mid-1970s, radical feminists had built large organizations, using grant money to support direct action, advocacy, and services for women. In conjunction, they created extensive community networks and institutions that fostered the development of a culture that aimed to embody feminist ideals. The relative abundance of resources permitted both feminist organizations and the "women's community" to develop enduring structures and to operate on a broader scale than in the movement's early years. The women's movement was not only successful in building a "world apart" during these years; it also was highly visible in mainstream culture and implemented programs that concretely affected policy and practice related to women, particularly at the state and local levels.

This boom was short-lived, however; external resources began to dry up in the late 1970s and virtually vanished in the 1980s. In the wake of shrinking opportunities, participants developed numerous ideas for how feminists should proceed. Some activists, mostly new entrants, argued that "internalized oppression" was the critical force holding women back; others focused on crisis management, alleviating the most pressing problems for women immediately through rape crisis centers and other direct services. Some worked to build coalitions with other social movements in order to resist the conservative backlash that targeted movements for peace, environmentalism, lesbians and gay men, and others as well as feminists. Many women's movement organizations folded, but feminist culture, which had never relied on external funding agencies, survived. In the antifeminist climate, the women's community served as a haven for both radical and liberal feminists who relied on the rejuvenation and political contacts they found at cultural events and women's bookstores. The women's movement survived not only through national organizations, but through the actions of individual movement veterans, the incorporation of feminism into other movements for social change, and local movement communities and cultural events.

A generation of activists was squeezed out of women's movement organizations in the 1980s by shrinking economic resources, strong opposition, and their own exhaustion. Yet these women, who had been core participants in the radical feminist movement during its peak, sustained their commitment in the face of opposition. In one sense, radical feminist veterans have been absorbed into mainstream society, taking jobs in universities, business, or government agencies. However, wherever they go they carry with them a commitment to the feminist transformation of society. The activists who were central to the radical women's movement in Columbus, Ohio, have continued to pursue feminist goals on the job and in their interactions with neighbors, friends, co-workers, and family members.

Core participants in the women's movement in the 1970s who continue to act on their feminist convictions today sustain feminism on more than an individual level; they help the women's movement as a whole to survive a hostile period. By carrying feminist concerns into mainstream institutions, they transform those institutions and also preserve the legacy of the women's movement for future waves of mobilization. The growth of women's studies programs within universities, shelters for battered women funded by mainstream sources such as local governments and the United Way, counseling for rape survivors within mental health centers, and even the focus on allegations of sexual harassment in the Supreme Court confirmation hearings for Clarence Thomas, result from the efforts of feminists—not only as activists outside "the system" but as players within it.

This study, in combination with others documenting the persistence of activist commitments, should definitively debunk the myth that activists in the movements of the 1960s have "sold out" in the 1990s.[2] Even as their participation in women's movement organizations has decreased, feminism remains an overarching guide to veterans' actions and understandings of the world. Activists who are bound together as a political generation in their early years remain a recognizable group over time. They remain connected to each other, view themselves as different from other groups, interpret women's lives in a feminist light, and continue to share important life experiences. Political generations are rooted in shared structural circumstances and formative experiences, as Mannheim suggested. Through interaction in social movement contexts, participants transform their shared experiences, structural constraints, and opportunities into the enduring system of beliefs, actions, and relationships that is collective identity.[3]

Of course, feminist veterans have been affected by years of experience in the women's movement, changes in their political and cultural surroundings, and their own aging. They have become more willing to work with people whose politics are different from their own, define feminism more broadly, and pursue feminist social change more as individuals than collectively. They have adopted new tactics in order to continue working toward feminist goals in unfriendly environments. But they have changed in ways that are consistent with their deeply held beliefs, rather than a repudiation of them.

In addition to the enduring collective identity of participants, the women's movement has also survived within other social movements in the 1980s and 1990s. Feminists have raised new issues, structured organizations differently, used innovative tactics, and conceptualized personal experiences as political problems, thus changing how other movements formulate and address issues.[4] When the radical women's movement resurged in the late 1960s, it challenged sexism not only in mainstream society, but also in the male-dominated New Left. Nevertheless, feminists remained concerned with peace, environmental protection, racism, class inequality, and U.S. military intervention in other countries. In the 1980s and early 1990s, feminist concern with these broader issues combined with opposition from a unified conservative movement to bring women's movement organizations and mixed-sex Left organizations closer together again, forming a feminist progressive coalition. In addition to reshaping the movements from which it grew, the feminist movement also helped create a range of newer movements that address questions of spirituality, personal growth through recovery from addictions or psychological restrictions, and the liberation of lesbians, gay men, bisexuals, and people with AIDS. These movements draw on the feminist view of the personal as political and the analysis of "internalized oppression" that developed in the women's movement of the late 1970s.

Lesbians and lesbian politics have been influential in all of these struggles and in the survival of radical feminism. Conflicts and tensions between lesbian and heterosexual women affected organizational dynamics, probably to an even greater extent in other cities than in Columbus. But lesbians' influence on feminism is about much more than the "gay–straight split." Theoretical analyses that explained "compulsory heterosexuality" as a means of enforcing male domination helped to place lesbian liberation squarely in the center of a feminist agenda.[5] As lesbian feminists developed a strong set of cultural institutions and lesbian feminist identity became increasingly separatist, an emphasis on "women-only space" gained popularity among many heterosexual feminists as well. Further, although I have focused on lesbian politics in radical feminist organizations, lesbians also provided substantial labor and influence to less militant groups as well. Shifts in lesbian feminist collective identity throughout the 1980s also had ramifications for the broader women's movement. For example, as AIDS pulled them into coalitions with men, some longtime lesbian feminists began to think of their identity as shared with gay men across gender boundaries. At the same time, a new cohort of lesbians defined themselves as "queer," forging links with gay men and others. Other lesbian feminists continued to see themselves as sharing more with heterosexual women than with gay men, but the partial reframing of lesbian identity fostered the growing links between feminism and other social movements. Lesbian time and effort, debates among lesbians over collective identity, and the cultural institutions built by lesbians all contributed immeasurably to the endurance of radical feminism in a period that was hostile to *all* women.

The radical feminist challenge, then, survives in mainstream

institutions, daily life, and other social movements. It also endures as part of the larger women's movement, both in feminist
culture and in the more externally directed protest that is still
visible, although less frequent than it was twenty years ago. My
assertion that radical feminism persists challenges both popular
and scholarly accounts of the movement's demise in the 1980s.
Popular authors have stereotyped the 1980s and 1990s as a "post
feminist" era and have suggested that organized feminism is
dead and that neither veterans of the women's movement nor
younger women are interested in protest.[6] Scholars have made a
somewhat different argument but have nonetheless contended
that the radical women's movement declined over the past decade or so because of internal organizational and ideological difficulties. In this view, all that remains of the radical feminist
legacy are apolitical and retreatist cultural institutions.[7]

I think, instead, that the women's movement community is a
direct, and political, heir of the radical feminist movement. It
has survived where externally oriented protest often could not.[8]
Cultural events sustain feminists' collective identity, recruit new
women to the movement, and provide a base from which participants organize other forms of protest. More directly, cultural
challenges undermine hegemonic ideology about gender by constructing new ways of being a woman that are visible to outsiders as well as insiders. Far from being nonpolitical, such efforts are central to the survival and impact of the women's
movement.

THE POLITICS OF CULTURE AND IDENTITY

"Identity politics," in which one's membership in social categories prompts and defines one's politics, have been variously celebrated and decried. Critics charge that identity politics restrict
political and cultural possibilities and freedom, simplifying

complex individual life histories, glossing over variations within groups, and fostering stultifying limits on "politically incorrect" dissent.[9] Such debates obscure the fact that identity is central to all social movements, whether they claim to be about identity or not, and dissent over the borders of identity categories exists within movements as well as outside them.

There is, in fact, a long tradition in American society of efforts to reform social institutions and inequalities by transforming individuals, ranging from Puritanism, through nineteenth-century reform efforts and utopian communities, to segments of the twentieth-century civil rights movement. Radical feminism is part of this tradition, and shares its strengths and limitations. In contemporary society, as traditional group definitions break down under the pressure of economic and cultural dislocation, defining collectivities becomes a central task of movements that aim to transform individuals as well as social structures.[10] Feminists have seized the opportunity to redefine the category of woman. In doing so, they alter both cultural definitions of gender categories and structural arrangements of gender stratification.

We are left to re-evaluate the distinction between structure and politics, the individual and the collective. It is inconsistent to argue on one hand that cultural hegemony is an important mode of domination, and on the other hand that cultural strategies of movements are apolitical. It is inconsistent to document the encroachment of social control into the very selves of dominated individuals, and yet view movements that seek to overturn "internalized oppression" as retreatist. In a society where domination is accomplished through both structural and cultural means, collectivities resist through both structural and cultural means.

As a result, viewing movements that focus on structural confrontation and those that emphasize personal transformation as separate is overly simplistic.[11] The radical women's movement bridges this gap itself, and has drawn together movements on either side. Activists in the environmental movement, for example, may also be part of the spirituality movement; peace activists may attend 12-step recovery meetings. The priestess of a Wiccan coven may also organize a demonstration at her state legislature for abortion rights. There are, of course, intense internal debates about the effectiveness of each tack, but the overlap between conventionally political movement organizations, alternative cultures, and personal growth movements is extensive.

Social movements, in other words, are about far more than organizations; they are also about identity, community, and culture. Veterans of the radical women's movement force us to reexamine our definition of what constitutes political action to include actions outside the realm of the state and conventional protest.[12] Their lives are political in everyday interactions and on the job, as well as in protest. Defining movements in terms of formal organizations tends to obscure the portions of challenges that go on outside confrontations with the State and seek cultural as well as structural change. If we look only at organizational activities and survival, we miss these dimensions of feminist activism, and would be forced to conclude that the radical women's movement was defunct by 1975 because its original organizations no longer existed.[13]

In contrast, I have shown that the radical women's movement survives in multiple forms and settings. The movement's endurance is visible when we define radical feminism in terms of collective identity. Tracing the threads of radical feminist collective identity over time captures the movement's subtle and stark transformations as well as its survival. Collective identity, I have argued, changes over time as new entrants to the movement continually redefine it. These shifts in collective identity are tied to another central theme of the book: political generations and micro-cohorts.

POLITICAL GENERATIONS AND MICRO-COHORTS
IN THE WOMEN'S MOVEMENT

The women's movement changed gradually throughout the 1970s as each micro-cohort adapted existing structures and strategies to changing external obstacles, took advantage of new resources as they became available, and made do as resources and political access shrank. As feminist organizations and the women's movement community grew larger and more established, new recruits took initial feminist demands for granted and emphasized new issues. The rise of lesbian feminism in the mid-1970s and the focus on issues of women of color and Third World women in the late 1970s were thus a result of the successes of the women's movement, rather than a sign of its failure. By discussing the transformations of feminist collective identity in detail, I hope to have shown that new directions were not necessarily a distraction from the central purpose of the women's movement. Rather, they emerged directly from the groundwork laid by the movement's founders.

If we accept the notion that each wave of participants constructs a different and lasting collective identity based on the movement context and mobilizing conditions when they enter the women's movement, we must rethink the position of newer feminists in the movement. Young women entering the movement in the 1980s and early 1990s faced a seeming lack of opportunity for feminist transformation, combined with the perception that the women's movement was staffed by their mothers' generation rather than by their own. Some—an early 1980s micro-cohort—defined themselves as postfeminist or as "nonideological feminists" as a result.[14] As the women's movement began to grow again in the late 1980s and early 1990s, a second incoming micro-cohort raised new issues and challenged what it means to be a woman and a feminist. Like the initiator micro-cohort who first organized feminist groups in the late 1960s, the newest feminists are articulating their own feminist agenda. This agenda draws on the legacy of the recent radical feminist movement, but also departs from it.

New activists, then, take the women's movement in directions that are quite different from those of the 1970s. It is not surprising that earlier activists are sometimes critical of or discouraged by feminist organizations of the 1980s and 1990s. Criticism of current feminist organizations by earlier activists stems in part from generational disagreements over the definition of "feminist." Conflicts among political generations in the women's movement are painful for all involved, and certainly detract from the effectiveness of feminist organizations. But the conflicts do not signify the degeneration of the movement, nor are they the result of aging or adolescent rebellion. Rather, they are an expected outcome of societal and movement change and grow from political generations' divergent experiences within and outside the women's movement.

But the conflicts are widespread. From longtime feminists' negative reviews of books by "twentysomething" feminists, to the young feminist Naomi Wolf's criticism of "old-style" feminism as rigid and hostile to men, political generations trade frequent barbs in the press.[15] In a movement often polarized along generational lines, it is perhaps risky or presumptuous for me, a "twentysomething feminist," to offer insights into the lives of longtime feminists. I confess trepidation at doing so. Yet the task of thinking, speaking, and listening across generational lines is critical to the longterm survival of the women's movement.

THE PERSISTENCE AND TRANSFORMATION OF SOCIAL MOVEMENTS

I began this study intending to contribute to sociological understandings of social movement continuity. I was primarily interested in how feminist activists of the 1970s had sustained their political commitments over time, and how as a result the women's movement as a whole had survived. As the research has progressed, however, I have come to believe that the question of how social movements endure is inseparable from the question of how they change.

It seems at first glance self-evident that lasting social movements undergo repeated transformations. Yet few authors have examined movement change in a systematic and theoretical way. Resource mobilization and political process theorists have focused on how prevailing political opportunity structures and available resources permit social movements to emerge and expand, and how changing funding sources and opportunities cause movement organizations to shift their structure, strategies, or focus.[16] But the broader question of how long-lived social movements change over decades and across generations is unanswered.

I cannot hope to have provided a complete answer to this question here. However, I will draw partial conclusions about how the women's movement in particular, and social movements in general, evolve over time. The generational approach to social movements that I have developed in this book focuses on the intersection of participant waves with social movement organizations and external resources and opportunities. Taking a generational approach necessitates looking at collective identity and defining politics broadly, as going beyond the State and formal organizations. I have argued that the transformation of participants is a lasting and powerful outcome of social movements, and that the ebb and flow of political generations are a way of understanding protest cycles.

Political generations are important to social movement continuity in three ways. First, the collective identity of a political generation remains consistent over time, as it has for women who participated in the feminist movement of the 1970s. Second, even when protest declines, a social movement continues to have an impact if a generation of movement veterans carry its key elements into societal institutions and other social movements. Institutions and innovations established by activists within these other settings serve not only as agents of change themselves but also as resources for the resurgence of a future wave of mobilization.

Third, a social movement changes as new participants enter the movement and redefine its collective identity. The continual entry of micro-cohorts at regular intervals produces gradual changes. Each micro-cohort constructs a collective identity that is shaped by its context, and therefore activists who enter during movement resurgence, growth, peak, and decline differ from each other. Despite the gradual shifts that occur continually within social movements, there are clearly sharper changes at certain points. At these times, a series of micro-cohorts converge into one political generation as their similarities to each other outweigh their differences from a distinct set of incoming micro-cohorts that make up a second political generation.

I propose the notion of social movement transition periods as a means of formalizing the idea that movements change relatively rapidly at particular points in their histories. Transition periods are marked by the entry of a new cohort of activists who differ from the old and by intergenerational conflict over the definition of the movement's collective identity. The late 1980s and early 1990s appear to be a period of transition for the women's movement. As a result of the changes in the movement, members of the various micro-cohorts that made up the 1970s political generation of feminists often feel a sense of alienation from and disagreement with the directions of the women's movement in the 1980s and 1990s. There are relatively few connections between the incoming political generation of the 1980s and 1990s and longtime feminists, and they have constructed collective identities that differ in key ways.

Conflict over the formulation of collective identity is not idiosyncratic to the women's movement, but reflects the characteristics of movements in transition. When the level of a movement's mobilization declines, former activists who retain their commitment to social change find new ways to act on their politics and seek to maintain the vision and version of the movement that they established. As long as new recruits remain few or uninfluential, the collective identity forged during the movement's peak receives little challenge. But as larger numbers of recruits enter a movement, assuming leadership positions in preexisting movement organizations or establishing new groups, they attempt to reformulate organizational goals and strategies, ideological interpretations, and movement culture. These changes, not surprisingly, produce intergenerational conflict. Yet, in order for a movement to shift to a higher level of mobilization, new participants must enter. The passing of social movements from one political generation to another thus becomes key to movement survival over the long haul. Such transitions are especially visible when mobilization grows, but their roots are often in the period preceding a phase of extensive activism. [17]

I have focused here on transitions during the women's movement of the 1980s and early 1990s, when the movement was at a relatively low level of mobilization. Similarly, the founding of SDS in 1962 marked a transition in the New Left that occurred during an abeyance period. [18] The Montgomery bus boycott and lunch counter sit-ins of the 1950s were a sign of a transition while the civil rights movement was in a relative lull. [19] The establishment of the President's Commission on the Status of Women in 1961 and the organizing that grew from it signified a transition from the postwar women's movement. [20] The notion of social movement transitions suggests that even movements in abeyance are not simply static, waiting in a sort of suspended animation to be revitalized.

Movements for social change are not reborn anew each time they resurge, and they do not necessarily die when they decline. [21] Rather, social movements are continuous and move from periods of peak mobilization into decline, abeyance, transition, and back to peak mobilization again. The entry and exit of political generations is central to an explanation of how and when social movements change. During transitions, movements are passed from one political generation to the next. Incoming activists adopt and redefine the collective identity associated with the movement, not without controversy. Social movement organizations are also passed on, staffed by a new cohort of activists, and redefined. If we are to understand how social movements endure and how they are transformed, we must understand the formation and persistence of political generations and the processes of intergenerational cooperation and conflict.

A complicated mix of factors have shaped the unfolding of the radical feminist challenge over the past twenty-five years. Successive micro-cohorts and political generations have entered and then struggled over and formulated definitions of feminism and perspectives on the world. They have sustained some women's movement organizations, let others die, and formed new ones. They have found new ways to act on their politics at work and in daily life. Simultaneously with generational dynamics, changes in the external context have reshaped the women's movement. Ties to other social movements have grown as opposition increased the need for allies, affecting both the women's movement and other movements. Political opposition and the widespread loss of resources during the 1980s shut down many women's movement organizations and channeled participants into new arenas. It is the intersection between the external context and generational dynamics of collective identity that shapes radical feminism's multiple forms and strategies as it moves into a third wave.

As feminists of all political generations enter the next century, they carry with them the legacy of the 1960s and 1970s wave of radical feminist protest. That legacy, with both its limitations and its strengths, is the foundation on which the ongoing radical women's movement builds. Longtime feminists and newcomers to the movement may sometimes disagree, but together they create the future of the struggle for women's equality and liberation.

APPENDIX

WOMEN'S MOVEMENT,
ORGANIZATIONS AND DATES,
COLUMBUS, OHIO

Organization	Affiliated With	Dates
Ohio Commission on the Status of Women (CSW) (nongovernmental)		1969–1977
Columbus–OSU Women's Liberation (WL)	Ohio State University	1970–1974
Columbus Women's Media Cooperative		1970–1973
Women's Studies Ad Hoc Committee	Ohio State University	1970–1975
National Organization for Women (NOW)		1971–
Women's Action Collective (WAC)		1971–1984
Women's Co-op Garage	WAC	1971–1977

(*Continued on next page*)

Women's Movement Organizations—*Continued*

Organization	Affiliated With	Dates
Legal Action Group	WAC	1971–1974
Women's Community Development Fund	WAC	1972–1982
Women Against Rape (WAR)	WAC	1972–
Lesbian Peer Support (LPS); *formerly* Gay Women's Peer Counseling	WAC Ohio State University/ WAC 1976–1979	1972–1979
Women's Publishing Group	WAC	1972–1975
Women's Health Action Collective	WAC	1972–1974 1978–1979
Women's Caucus of the Ohio State Community	Ohio State University	1972–1975
Coalition for the Ratification of the ERA		1972–1974
Single Mothers' Support Group	WAC	1973–1977
Association of Women Students (AWS)	Ohio State University	1973–
Women's Broadcasting Group	WAC	1974–1975
Womansong (newspaper)	WAC	1974–1979
Fan the Flames Feminist Bookstore	WAC	1974–
Central Ohio Lesbians	Ohio State University	1974–1977
Coalition for the Implementation of the ERA		1974–1977
Task Force for the Implementation of the ERA	State of Ohio	1974–1975

(*Continued*)

Organization	*Affiliated With*	*Dates*
Ohio State University Center for Women's Studies	Ohio State University	1975–
Women's Programming Advisory Committee (WPAC)	Ohio State University	1976–
Women's Music Union		1976–1990
Women's Research and Policy Development Center (WRPDC)		1976–1978
United People for Women's Achievement, Research, and Development (UPWARD)		1976–1977
International Women's Year Planning Committee		1976–1977
National Abortion Rights Action League (NARAL)	NARAL (national)	1977–
Women's Information Center	State of Ohio	1977–
Feminists in Self-Defense Training (FIST)		1978–1981
Metropolitan Women's Center		1978–1981
Center for New Directions (displaced homemakers)		1978–
Ohio Women, Inc.		1978–
Women's Outreach for Women (WOW)		1983–

NOTES

INTRODUCTION

1. I use the terms "radical" and "liberal" to describe two loosely divided, overlapping arms of the women's movement. I have adopted these terms reluctantly, although I think they imply a more clear-cut division than ever existed, because the terms "radical" and "liberal" were used by participants to describe themselves. As I discuss in later chapters, activists distinguished between radicals and liberals even when they worked together. Their self-identification seems the most appropriate term to use.

2. Robert C. Liebman and Robert Wuthnow, *The New Christian Right* (New York: Aldine, 1983).

3. Susan Faludi, *Backlash: The Undeclared War on American Women* (New York: Crown, 1991).

4. Susan Bolotin, "Views from the Post-Feminist Generation," *New York Times Magazine,* October 17, 1982, pp. 29–31, 103–116; Gloria Steinem, "Why Younger Women Are More Conservative," in *Outrageous Acts and Everyday Rebellions* (New York: Holt, Rinehart and Winston, 1983), pp. 211–218; Judith Stacey, "Sexism by a Subtler Name? Postindustrial Conditions and Postfeminist Consciousness in the Silicon Valley," *Socialist Review* 17, no. 6 (1987): 7–28; Barbara Ehrenreich, "The Next Act," *Ms.,* December 1988, pp. 32–33.

5. A few high-profile cases provided fodder for such claims: Jerry Rubin, former YIPPIE leader and Chicago 7 defendant, became a stockbroker; Eldridge Cleaver, former Black Panther, declared himself a born-again Christian; Tom Hayden, a leader in Students for a Democratic Society (SDS) and Chicago 7 defendant, sought and won election to the California State Assembly.

6. See Beth Schneider, "Political Generations in the Contemporary Women's Movement," *Sociological Inquiry* 58 (1988): 4–21.

7. Ibid.

8. See, e.g., Jo Freeman, *The Politics of Women's Liberation* (New York: David McKay, 1975); Sara Evans, *Personal Politics: The Roots of Women's Liberation in the Civil Rights Movement and the New Left* (New York: Knopf, 1979); Barbara Ryan, *Feminism and the Women's Movement* (New York: Routledge, 1992); Alice Echols, *Daring to Be Bad: Radical Feminism in America 1967–1975* (Minneapolis: University of Minnesota Press, 1989); Joan Cassell, *A Group Called Women: Sisterhood and Symbolism in the Feminist Movement* (New York: David McKay, 1977). Yet much nationally significant activism began at the grassroots level, pointing to the need for local studies. See Maurice Isserman, *If I Had a Hammer: The Death of the Old Left and the Birth of the New Left* (New York: Basic Books, 1987).

9. The second wave of the women's movement emerged in the late 1960s, succeeding the first wave of suffrage organizing in the early part of the century.

10. This vignette is drawn from an interview conducted by Kim Dill in "Feminism in the Nineties: The Influence of Collective Identity and Community on Young Feminist Activists" (M.A. thesis, The Ohio State University, 1991).

11. The unprocessed papers of the Women's Action Collective are housed at the Ohio Historical Society in Columbus, Ohio. The Ohio State University Archives in Columbus, Ohio, houses records of campus-based organizations. I also had access to the personal papers of some participants.

12. The interview with the key informant from the Association of Women Students was conducted by Kim Dill during her research on young feminists for "Feminism in the Nineties." Three key informants from the Women's Information Center, Women's Outreach for Women, and OSU's Center for Women's Studies were among the 34

respondents who were participants in the women's movement during the 1970s. These women provided information about their groups in the 1980s in the course of their interviews, but I did not conduct separate interviews with them in their capacity as key informants. In all, I conducted 7 separate interviews with key informants in addition to the 34 interviews discussed above.

13. Nineteen women (56 percent) held graduate or professional degrees, 6 (18 percent) had some graduate school, 8 (23 percent) held bachelor's degrees, and 1 (3 percent) had a high school diploma and some college education.

14. One woman worked part time as a clerical worker, and another worked as a printer. One woman's occupation was unknown.

15. In a few cases it has been impossible to make the source of a comment unrecognizable to other members of the Columbus women's movement. I have minimized such cases and have removed any potentially damaging or sensitive material from recognizable quotations.

16. Doug McAdam, *Freedom Summer* (New York: Oxford University Press, 1988), and Jack Whalen and Richard Flacks, *Beyond the Barricades: The Sixties Generation Grows Up* (Philadelphia: Temple University Press, 1989) document the distress of New Left and civil rights activists during the same period.

17. Dill, "Feminism in the Nineties."

18. See Schneider, "Political Generations."

19. Verta Taylor, "Social Movement Continuity: The Women's Movement in Abeyance," *American Sociological Review* 54 (1989): 771.

20. Alberto Melucci, *Nomads of the Present: Social Movements and Individual Needs in Contemporary Society* (Philadelphia: Temple University Press, 1989).

21. Political generations theory originates with Karl Mannheim, "The Problem of Generations," in *Essays on the Sociology of Knowledge,* ed. Paul Kecskemeti (London: Routledge and Kegan Paul, 1952 [1926]), pp. 276–332. Recent works include Vern L. Bengston, "Time, Aging, and the Continuity of Social Structure: Themes and Issues in Generational Analysis," *Journal of Social Issues* 30, no. 2 (1974): 1–29; Richard G. Braungart, "The Sociology of Generations and Student Politics: A Comparison of the Functionalist and Generation Unit Models," *Journal of Social Issues* 30, no. 2 (1974): 31–54; Richard G. Braungart and Margaret M. Braungart, "Life Course and

Generational Politics," *Journal of Political and Military Sociology* 12, no. 1 (1984): 1–8; Schneider, "Political Generations." These recent works emphasize Mannheim's concept of the generation unit, a subset of an age group that shares both experiences and political allegiances.

22. See, e.g., Braungart and Braungart, "Life Course and Generational Politics"; Howard Schumann and Jacqueline Scott, "Generations and Collective Memories," *American Sociological Review* 54 (1989): 359–381; M. Kent Jennings and Richard G. Niemi, *Generations and Politics: A Panel Study of Young Adults and Their Parents* (Princeton: Princeton University Press, 1981); M. Kent Jennings, "Residues of a Movement: The Aging of the American Protest Generation," *American Political Science Review* 81 (1987): 367–382; Stephen I. Abramowitz and Alberta J. Nassi, "Keeping the Faith: Psychological Correlates of Activism Persistence into Middle Adulthood," *Journal of Youth and Adolescence* 10 (1981): 507–523.

23. Alain Touraine proposes a similar focus on "structure in action," although the origins and development of his approach are quite different from mine. See especially *The Voice and the Eye* (New York: Cambridge University Press, 1981).

24. William Gamson, "The Social Psychology of Collective Action," in *Frontiers of Social Movement Theory*, ed. Aldon Morris and Carol Mueller (New Haven: Yale University Press, 1992), pp. 53–76. Doug McAdam, John McCarthy, and Mayer Zald, "Social Movements," in *Handbook of Sociology*, ed. Neil J. Smelser (Newbury Park, Calif.: Sage Publications, 1988), pp. 695–737.

25. The term "women's movement community" is drawn from Steven M. Buechler, *Women's Movements in the United States* (New Brunswick, N.J.: Rutgers University Press, 1990).

26. Touraine, *The Voice and the Eye.*

27. See Evans, *Personal Politics,* and Freeman, *Politics,* for accounts of the emergence of women's liberation.

28. See n1.

29. For a description of NOW, see Ryan, *Feminism and the Women's Movement.*

30. Freeman, *Politics,* pp. 130–142; Echols, *Daring to Be Bad,* ch. 5.

31. For more detailed discussion of the centralized national organizations, see Ryan, *Feminism and the Women's Movement* on NOW, and

Suzanne Staggenborg, *The Pro-Choice Movement* (Oxford: Oxford University Press, 1991), on NARAL and other organizations working for abortion rights.

32. See Patricia Hill Collins, *Black Feminist Thought* (New York: Routledge, 1991) for a detailed discussion of African American women's pursuit of social change through what she calls "the struggle for group survival." Her formulation has influenced mine.

33. Alessandro Pizzorno, "Political Science and Collective Identity in Industrial Conflict," in *The Resurgence of Class Conflict in Western Europe Since 1968,* ed. Colin Crouch and Alessandro Pizzorno (New York: Holmes and Meier, 1978); Jean L. Cohen, "Strategy or Identity: New Theoretical Paradigm and Contemporary Social Movements," *Social Research* 52 (1985): 663–716; Alberto Melucci, "The Symbolic Challenge of Contemporary Movements," *Social Research* 52 (1985): 781–816; Melucci, *Nomads of the Present;* Claus Offe, "New Social Movements: Challenging the Boundaries of Institutional Politics," *Social Research* 52 (1985): 817–868; Bert Klandermans and Sidney Tarrow, "Mobilization into Social Movements: Synthesizing European and American Approaches," in *From Structure to Action: Comparing Movement Participation Across Cultures, International Social Movement Research,* vol. 1, ed. Bert Klandermans, Hanspeter Kriesi, and Sidney Tarrow (Greenwich, Conn.: JAI Press, 1988), pp. 1–38.

34. On the temperance movement, see Barbara Epstein, *The Politics of Domesticity* (Middletown, Conn.: Wesleyan University Press, 1986), and Ruth Bordin, *Women and Temperance* (Philadelphia: Temple University Press, 1981).

35. Anthony Giddens, *Modernity and Self-Identity: Self and Society in the Late Modern Age* (Palo Alto, Calif.: Stanford University Press, 1991); Jürgen Habermas, *The Theory of Communicative Action,* vol. 2: *Lifeworld and System: A Critique of Functionalist Reason* (Boston: Beacon Press, 1987); Michel Foucault, *Discipline and Punish* (New York: Vintage, 1977); Michel Foucault, *The History of Sexuality,* vol. 1 (London: Penguin, 1979).

36. Habermas, *Theory,* terms the extension of State control the "colonization of lifeworld by system."

37. Robert Wuthnow, *Communities of Discourse: Ideology and Social Structure in the Reformation, the Enlightenment, and European Socialism* (Cambridge, Mass.: Harvard University Press, 1989).

38. Much of this builds on resource mobilization theory as John McCarthy and Mayer Zald initially formulated it in John D. McCarthy and Mayer N. Zald, *The Trend of Social Movements in America* (Morristown, N.J.: General Learning Press, 1973), and John D. McCarthy and Mayer N. Zald, "Resource Mobilization and Social Movements: A Partial Theory," *American Journal of Sociology* 82 (1987): 1212–1241, and on political process approaches developed by Charles Tilly, *From Mobilization to Revolution* (Reading, Mass.: Addison-Wesley, 1978), and Doug McAdam, *Political Process and the Development of Black Insurgency* (Chicago: University of Chicago Press, 1982). The resource mobilization and political process approaches originally de-emphasized group grievances and the processes of defining ideology and identity, and focused instead on the internal dynamics of formal organizations and their interactions with the state and elites. Jo Freeman's resource mobilization analysis of the women's movement, "Mobilization and Strategy: A Model for Analyzing Social Movement Organization Actions," in *The Dynamics of Social Movements,* ed. Mayer N. Zald and John D. McCarthy (Cambridge, Mass.: Winthrop, 1979), was quite influential.

More recently, there has been a revival of interest in cultural theory among scholars of social movements, including many who come from the resource mobilization and political process perspectives. This work retains the insight from both perspectives that the resources and structures of organizations and their political contexts shape movements' paths and outcomes, but adds a direct concern with meaning. See Myra Marx Ferree and Frederick D. Miller, "Mobilization and Meaning: Some Social-Psychological Contributions to the Resource Mobilization Perspective on Social Movements," *Sociological Inquiry* 55 (1985): 38–61; David A. Snow, E. Burke Rochford, Jr., Steven K. Worden, and Robert D. Benford, "Frame Alignment Processes, Micromobilization, and Movement Participation," *American Sociological Review* 51 (1986): 464–481; Rick Fantasia, *Cultures of Solidarity* (Berkeley: University of California Press, 1988); Sidney Tarrow, *Democracy and Disorder* (New York: Oxford University Press, 1989); Aldon Morris and Carol Mueller, eds., *Frontiers of Social Movement Theory* (New Haven: Yale University Press, 1992); and Hank Johnston and Bert Klandermans, eds., *Social Movements and Culture* (Minneapolis: University of Minnesota Press, forthcoming, 1995). For an expanded treatment of the theoretical issues regarding the culture of the women's movement, see Verta Taylor and Nancy Whittier, "Analytical Approaches to Social Movement Culture: The U.S. Women's Movement," in Johnston and Klandermans, eds., *Social Movements and Culture*.

39. This formulation is similar to the definition in McCarthy and Zald, "Resource Mobilization," of a social movement as a "preference structure" in the general population, as distinguished from social movement organizations that seek to implement those preferences.

40. Tarrow, *Democracy and Disorder;* Taylor, "Social Movement Continuity."

41. See, e.g., Molly Andrews, *Lifetimes of Commitment: Aging, Politics, Psychology* (Cambridge: Cambridge University Press, 1991); McAdam, *Freedom Summer;* Whalen and Flacks, *Beyond the Barricades*.

42. For an example of a movement that failed to attract new members, see the discussion of the stagnation of the National Woman's Party after World War II in Leila J. Rupp and Verta Taylor, *Survival in the Doldrums: The American Women's Rights Movement, 1945 to the 1960s* (New York: Oxford University Press, 1987).

CHAPTER 1 :: RADICAL FEMINISM IN COLUMBUS, OHIO

1. Steven M. Buechler, *Women's Movements in the United States* (New Brunswick, N.J.: Rutgers University Press, 1990).

2. Alberto Melucci, *Nomads of the Present: Social Movements and Individual Needs in Contemporary Society* (Philadelphia: Temple University Press, 1989).

3. Buechler, *Women's Movements*.

4. Jo Freeman, *The Politics of Women's Liberation* (New York: David McKay, 1975); Sara Evans, *Personal Politics: The Roots of Women's Liberation in the Civil Rights Movement and the New Left* (New York: Knopf, 1979).

5. Women's Herstory Microfilm Collection, Herstory 1, Reel 20, OSU-*Women's Liberation Newsletter,* issue 1, 1971.

6. Ibid.

7. Ohio Historical Society [OHS], Columbus, Ohio, Women's Action Collective Papers, Box 3, Historical, Karen Quinn, Columbus–OSU Women's Liberation Demands. The collection is not invento-

ried, and thus files and their locations are not orderly. Subsequent citations from this collection will be in the following form: OHS, box number, file name, subfile name (if any), title of document (if any).

8. OHS, B3, Historical, "Columbus–OSU Women's Liberation Newsletter, Issue 1, 1971."

9. One organizer estimated that six hundred children attended, but the figure is impossible to verify.

10. OHS, B3, Historical, "Columbus–OSU Women's Liberation Newsletter," April 8, 1971.

11. OHS, B3, Children, letter from Marcia Clark to OSU Women's Liberation Movement, December 12, 1972.

12. OHS, B3, Historical, "Columbus–OSU Women's Liberation Newsletter, Issue 1, 1971."

13. Cindy Wilkey, "The Role of Women in Local Radical Organizations" (paper, The Ohio State University, n.d.).

14. Ohio State University [OSU] Archives, Accession number 127/88 (9/c-17), Box 1, "WSGA Budgets and Financial Statements," WSGA Statements of Income and Expense (Schedule 1), academic years 1964/65 through 1971/72.

15. OSU Archives, Accession number 127/88 (9/c-17), Box 1, "History of AWS," *Report of the Committee on the Role and Relevancy of the Women's Self-Government Association, 1970.*

16. OSU Archives, Accession number 127/88 (9/c-17), Box 1, "WSGA Budgets and Financial Statements," WSGA Statements of Income and Expense (Schedule 1), June 30, 1971–June 30, 1972 and June 30, 1972–June 30, 1973. The appropriation in 1971/72 was $4,595, and in 1972/73 had dropped to $2,375.

17. Mary Haller, "Decline of a Social Movement Organization: The Women's Action Collective" (paper, The Ohio State University, 1984).

18. Women's Action Collective, "Women's Action Collective, Columbus, Ohio, Condensed Organizational History," 1977, personal files of Mary Haller, Columbus, Ohio.

19. Ibid.

20. On Chicago, see Margaret Strobel, "The Chicago Women's Liberation Union," paper presented at the Workshop on Feminist Organizations, Washington, D.C., February 14–16, 1992. On the Twin Cities Women's Union, see Marcia Neff, "'Still Ain't Satisfied': Lega-

cies of the 1970s Socialist Feminist Movement in Minneapolis/St. Paul," paper presented at the Berkshire Conference on Women's History, Vassar College, June 13, 1993. Information on the Twin Cities Female Liberation Group, Ann Arbor, Iowa City, and Madison comes from the Women's Herstory Microfilm Collection, Herstory 1, Reel 15, Minneapolis/St. Paul, *Female Liberation Group Newsletter*, 1969–1971; Herstory 2, Reel 6, Ann Arbor, *Her Self: Community Women's Newspaper*, 1972–1973; Herstory 1, Reel 1, and Herstory 1 Update, Reel 1, and Herstory 1 Continuing Update, Reel 1, Iowa City, *Ain't I A Woman*, 1970–1974; Herstory 2 Update, Madison, *Whole Woman*, 1973–1974.

21. Maren Carden, *The New Feminist Movement* (New York: Russell Sage, 1974); Myra Marx Ferree and Beth B. Hess, *Controversy and Coalition: The New Feminist Movement* (Boston: Twayne, 1985); Jane Mansbridge, *Why We Lost the ERA* (Chicago: University of Chicago Press, 1986); Buechler, *Women's Movements;* Suzanne Staggenborg, *The Pro-Choice Movement* (New York: Oxford University Press, 1991).

22. Barbara Ryan, *Feminism and the Women's Movement* (New York: Routledge, 1992).

23. "Women's Action Collective Condensed Organizational History," personal files of Mary Haller, Columbus, Ohio.

24. OHS, Box 3, Automechanics, *The Lantern*, 1973.

25. OSU Archives, Accession number 102/90 (9/c-17), Box 1, "Women's Programming Advisory Committee," WPAC Minutes, September 28, 1977.

26. The term "social movement community" is drawn from Buechler, *Women's Movements*, p. 42.

27. OSU Archives, Accession number 127/88 (9/c-17), Box 1, "Student Intern Reports," letter and report from Rusty Belote, Coordinator of Women's Services, to Dr. Richard Armitage, Vice President for Student Services, March 7, 1977.

28. OSU Archives, Accession number 133/85 (9/c-17), Box 1, "Women's Programs—Office of Student Services: Planning," letter from Beth McNeer for the Campus Wide Women's Services Group to Dr. Richard Armitage, Vice President, Office of Student Services, and Dr. Robert Archibald, Director, Counseling and Consultation Services, May 9, 1975.

29. OSU Archives, Accession number 127/88 (9/c-17), Box 1,

"Student Intern Reports," letter and report from Rusty Belote, Coordinator of Women's Services, to Dr. Richard Armitage, Vice President for Student Services, March 7, 1977.

30. Women's Herstory Microfilm Collection, Herstory 1, Herstory 1 Update, Herstory 2, Minneapolis–St. Paul, *Female Liberation Newsletter*, 1969–1971; *Goldflower*, 1971–1973; and *So's Your Old Lady*, 1973.

31. Herstory, Herstory 1, Reel 1; Herstory 1 Update, Reel 1; Herstory 1 Continuing Update, Reel 1, *Ain't I A Woman*, 1970–1974.

32. Herstory, Herstory 2, Reel 6; Herstory 2 Update, Reel 3, Ann Arbor, Michigan, *Her Self: Community Women's Newspaper*, 1972–1974.

33. Jo Freeman, *Politics,* made this point in her pioneering work on the women's movement. She termed the branches "older" and "younger," and argued that their main differences were the networks from which they grew and their style.

34. *WAC Newsletter,* April 1979, personal files of Debbie Chalfie, Washington, D.C.

35. *WAC Newsletter,* November 1979, personal files of Debbie Chalfie.

36. *WAC Newsletter,* March 1981, personal files of Debbie Chalfie.

37. Ryan, *Feminism and the Women's Movement.*

38. Verta Taylor and Nancy Whittier, "The New Feminist Movement," in *Feminist Frontiers III,* ed. Laurel Richardson and Verta Taylor (New York: McGraw-Hill, 1993), pp. 533–548

39. OHS, B5, Annual meeting 1981, Bylaws, Purpose and Policy section, Article II, revised July 1977.

40. *WAC Newsletter,* September 1979, p. 2, personal files of Debbie Chalfie.

41. OHS, B5, Annual Meeting 1981, WAR annual report.

42. *WAC Newsletter,* July/August 1979, September 1979, personal files of Debbie Chalfie.

43. Haller, "Decline."

44. Alice Echols, *Daring to Be Bad: Radical Feminism in America 1967–1975* (Minneapolis: University of Minnesota Press, 1989).

45. Sara Evans and Harry Boyte, *Free Spaces: The Sources of Democratic Change in America* (New York: Harper and Row, 1986).

46. Verta Taylor and Leila J. Rupp, "Women's Culture and the

Survival of the Women's Movement: A Reconsideration of Cultural Feminism," *Signs* 19 (1993): 32–61.

47. Aldon Morris, "Political Consciousness and Collective Action," in *Frontiers of Social Movement Theory*, ed. Aldon Morris and Carol Mueller (New Haven: Yale University Press, 1992), pp. 351–373.

48. Barbara Ryan, in *Feminism and the Women's Movement*, pp. 160–161, also identifies "what is radical?" as a key issue in the study of the contemporary women's movement.

CHAPTER 2 :: THE EVOLUTION OF
RADICAL FEMINIST IDENTITY

1. Joan Cassell, *A Group Called Women: Sisterhood and Symbolism in the Feminist Movement* (New York: David McKay, 1977).

2. Verta Taylor and Nancy Whittier, "Collective Identity and Lesbian Feminist Mobilization," in *Frontiers of Social Movement Theory*, ed. Aldon Morris and Carol Mueller (New Haven: Yale University Press, 1992).

3. E. P. Thompson makes this point in *The Making of the English Working Class* (New York: Vintage, 1966).

4. Sara Evans, *Personal Politics: The Roots of Women's Liberation in the Civil Rights Movement and the New Left* (New York: Knopf, 1979).

5. Ohio Historical Society [OHS], Columbus, Ohio, Women's Action Collective Papers, Box 3, Historical, Karen Quinn, *Columbus–OSU Women's Liberation Newsletter*, November 5, 1970.

6. Carol Anne Douglas, "Review of Alice Echols, *Daring to Be Bad*," *Off Our Backs* 20 (April 1990): 16–17.

7. Alice Echols, *Daring to Be Bad: Radical Feminism in America 1967–1975* (Minneapolis: University of Minnesota Press, 1989), ch. 2.

8. Maren Carden, *The New Feminist Movement* (New York: Russell Sage, 1974); Myra Marx Ferree and Elizabeth B. Hess, *Controversy and Coalition: The New Feminist Movement* (Boston: Twayne, 1985), chs. 5–6; Steven M. Buechler, *Women's Movements in the United States* (New Brunswick, N.J.: Rutgers University Press, 1990), ch. 2.

9. Ferree and Hess, *Controversy and Coalition*, chs. 5–6; Barbara

Ryan, *Feminism and the Women's Movement* (New York: Routledge, 1992).

10. See Jill Johnston, *Lesbian Nation: The Feminist Solution* (New York: Simon and Schuster, 1973); Radicalesbians, "The Woman-Identified Woman," in *Radical Feminism,* ed. Anne Koedt, Ellen Levine, and Anita Rapone (New York: Quadrangle, 1973), pp. 240–245; Ti-Grace Atkinson, *Amazon Odyssey* (New York: Link Books, 1974); Nancy Myron and Charlotte Bunch, *Lesbianism and the Women's Movement* (Baltimore: Diana Press, 1975).

11. Women's Action Collective Statement of Philosophy, adopted by consensus May 21, 1974, personal files of Teri Wehausen, Columbus, Ohio.

12. *WAC Newsletter,* August 1977, personal files of Debbie Chalfie, Washington, D.C.

13. WAC Statement of Philosophy.

14. *WAC Newsletter,* November/December 1976, personal files of Debbie Chalfie.

15. *WAC Newsletter,* April/May 1977, June 1977, personal files of Debbie Chalfie.

16. "Outline for sessions," personal files of Teri Wehausen.

17. Buechler, *Women's Movements.*

18. *WAC Newsletter,* September/October 1976, personal files of Debbie Chalfie.

19. OHS, B7, Minutes of Struggle Session #1, Lesbian separatism, September 12, 1981.

20. E. T. Beck, *Nice Jewish Girls: A Lesbian Anthology* (Watertown, Mass.: Persephone, 1980); Cherrie Moraga and Gloria Anzaldua, *This Bridge Called My Back: Writings by Radical Women of Color* (Watertown, Mass.: Persephone, 1981); Gloria T. Hull, Patricia Bell Scott, and Barbara Smith, *But Some of Us Are Brave: Black Women's Studies* (New York: Feminist Press, 1982); Barbara Smith, ed., *Home Girls: A Black Feminist Anthology* (New York: Kitchen Table Women of Color Press, 1983).

21. OHS, B7, Minutes of Struggle Session #2, Mass vs. elite movement, October 24, 1981, and Struggle Session #3, Racism–Minority Women, November 22, 1981; Process Narrative of Struggle Session #4, Mass vs. elite, Part 2, n.d.; all in personal files of Teri Wehausen.

22. OHS, B7, Minutes of Struggle Session #3, November 22, 1981.

23. *WAC Newsletter*, September/October 1982, personal files of Teri Wehausen.

24. *WAC Newsletter*, November/December 1982, p. 9, personal files of Teri Wehausen.

25. *WAC Newsletter*, November/December 1982, p. 9, personal files of Teri Wehausen.

26. Ferree and Hess, *Controversy and Coalition*, ch. 6; Ryan, *Feminism and the Women's Movement*, ch. 9.

27. Jo Freeman, *The Politics of Women's Liberation* (New York: David McKay, 1975); Cassell, *A Group Called Women;* Carden, *New Feminist;* Echols, *Daring to Be Bad;* Evans, *Personal Politics.*

CHAPTER 3 :: CHANGERS AND THE CHANGED

Acknowledgment: The Changer and the Changed is the title of a record album by Cris Williamson, Olivia Records, 1975. Thanks to Cris Williamson for permission to use it here.

1. C. Wright Mills, *The Sociological Imagination* (London: Oxford University Press, 1959). Doug McAdam, "The Biographical Consequences of Activism," *American Sociological Review* 54 (1989): 744–760, makes this point in his work on participants in Freedom Summer.

2. The lifecycle approach includes what has been termed the functionalist or Eisenstadt–Parsons model developed by N. S. Eisenstadt, *From Generation to Generation* (Glencoe: Free Press, 1956); Talcott Parsons, "Youth in the Context of American Society," in *Youth: Change and Challenge,* ed. E. H. Erikson (New York: Basic Books, 1963); Richard Braungart, "The Sociology of Generations and Student Politics: A Comparison of the Functionalist and Generation Unit Models," *Journal of Social Issues* 30, no. 2 (1974): 31–54. It also includes lifecourse theory. See Mathilda White Riley, "Aging and Social Change, and the Power of Ideas," *Daedalus* 107, no. 4 (1978): 39–52; Daniel J. Levinson, *The Seasons of a Man's Life* (New York: Russell Sage, 1978); Richard Braungart, "Historical Generations and Generation Units: A Global Pattern of Youth Movements," *Journal of Political and*

Military Sociology 12, no. 1 (1984): 113–136; Jill K. Kiecolt, "Age and Political Sophistication: A Cohort Analysis," *Journal of Political and Military Sociology* 15, no. 1 (1987): 47–59. Although these approaches are not identical, they both rest on a biological model of aging and the varying developmental tasks associated with each age to explain the emergence of protest among youth and of generational conflict. The functionalist strain holds that because youths are not yet integrated into society, generational conflict occurs as the young seek power and change within social institutions while their elders seek to maintain the status quo. The lifecourse model argues that the developmental characteristics of youth (including initial awareness of political issues and events, feeling of connection or commitment to politics, criticism of society and politics, and a striving for independence) make them prone to participation in social movements and protest. Representative of this approach are Erik H. Erikson, *Identity: Youth and Challenge* (New York: Basic Books, 1968); Lewis Feuer, *The Conflict of Generations: The Character and Significance of Student Movements* (New York: Basic Books, 1969); Margaret Braungart, "Aging and Politics," *Journal of Political and Military Sociology* 12, no. 1 (1984): 79–98.

3. In addition, as Beth Schneider points out in "Political Generations in the Contemporary Women's Movement," *Sociological Inquiry* 58 (1988): 4–21, the lifecycle perspective assumes a fixed set of stages through which individuals pass as they age, and neglects differences of class, race, ethnicity, and gender in the "stages" of the lifecycle.

4. John D. McCarthy and Mayer N. Zald, "Resource Mobilization and Social Movements: A Partial Theory," *American Journal of Sociology* 82 (1977): 1212–1241; Charles Tilly, *From Mobilization to Revolution* (Reading, Mass.: Addison-Wesley, 1978); Doug McAdam, *Political Process and the Development of Black Insurgency* (Chicago: University of Chicago Press, 1982); J. Craig Jenkins, "Resource Mobilization Theory and the Study of Social Movements," *Annual Review of Sociology* 9 (1983): 527–553.

5. Karl Mannheim, "The Problem of Generations," in *Essays on the Sociology of Knowledge,* ed. Paul Kecskemeti (London: Routledge and Kegan Paul, 1952), pp. 276–332; Vern L. Bengston, "Time, Aging, and the Continuity of Social Structure: Themes and Issues in Generational Analysis," *Journal of Social Issues* 30, no. 2 (1974): 1–29; R. Braungart, "Sociology of Generations"; Richard Braungart and Marga-

ret Braungart, "Life Course and Generational Politics," *Journal of Political and Military Sociology* 12, no. 1 (1984): 1–8; Schneider, "Political Generations."

6. Robert Ross, "Generational Change and Primary Groups in a Social Movement," in *Social Movements of the Sixties and Seventies*, ed. Jo Freeman (New York: Longman, 1983), pp. 177–189.

7. Braungart and Braungart, "Life Course and Generational Politics," p. 2.

8. Mannheim, "Problem of Generations," pp. 297–298. A recent study of different age cohorts' "collective memories" of national or world events or changes provides support for this view: Howard Schuman and Jacqueline Scott, "Generations and Collective Memories," *American Sociological Review* 54 (1989): 359–381.

9. As Braungart and Braungart, "Life Course and Generational Politics," point out, it is Mannheim's notion of "generation unit," a group within a generation that shares a political outlook, that is today termed a political generation. Norman Ryder, "The Cohort as a Concept in the Study of Social Change," *American Sociological Review* 30 (1965): 843–861; Ross, "Generational Change"; and Schneider, "Political Generations," all point to factors other than age as determinants of political generation or cohort membership.

10. Ryder, "Cohort as a Concept."

11. Ross, "Generational Change"; Schneider, "Political Generations."

12. N. J. Demerath, Gerald Marwell, and Michael Aiken, *Dynamics of Idealism: White Activists in a Black Movement* (San Francisco: Jossey-Bass, 1971); James Fendrich and Alison Tarleau, "Marching to a Different Drummer: Occupational and Political Correlates of Former Student Activists," *Social Forces* 52 (1973): 245–253; James Fendrich, "Activists Ten Years Later: A Test of Generational Unit Continuity," *Journal of Social Issues* 30, no. 3 (1974): 95–118; James Fendrich, "Keeping the Faith or Pursuing the Good Life: A Study of the Consequences of Participation in the Civil Rights Movement," *American Sociological Review* 42 (1977): 144–157; James Fendrich and Kenneth Lovoy, "Back to the Future: Adult Political Behavior of Former Student Activists," *American Sociological Review* 53 (1988): 780–784; Doug McAdam, *Freedom Summer* (New York: Oxford University Press, 1988); McAdam, "Biographical Consequences"; James Max Fendrich

and Robert W. Turner, "The Transition from Student to Adult Politics," *Social Forces* 67 (1989): 1049–1057.

13. Alberta J. Nassi and Stephen I. Abramowitz, "Transition or Transformation? Personal and Political Development of Former Berkeley Free Speech Movement Activists," *Journal of Youth and Adolescence* 8 (1979): 21–35; Stephen I. Abramowitz and Alberta J. Nassi, "Keeping the Faith: Psychological Correlates of Activism Persistence Into Middle Adulthood," *Journal of Youth and Adolescence* 10 (1981): 507–523.

14. Jack Whalen and Richard Flacks, *Beyond the Barricades: The Sixties Generation Grows Up* (Philadelphia: Temple University Press, 1989).

15. M. Kent Jennings and Richard G. Niemi, *Generations and Politics: A Panel Study of Young Adults and Their Parents* (Princeton: Princeton University Press, 1981); Dean Hoge and Teresa Ankney, "Occupations and Attitudes of Former Student Activists 10 Years Later," *Journal of Youth and Adolescence* 11 (1982): 355–371; M. Kent Jennings, "Residues of a Movement: The Aging of the American Protest Generation," *American Political Science Review* 81 (1987): 367–382.

16. Joyce M. Mushaben, "Anti Politics and Successor Generations: The Role of Youth in the West and East German Peace Movements," *Journal of Political and Military Sociology* 12, no. 1 (1984): 191–201.

17. The few studies that do not find cohort effects are based on survey data and focus primarily on voting patterns, suggesting that political generations are characterized by more fundamental or specific differences in political outlook rather than by broad differences in voting patterns. See Seymour Martin Lipset and Everett Carl Ladd, "The Political Future of Activist Generations," in *The New Pilgrims*, ed. Phillip G. Altback and Robert S. Laufer (New York: David McKay, 1972), pp. 63–84; Kiecolt, "Age and Political Sophistication."

18. Fendrich and Lovoy, "Adult Political Behavior."

19. Fendrich, "Pursuing the Good Life."

20. Hoge and Ankney, "Occupations and Attitudes."

21. McAdam, "Biographical Consequences."

22. The finding about marriage is reported in Hoge and Ankney, "Occupations and Attitudes," and McAdam, "Biographical Consequences." These studies have noted some changes in their subjects.

Hoge and Ankney, and Whalen and Flacks, *Beyond the Barricades,* find that activists are more likely to be involved with community than national politics. Nassi and Abramowitz, "Transition or Transformation"; Jennings and Niemi, *Generations and Politics;* and Fendrich and his colleagues suggest that radicals have mellowed or moderated in ideology; McAdam, *Freedom Summer,* adds that they are less active in social movements than they were in the 1960s.

23. The line between collective and individual identity is blurry in this case. Collective identity is a property of a group, a definition of a category of persons such as "feminists." Boundaries refer to and establish the perimeter of that group and keep others out; consciousness is the definition of that group in a politicized way and an explanation of its position in the social structure. These are constructed at the group level. At the same time, individuals who are part of a politicized collectivity internalize the collective identity in varying degrees, making it part of their individual social identities.

24. Madeleine Kimmich, *America's Children: Who Cares?* (Washington, D.C.: Urban Institute, 1985); Joyce Gelb and Marian Lief Palley, *Women and Public Policies* (Princeton: Princeton University Press, 1982).

25. Gelb and Palley, *Women and Public Policies.*

26. Kimmich, *America's Children.*

27. Gelb and Palley, *Women and Public Policies,* p. 40.

28. Doug Imig, "Resource Mobilization and the Survival Tactics of Poverty Advocacy Groups," *Western Political Science Quarterly* 45 (1992): 501–520; Jean Potuchek, "The Context of Social Service Funding: The Funding Relationship," *Social Science Review* 11 (1986): 435–450.

29. Potuchek, "Social Service Funding."

30. Gelb and Palley, *Women and Public Policies.*

31. Martha Burt and Karen Pittman, *Testing the Social Safety Net: The Impact of Changes in Support Programs During the Reagan Administration* (Washington, D.C.: Urban Institute, 1985).

32. Jilda M. Aliotta, "The Unfinished Feminist Agenda: The Shifting Forum," *Annals of the American Academy of Political and Social Science* 515 (May 1991): 140–150.

33. Aliotta, "Unfinished Feminist Agenda"; Anne Costain, *Inviting Women's Rebellion* (Baltimore: Johns Hopkins University Press, 1992).

34. Janet Clark, "Getting There: Women in Political Office," *Annals of the American Academy of Political and Social Science* 515 (May 1991): 68.

35. Ibid.

36. Ibid.

37. Rita Mae Kelly, Michelle A. Saint-Germain, and Jody D. Horn, "Female Public Officials: A Different Voice?" *Annals of the American Academy of Political and Social Science* 515 (May 1991): 82, 83.

38. Carol Mueller, "The Gender Gap and Women's Political Influence," *Annals of the American Academy of Political and Social Science* 515 (May 1991): 23–37.

39. David Meyer, "Institutionalizing Dissent: The United States Structure of Political Opportunity and the End of the Nuclear Freeze Movement," *Sociological Forum* 8 (June 1993): 157–180.

40. The term is drawn from Janet Boles, "Form Follows Function: The Evolution of Feminist Strategies," *Annals of the American Academy of Political and Social Science* 515 (May 1991): 38–49.

41. Mary Katzenstein, "Feminism Within American Institutions: Unobtrusive Mobilization in the 1980s," *Signs* 16 (1990): 27–54.

42. Boles, "Form Follows Function"; Susan Bolotin, "Views from the Post Feminist Generation," *New York Times Magazine,* October 17, 1982, pp. 29–31, 103–116.

43. For a thorough discussion of oppositional consciousness, see the essays in Morris and Mueller, eds., *Frontiers of Social Movement Theory* (New Haven: Yale University Press, 1992), especially the concluding essay by Morris.

44. Jo Freeman, *The Politics of Women's Liberation* (New York: David McKay, 1975); Joan Cassell, *A Group Called Women: Sisterhood and Symbolism in the Feminist Movement* (New York: David McKay, 1977); Alice Echols, *Daring to Be Bad: Radical Feminism in America 1967–1975* (Minneapolis: University of Minnesota Press, 1989).

45. See Table 2 in Chapter 1 for a list of such groups.

46. Leila J. Rupp, personal correspondence.

47. Myra Marx Ferree and Frederick D. Miller, "Mobilization and Meaning: Some Social-Psychological Contributions to the Resource Mobilization Perspective on Social Movements," *Sociological Inquiry* 55 (1985): 38–61.

48. Dinesh D'Souza, *Illiberal Education: The Politics of Race and Sex on Campus* (New York: Free Press, 1991).

49. Verta Taylor and Nancy Whittier, "Collective Identity and Lesbian Feminist Mobilization," in Mueller and Morris, eds., *Frontiers*, pp. 104–129.

50. Laurel Richardson, *Dynamics of Sex and Gender*, 3rd ed. (New York: Harper and Row, 1988).

51. Leila J. Rupp and Verta Taylor, *Survival in the Doldrums: The American Women's Rights Movement, 1945 to the 1960s* (New York: Oxford University Press, 1987); Verta Taylor, "Social Movement Continuity: The Women's Movement in Abeyance," *American Sociological Review* 54 (1989): 761–775.

52. Barbara Ryan, "Ideological Purity and Feminism: The U.S. Women's Movement from 1966–1975," *Gender and Society* 3 (1989): 239–257, reports a similar complaint from a few heterosexual women.

53. Susan Cavin, "The Invisible Army of Women: Lesbian Social Protests, 1969–1988," in *Women and Social Protest*, ed. Guida West and Rhoda Blumberg (New York: Oxford University Press, 1990), pp. 321–332.

54. Jan Clausen, "My Interesting Condition," *Out/Look* 2 (1990): 11–21; Holly Near, *Fire in the Rain, Singer in the Storm* (New York: Morrow, 1990), ch. 12.

55. This was apparent when I was trying to locate interview subjects; it was easy to get names and phone numbers from respondents. McAdam reports a similarly dense and enduring network among participants in Freedom Summer, in *Freedom Summer*.

56. McAdam, *Freedom Summer*, ch. 6; Whalen and Flacks, *Beyond the Barricades*, ch. 4.

57. Taylor and Whittier, "Collective Identity."

CHAPTER 4 :: KEEPING THE FAITH

1. See, e.g., Sidney Tarrow, "National Politics and Collective Action," *Annual Review of Sociology* 14 (1988): 421–440; Charles Tilly, *From Mobilization to Revolution* (Reading, Mass.: Addison-Wesley, 1978); John D. McCarthy and Mayer N. Zald, *The Trend of Social*

Movements in America (Morristown, N.J.: General Learning Press, 1973); Doug McAdam, John McCarthy, and Mayer Zald, "Social Movements," in *Handbook of Sociology*, ed. Neil J. Smelser (Newbury Park, Calif.: Sage Publications, 1988), pp. 695–737.

2. Patricia Hill Collins, *Black Feminist Thought* (Boston: Routledge, 1991).

3. The latter have been termed "submerged networks" and the "latent" phase of movements by Alberto Melucci, "The Symbolic Challenge of Contemporary Movements," *Social Research* 52 (1985): 781–816; Alberto Melucci, *Nomads of the Present: Social Movements and Individual Needs in Contemporary Society* (Philadelphia: Temple University Press, 1989); they are referred to as "negotiation" or the politicization of everyday life by Verta Taylor and Nancy Whittier, "Collective Identity and Lesbian Feminist Mobilization," in *Frontiers of Social Movement Theory*, ed. Aldon Morris and Carol Mueller (New Haven: Yale University Press, 1992); and as personalized politics by Paul Lichterman, "When Is the Personal Political? Class, Culture, and Political Style in U.S. Grassroots Environmentalism," paper presented at the American Sociological Association, Pittsburgh, August 20–24, 1992. Also see Verta Taylor and Nicole Raeburn, "Identity Politics as High-Risk Activism: Career Consequences for Lesbian, Gay, and Bisexual Sociologists," *Social Problems*, forthcoming, 1995.

4. The concept draws on the work of Diane Rothbard Margolis, "Redefining the Situation: Negotiations on the Meaning of Woman," *Social Problems* 32 (1985): 332–347, in which she discusses ways that women negotiate the identity "woman" in public and private settings. The application of this work to social movements is discussed further in Taylor and Whittier, "Collective Identity."

5. This figure would undoubtedly be larger for women who were more peripheral participants in the 1970s movement.

6. The age cohort into which most respondents fell was 35 to 44 in 1986. Cynthia Taeuber, ed., *Statistical Handbook on Women in America* (Phoenix, Ariz.: Oryx Press, 1991), p. 92.

7. U.S. Department of Commerce, Economics and Statistics Administration, and Bureau of the Census, *Statistical Abstract of the United States 1993*, 113th edition (Lanham, Md.: Bernan Press, 1993), p. 409. Even within the professional and managerial category, the re-

spondents are not in the traditionally female professions such as nursing or elementary/secondary teaching.

8. See, e.g., Dinesh D'Souza, *Illiberal Education: The Politics of Race and Sex on Campus* (New York: Free Press, 1991); Roger Kimball, *Tenured Radicals: How Politics Has Corrupted Our Higher Education* (New York: Harper and Row, 1990).

9. Hester Eisenstein, *Gender Shock: Practicing Feminism on Two Continents* (Boston: Beacon Press, 1991); Drude Dahlerup, "Comparing the Effect of the New Women's Movement in Various Countries," paper presented to the ECPR Planning Session on Requirements for the Comparative Study of Women in European Politics: Theories, Methodologies, Data and Resources, Bochum, Denmark, April 2–7, 1990.

10. Janet Boles, "Form Follows Function: The Evolution of Feminist Strategies," *Annals of the American Academy of Political and Social Science* 515 (May 1991): 38–49.

11. Wini Breines, *Community and Organization in the New Left 1962–68* (New York: Praeger, 1982), makes this point about the New Left. The women's movement carried on this tradition, making prefigurative politics even more central to organizational structure and practices and developing an elaborate alternative "feminist structure." See Barbara Epstein, *Political Protest and Cultural Revolution: Nonviolent Direct Action in the 1970's and 1980's* (Berkeley: University of California Press, 1991), for an excellent discussion of this point.

12. Sara Evans, *Born for Liberty: A History of Women in America* (New York: Free Press, 1989), p. 103.

13. Susan Brownmiller, *Femininity* (New York: Fawcett Columbine, 1984); Holly Devor, *Gender Blending* (Bloomington: Indiana University Press, 1989).

14. Quoted in Vera Whisman, "Identity Crisis: Who Is a Lesbian Anyway?" in *Sisters, Sexperts, Queers: Beyond the Lesbian Nation,* ed. Arlene Stein (New York: Plume, 1993), p. 47.

15. Breines, *Community and Organization.*

16. Ti-Grace Atkinson, *Amazon Odyssey* (New York: Link Books, 1974), for example, asked in a classic analogy, "Can you imagine a Frenchman, serving in the French army from 9 A.M. to 5 P.M., then trotting 'home' to Germany for supper overnight?" (p. 11).

17. See Taylor and Whittier, "Collective Identity," for a discussion

of this wing of contemporary lesbian feminist communities. For recent examples of lesbian feminist writing, see Sarah Lucia Hoagland, *Lesbian Ethics: Toward New Value* (Palo Alto, Calif.: Institute for Lesbian Studies, 1988), and Sarah Lucia Hoagland and Julia Penelope, *For Lesbians Only* (London: Only Women Press, 1988).

18. See Jo Freeman, *The Politics of Women's Liberation* (New York: David McKay, 1975); Joan Cassell, *A Group Called Women: Sisterhood and Symbolism in the Feminist Movement* (New York: David McKay, 1977); and Deborah Goleman Wolf, *The Lesbian Community* (Berkeley: University of California Press, 1979), for further discussion of how women's movement groups contributed to lesbian identity formation.

19. *Statistical Abstract*, p. 102. The available figures on women's marital status are for 1990 and are broken down by age in five-year increments. I have aggregated the categories from the age of 35 years to 54 years, which includes all but two of the women I interviewed (both of whom are in their eighties). The percentage of white women married in each of the categories is: age 35–39, 91.4 percent; age 40–44, 93.4 percent; age 45–49, 95.1 percent, age 50–54, 96.1 percent.

20. *Statistical Abstract*, p. 80. Calculated based on (1) number and percentage of ever-married women between the ages of 34 and 44 who are childless; (2) number and percentage of never-married women between the ages of 34 and 44 who are childless.

21. Most of the lesbians I interviewed joined the women's movement and came out when they were in their early twenties, so they had not previously been married.

22. Linda Gordon, "Functions of the Family," in *Voices from Women's Liberation,* ed. Leslie B. Tanner (New York: Signet, 1970), pp. 181–188; Beverly Jones, "The Dynamics of Marriage and Motherhood," in *Sisterhood Is Powerful,* ed. Robin Morgan (New York Vintage, 1970), pp. 49–66; Evelyn Leo, "Dependency in Marriage: Oppression in Middle-class Marriage," in Tanner, ed., *Voices from Women's Liberation,* pp. 235–237; Rita Van Lew, "Producing Society's Babies," ibid., pp. 193–198; Adrienne Rich, "Compulsory Heterosexuality and Lesbian Existence," *Signs* 5 (1980): 631–660.

23. Betty Friedan, *The Second Stage* (New York: Summit, 1981).

24. See Lindsay Van Gelder, "Grown-up Children of Feminist Mothers—What They Think of It All," *Ms.,* April 1983, pp. 44–45, 90, for an expansion of this argument.

CHAPTER 5 :: UNITED WE STAND

1. Judith Hole and Ellen Levine, *Rebirth of Feminism* (New York: Quadrangle, 1971); Jo Freeman, *The Politics of Women's Liberation* (New York: David McKay, 1975); Sara Evans, *Personal Politics: The Roots of Women's Liberation in the Civil Rights Movement and the New Left* (New York: Knopf, 1979).

2. See David Meyer and Nancy Whittier, "Social Movement Spillover," *Social Problems* 41 (1994): 277–298, for an expanded treatment of the mechanisms of movement-to-movement influence.

3. Meyer and Whittier, "Spillover."

4. John D. McCarthy and Mayer N. Zald, "Resource Mobilization and Social Movements: A Partial Theory," *American Journal of Sociology* 82 (1977): 1212–1241. McCarthy and Zald recognized linkages among diverse organizations within a single movement (using the notion of social movement industry) and among all movement organizations, whether cooperating or competing (the concept of social movement sector).

5. Suzanne Staggenborg, "Stability and Innovation in the Women's Movement," *Social Problems* 36 (1989): 75–92.

6. Steven M. Buechler, *Women's Movements in the United States* (New Brunswick, N.J.: Rutgers University Press, 1990), p. 42.

7. Todd Gitlin, *The Sixties* (New York: Bantam, 1987); Doug McAdam, *Freedom Summer* (New York: Oxford University Press, 1988).

8. Meyer and Whittier, "Spillover."

9. Clearly, there are other social movement communities as well as the progressive community. Conservatives participate in connected social movements, including antiabortion, support for prayer in the schools, support for the death penalty, opposition to affirmative action, opposition to gay and lesbian rights, and so forth. In addition, historians and sociologists studying the women's movement of the late 1800s and early 1900s have documented connections and mutual influence between the suffrage, women's club, and temperance movements. See Naomi Rosenthal, Meryl Fingrutd, Michele Ethier, Roberta Karant, and David McDonald, "Social Movements and Network Analysis: A Case Study of Nineteenth Century Women's Reform in New York State," *American Journal of Sociology* 90 (1985): 1022–1055;

Ruth Bordin, *Women and Temperance* (Philadelphia: Temple University Press, 1981).

10. Hole and Levine, *Rebirth of Feminism;* Freeman, *Politics;* Evans, *Personal Politics;* John D'Emilio, *Sexual Politics, Sexual Communities* (Chicago: University of Chicago Press, 1983); Barry D. Adam, *The Rise of a Gay and Lesbian Movement* (Boston: Twayne, 1987); Gitlin, *The Sixties;* Jack Whalen and Richard Flacks, *Beyond the Barricades: The Sixties Generation Grows Up* (Philadelphia: Temple University Press, 1987); McAdam, *Freedom Summer.*

11. Meyer and Whittier, "Spillover."

12. Ibid.

13. Evans, *Personal Politics.*

14. Cindy Wilkey, "The Impact of the Radical Women's Movement on the New Left, 1966–1971" (M.A. thesis, The Ohio State University, 1990), documents the response of men in SDS to the emergence of women's liberation.

15. Robert C. Liebman and Robert Wuthnow, *The New Christian Right* (New York: Aldine, 1983).

16. In the 1980s and early 1990s, progressive social movements in Columbus and nationwide organized around a variety of issues. Groups like the Nuclear Freeze, Committee for a Sane Nuclear Policy (SANE), Campaign for Nuclear Disarmament, the Clamshell Alliance, and the Livermore Action Group opposed nuclear power and supported nuclear disarmament. See David Meyer, *A Winter of Discontent: The Nuclear Freeze and American Politics* (New York: Praeger, 1990); Barbara Epstein, *Political Protest and Cultural Revolution: Nonviolent Direct Action in the 1970's and 1980's* (Berkeley: University of California Press, 1991). The Committee in Solidarity with the People of El Salvador (CISPES), the Latin American Solidarity Committee, and a variety of local peace groups opposed U.S. intervention in El Salvador, Nicaragua, Grenada, Panama, and Iraq. Socialist organizations (including the Socialist Workers' Party, the Revolutionary Communist Party, the International Socialist Organization, and the Young Socialist Alliance) continued to recruit and educate members. An antiapartheid movement emerged on college campuses and elsewhere in the mid-1980s, seeking disinvestment in companies that did business in South Africa. Movements of numerous racial and ethnic minorities arose, including African Americans, Chicana/os, Latina/os, Native

Americans, and Asians, as did a small movement of whites opposing racism. The animal rights movement grew to be large and visible, with such organizations as People for the Ethical Treatment of Animals; see Lake Jagger, "The Animal Rights Movement and Social Movement Theory" (paper, The Ohio State University, 1991). Environmental groups addressed issues including pesticide use, toxic waste, oil spills, and recycling, with a huge Earth Day celebration in 1990 resulting in much popular discussion of environmental issues and the growth of "green consumerism."

17. *WAC Newsletter*, January 1978, July 1978, personal files of Debbie Chalfie, Washington, D.C.

18. *WAC Newsletter*, January 1980, December 1980, personal files of Debbie Chalfie; Ohio Historical Society [OHS], B5, Annual Meeting 1981, WAC Annual Report, 1980/81.

19. Information on the El Salvador vigil: Letter to WAC members from Lisa Hurtubise and Jan Brittan, March 12, 1981, personal files of Debbie Chalfie. Information on the Feminist Celebration for Life: *WAC Newsletter*, May 1981, personal files of Debbie Chalfie; and *WAC Newsletter*, June 1981, personal files of Teri Wehausen, Columbus, Ohio.

20. *WAC Newsletter*, June 1981, personal files of Teri Wehausen.

21. *WAC Newsletter*, July/August 1982, personal files of Teri Wehausen.

22. *New York Times*, January 18, 1991.

23. See Meyer and Whittier, "Spillover," for a more detailed discussion of the impact of the women's movement on the peace movement.

24. Alice Cook and Gwyn Kirk, *Greenham Women Everywhere* (London: Pluto Press, 1983); Puget Sound Women's Peace Camp Participants, *We Are Ordinary Women: A Chronicle of the Puget Sound Women's Peace Camp* (Seattle: Seal Press, 1985); Carol Jacobson, "Peace by Piece: The Creative Politics of Greenham Common Women's Peace Camp," *Heresies* 20, nos. 4/5 (1985/86): 60–65.

25. Epstein, *Political Protest*.

26. Jacobson, "Peace by Piece."

27. Rhoda Linton and Michele Whitham, "With Mourning, Rage, Empowerment, and Defiance: The 1981 Women's Pentagon Action," *Socialist Review* 12 (May 1982): 11; Annie Popkin and Gary Delgado, "Mobilizing Emotions: Organizing the Women's Pentagon Action:

Interview with Donna Warnack," *Socialist Review* 12 (May 1982): 37; Meyer, *Winter of Discontent*.

28. Diana Russell, *Exposing Nuclear Phallacies* (New York: Pergamon, 1989).

29. Margot Adler, *Drawing Down the Moon: Witches, Druids, Goddess-Worshippers, and Other Pagans in America Today* (Boston: Beacon Press, 1986); Lindsay Van Gelder, "It's Not Nice to Mess with Mother Nature," *Ms.*, January/February 1989, pp. 60–63.

30. Epstein, *Political Protest*.

31. *WAC Newsletter*, September/October 1982, November/December 1982, personal files of Teri Wehausen.

32. *WAC Newsletter*, November/December 1982, personal files of Teri Wehausen.

33. Adam, *Gay and Lesbian Movement*; Phyllis Gorman, "The Ohio AIDS Movement" (Ph.D. dissertation, The Ohio State University, 1992).

34. Adam, *Gay and Lesbian Movement*.

35. Ibid.

36. Ibid.

37. Alice Echols, *Daring to Be Bad: Radical Feminism in America 1967–1975* (Minneapolis: University of Minnesota Press, 1989), ch. 5; Lilian Faderman, *Odd Girls and Twilight Lovers: A History of Lesbian Life in Twentieth Century America* (New York: Columbia University Press, 1991), ch. 8; Del Martin and Phyllis Lyon, *Lesbian/Woman* (New York: Bantam, 1972).

38. For example, in 1977 Lesbian Peer Support circulated a petition in support of lesbian and gay rights that was sponsored by the National Gay Task Force. *WAC Newsletter*, July 1977, personal files of Debbie Chalfie.

39. Central Ohio Lesbians letter, November 17, 1977, personal files of Chris Guarnieri, Cleveland Heights, Ohio.

40. Adam, *Gay and Lesbian Movement*.

41. Ibid.

42. Randy Shilts, *And the Band Played On: People, Politics, and the AIDS Epidemic* (New York: St. Martin's Press, 1987); Susan Cavin, "The Invisible Army of Women: Lesbian Social Protests, 1969–1988," in *Women and Social Protest*, ed. Guida West and Rhoda Blumberg (New York: Oxford University Press, 1990), pp. 321–332.

43. Linda Anderson and Samantha Winchester, "AIDS: Between Rubber and Reason," *Off Our Backs* 18 (April 1988): 20.

44. Mike Kehlmeier, "Militant Gay Group Demands Attention," *Clintonville {Ohio} Booster,* August 21, 1991, p. 24.

45. Alexander Chee, "A Queer Nationalism," *Out/Look* 11 (1991): 15–19.

46. Maria Maggenti, "Women as Queer Nationals," *Out/Look* 11 (Winter 1991): 20–23.

47. Urvashi Vaid, "Let's Put Our Own House in Order," *Out/Look* 14 (Fall 1991): 55–57.

48. Maggenti, "Women as Queer Nationals."

49. Adler, *Drawing Down the Moon.*

50. Robert Murphy, "The Neo-Pagans Celebrate Rites of the Earth," *Utne Reader* 48 (November/December 1991): 22–26.

51. Anthony Brandt, "Do Kids Need Religion?" *Utne Reader* 43 (January/February 1991): 84–88; Rick Fields, "America's Lively Spiritual Supermarket," ibid., pp. 76–77.

52. For examples see: E. T. Beck, *Nice Jewish Girls: A Lesbian Anthology* (Watertown, Mass.: Persephone, 1980); Rosemary Ruether, *Sexism and God-Talk* (Boston: Beacon Press, 1983); Clarissa Atkinson, Constance Buchanan, and Margaret Miles, *Immaculate and Powerful: The Female in Sacred Image and Reality* (Boston: Beacon Press, 1985); Beverly Wildung Harrison, *Making the Connection: Essays in Feminist Social Ethics* (Boston: Beacon Press, 1985).

53. Charlene Spretnak, "Introduction," in *The Politics of Women's Spirituality: Essays on the Rise of Spiritual Power Within the Feminist Movement,* ed. Charlene Spretnak (New York: Anchor Press, 1982), pp. xi–xxx.

54. Gina Foglia and Dorit Wolffberg, "Spiritual Dimensions of Feminist Anti-Nuclear Activism," in Spretnak, ed., *Politics of Women's Spirituality,* pp. 446–461; Spretnak, "Introduction"; Adler, *Drawing Down the Moon;* Epstein, *Political Protest;* Gretchen Matteson, "Recruitment and Conversion in a Religious Social Movement" (M.A. thesis, The Ohio State University, 1988). For examples of publications, see Mary Daly, *Gyn/Ecology: The Metaethics of Radical Feminism* (Boston: Beacon Press, 1978); Mary Daly, *Pure Lust: Elemental Feminist Philosophy* (Boston: Beacon Press, 1984); Starhawk, *The Spiral Dance: A Re-*

birth of the Ancient Religion of the Great Goddess (San Francisco: Harper and Row, 1979); Starhawk, *Dreaming the Dark: Magic, Sex, and Politics* (Boston: Beacon Press, 1982); Hallie Austen Inglehart, *Woman Spirit: A Guide to Women's Wisdom* (San Francisco: Harper and Row, 1983).

55. Because the Wiccan movement is decentralized and not publicly visible, it is not possible to estimate the number or size of covens in Columbus. Based on information in Amber Ault, "Witches, Wicca, and Revitalization" (M.A. thesis, The Ohio State University, 1989); Matteson, "Recruitment"; and my own participant observation in the Columbus women's movement, I am aware of at least three all-women covens in the area, ranging in size from fewer than ten members to around twenty-five. Larger numbers of women participate in rituals on special occasions such as the Solstices or Equinoxes. There may be additional covens of which I am not aware.

56. *WAC Newsletter,* November/December 1982, p. 9, personal files of Teri Wehausen.

57. Sally Binford, "Myths and Matriarchies," in Spretnak, ed., *Politics of Women's Spirituality,* pp. 541–549.

58. Adler, *Drawing Down the Moon;* Katy Butler, "Spirituality and Therapy: Toward a Partnership," *Utne Reader* 43 (January/February 1991): 75–83. For an example drawing on the Judeo-Christian tradition, see Marianne Williamson, *A Woman's Worth* (New York: Random House, 1993).

59. Fields, "Spiritual Supermarket."

60. Ibid.; Robert Bly, *Iron John: A Book About Men* (Reading, Mass.: Addison-Wesley, 1990).

61. See Alice Jardine and Paul Smith, eds., *Men in Feminism* (New York: Methuen, 1987).

62. For examples see: Claudia Black, *It Will Never Happen to Me: Children of Alcoholics* (Denver: MAC Publishing, 1981); Jean Swallow, *Out from Under: Sober Dykes and Our Friends* (San Francisco: Harper and Row, 1983); Anne Wilson Schaef, *Co-Dependence: Misunderstood—Mistreated* (San Francisco: Harper and Row, 1986); Anne Wilson Schaef, *When Society Becomes an Addict* (San Francisco: Harper and Row, 1988); Robin Norwood, *Women Who Love Too Much: When You Keep Wishing and Hoping He'll Change* (New York: Jeremy Tarcher, 1985); Janet Geringer Woititz, *Struggle for Intimacy* (Pompano Beach, Fla.: Health

Communications, 1985); Harriet Lerner, *The Dance of Anger: A Woman's Guide to Changing the Patterns of Intimate Relationships* (New York: Harper and Row, 1986); Ellen Bass and Laura Davis, *The Courage to Heal: A Guide for Women Survivors of Child Sexual Abuse* (New York: Harper and Row, 1988); Sue E. Blume, *Secret Survivors: Uncovering Incest and Its Aftereffects in Women* (New York: Ballantine Books, 1990).

63. Wendy Simonds, *Women and Self Help Culture* (New Brunswick, N.J.: Rutgers University Press, 1992).

64. Swallow, *Out from Under*; Lindsay Van Gelder, "Dependencies of Independent Women," *Ms.*, February 1987, pp. 73–75; Ellen Herman, "The Twelve Step Program: Cover or Cure?" *Out/Look* (Summer 1988): 11–13; Beth Freeman, "The Twelve Steps Anonymous," *Off Our Backs* 19 (March 1989): 20–21.

65. *WAC Newsletter*, March 1980, April 1980, personal files of Debbie Chalfie.

66. *WAC Newsletter*, May 1981, personal files of Debbie Chalfie; OHS, B5, Annual Report, 1981/82.

67. *WAC Update*, April 1, 1981, personal files of Debbie Chalfie.

68. It is not possible to estimate accurately the proportion of activists and participants in the recovery movement who were involved in the women's movement of the 1960s and 1970s, because of informal and shifting membership and the mandate of anonymity in 12-step groups.

69. Schaef, *Codependence*; Schaef, *Society*; Bass and Davis, *The Courage to Heal*.

70. Carpe Diem opened in 1991 and had closed by 1993.

71. Verta Taylor, "Self-Labeling and Women's Mental Health: Postpartum Illness and the Reconstruction of Motherhood," *Sociological Focus* 27, no. 2 (1994).

72. See Chapters 2 and 6 for a lengthier discussion of internalized oppression.

73. Herman, "Twelve Step"; Freeman, "Twelve Steps."

74. Wendy Kaminer, *I'm Dysfunctional, You're Dysfunctional* (Reading, Mass.: Addison-Wesley, 1992).

75. Meyer and Whittier, "Spillover."

76. Judith Rollins, *Between Women: Domestics and Their Employers* (Philadelphia: Temple University Press, 1985). See also bell hooks,

Sisters of the Yam: Black Women and Self-Recovery (Boston: South End Press, 1993); Gloria Steinem, *Revolution from Within* (Boston: Little, Brown, 1992).

CHAPTER 6 :: FEMINISTS IN THE "POSTFEMINIST" AGE

1. Leila J. Rupp and Verta Taylor, *Survival in the Doldrums: The American Women's Rights Movement, 1945 to the 1960s* (New York: Oxford University Press, 1987); Maurice Isserman, *If I Had a Hammer: The Death of the Old Left and the Birth of the New Left* (New York: Basic Books, 1987); Kate Weigand, "Vanguards of Women's Liberation: The Contributions of the Old Left to the Women's Movement of the 1960's," paper presented at Towards a History of the 1960's conference, State Historical Society of Wisconsin, Madison, April 29, 1993.

2. Verta Taylor, "Social Movement Continuity: The Women's Movement in Abeyance," *American Sociological Review* 54 (1989): 761–775.

3. Aldon Morris, *The Origins of the Civil Rights Movement: Black Communities Organizing for Change* (New York: Free Press, 1984).

4. Rupp and Taylor, *Survival;* and Morris, *Origins,* make this clear.

5. Rupp and Taylor, *Survival;* Taylor, "Social Movement Continuity."

6. See Janet Boles, "Form Follows Function: The Evolution of Feminist Strategies," *Annals of the American Academy of Political and Social Science* 515 (May 1991): 38–49, on women's policy networks at local and national levels.

7. On self-help and recovery, see Wendy Simonds, *Women and Self Help Culture* (New Brunswick, N.J.: Rutgers University Press, 1992); and Wendy Kaminer, *I'm Dysfunctional, You're Dysfunctional* (Reading, Mass.: Addison-Wesley, 1992). On postpartum depression, see Verta Taylor, "Self-Labeling and Women's Mental Health: Postpartum Illness and the Reconstruction of Motherhood," *Sociological Focus* 27, no. 2 (1994).

8. On N A R A L and the pro-choice movement, see Suzanne Staggenborg, *The Pro-Choice Movement* (New York: Oxford University Press, 1991). On N O W, see Barbara Ryan, *Feminism and the Women's Movement* (New York: Routledge, 1992); Jane Mansbridge, *Why We Lost the*

ERA (Chicago: University of Chicago Press, 1986). For overviews, see Myra Marx Ferree and Beth B. Hess, *Controversy and Coalition: The New Feminist Movement* (Boston: Twayne, 1985); Steven M. Buechler, *Women's Movements in the United States* (New Brunswick, N.J.: Rutgers University Press, 1990); and Flora Davis, *Moving the Mountain* (New York: Simon and Schuster, 1991).

9. This formulation draws on the distinction made by Janet Boles, "Form Follows Function," between a national women's rights lobby and "local women's policy networks." See K. J. Tierney, "The Battered Women Movement and the Creation of the Wife Beating Problem," *Social Problems* 29 (1982): 207–220, and Patricia Gagne, "The Battered Women's Movement in the 'Post Feminist' Era" (Ph.D. dissertation, The Ohio State University, 1993), on battered women; and see Nancy Matthews, *Confronting Rape: The Feminist Anti-Rape Movement and the State* (New York: Routledge, 1994) on the antirape movement. Verta Taylor and Nancy Whittier, "The New Feminist Movement," in *Feminist Frontiers III,* ed. Laurel Richardson and Verta Taylor (New York: McGraw-Hill, 1993), provide an overview.

10. On changes in the structure of NOW and its adoption of "radical feminist" goals and ideology, see Ryan, *Feminism and the Women's Movement,* ch. 6. On the institutionalization of radical feminist organizations, see especially Matthews, *Moving Onto the Terrain of the State.*

11. Ryan, *Feminism and the Women's Movement,* chs. 5 and 6; Davis, *Moving the Mountain,* ch. 18.

12. Ryan, *Feminism and the Women's Movement,* pp. 140–144; Davis, *Moving the Mountain,* ch. 19.

13. Carol Mueller, "Collective Consciousness, Identity Transformation and the Rise of Women in Public Office in the United States," in *The Women's Movements of the United States and Western Europe,* ed. M. F. Katzenstein and C. M. Mueller (Philadelphia: Temple University Press, 1987), pp. 89–108; Ryan, *Feminism and the Women's Movement.*

14. Staggenborg, *Pro-Choice Movement,* p. 138; Ryan, *Feminism and the Women's Movement,* p. 145.

15. Zillah Eisenstein, *The Radical Future of Liberal Feminism* (New York: Longman, 1981).

16. Jo Freeman, *The Politics of Women's Liberation* (New York: David McKay, 1975), ch. 2; Ryan, *Feminism and the Women's Movement,* ch. 3.

17. Boles, "Form Follows Function."

18. As this book went to press, Women Against Rape had just announced that it was in serious financial trouble and might have to fold, passing on responsibility for the Rape Crisis Line to another organization. Felix Hoover, "Rape Crisis Line in Jeopardy," *Columbus Dispatch*, August 25, 1994.

19. The Women's Information Center became the Women's Policy and Research Commission in 1991, permitting it to advocate policy change as well as collect information.

20. The Child Assault Prevention Project has been the center of considerable controversy among participants in the 1970s Columbus women's movement. A split between its early members led to a bitter court fight over rights to documents written by the Women Against Rape collective. Although the dispute was thrown out of court, in effect giving the literature rights to the project's current leaders, many respondents believed this was not the correct decision. Others were generally disturbed by the nastiness of the conflict and by the combatants' reliance on the "patriarchal legal system" to resolve their dispute.

21. Verta Taylor and Nancy Whittier, "Collective Identity and Lesbian Feminist Mobilization," in *Frontiers of Social Movement Theory*, ed. Aldon Morris and Carol Mueller (New Haven: Yale University Press, 1992).

22. Verta Taylor and Leila J. Rupp, "Women's Culture and the Survival of the Women's Movement: A Reconsideration of Cultural Feminism," *Signs* 19 (1993): 32–61.

23. Taylor and Whittier, "New Feminist Movement."

24. Sample list of gatherings drawn from the *Lesbian Connection*, Fall 1991.

25. Denyse Lockard, "The Lesbian Community: An Anthropological Approach," in *Many Faces of Homosexuality*, ed. Evelyn Blackwood (New York: Harrington Park Press, 1986), pp. 83–95.

26. Taylor and Rupp, "Women's Culture."

27. See Alice Echols, *Daring to Be Bad: Radical Feminism in America 1967–1975* (Minneapolis: University of Minnesota Press, 1989), for a negative view of this process in some East Coast cities.

28. Nancy Chodorow, *The Reproduction of Mothering: Psychoanalysis and the Sociology of Gender* (Berkeley: University of California Press, 1978); Mary Daly, *Gyn/Ecology: The Metaethics of Radical Feminism* (Boston: Beacon Press, 1978); Mary Daly, *Pure Lust: Elemental Feminist*

Philosophy (Boston: Beacon Press, 1984); Carol Gilligan, *In a Different Voice* (Cambridge, Mass.: Harvard University Press, 1982); Marilyn Frye, *The Politics of Reality: Essays in Feminist Theory* (Trumansburg, N.Y.: Crossing Press, 1983); Susan Cavin, *Lesbian Origins* (San Francisco: Ism Press, 1985); Sonia Johnson, *Going Out of Our Minds: The Metaphysics of Liberation* (Freedom, Calif.: Crossing Press, 1987); and Sarah Lucia Hoagland, *Lesbian Ethics: Toward New Value* (Palo Alto, Calif.: Institute for Lesbian Studies, 1988).

29. Kim Dill, "Feminism in the Nineties: The Influence of Collective Identity and Community on Young Feminist Activists" (M.A. thesis, The Ohio State University, 1991).

30. Arlene Stein, ed., *Sisters, Sexperts, Queers: Beyond the Lesbian Nation* (New York: Plume, 1993); Arlene Stein, "All Dressed Up, but No Place to Go? Style Wars and the New Lesbianism," *Out/Look* 1, no. 4 (Winter 1989): 34–42.

31. See Ann Snitow, Christine Stansell, and Sharon Thompson, eds., *Powers of Desire: The Politics of Sexuality* (New York: Monthly Review Press, 1983); and Carol S. Vance, ed., *Pleasure and Danger: Exploring Female Sexuality* (Boston: Routledge and Kegan Paul, 1984), for accounts of the conference and writings on the "sex debates," mostly from the perspective of sex radicalism. For a more recent perspective, see Dorothy Allison, *Skin* (Ithaca, N.Y.: Firebrand, 1994).

32. Field notes: Columbus, Ohio, January 24, 1991, dance fundraiser for Take Back the Night; Columbus, Ohio, May 18, 1991, Take Back the Night march. The quotation about anger is paraphrased but is very close to the original wording and accurately recounts the gist of the original comment.

33. Echols, *Daring to Be Bad.*

34. Dill, "Feminism in the Nineties."

35. Beth Schneider, "Political Generations in the Contemporary Women's Movement," *Sociological Inquiry* 58 (1988): 4–21.

CHAPTER 7 :: THE NEXT WAVE

1. Beth Schneider, "Political Generations in the Contemporary Women's Movement," *Sociological Inquiry* 58 (1988): 4–21.

2. Susan Bolotin, "Views from the Post-Feminist Generation," *New*

York Times Magazine, October 17, 1982, pp. 29–31, 103–116; Judith Stacey, "Sexism by a Subtler Name? Postindustrial Conditions and PostFeminist Consciousness," *Socialist Review* 17, no. 6 (1987): 7–28; Barbara Ryan, *Feminism and the Women's Movement* (New York: Routledge, 1992).

3. Claire M. Renzetti, "New Wave or Second Stage? Attitudes of College Women Toward Feminism," *Sex Roles* 16, nos. 5/6 (1987): 265–277; Schneider, "Political Generations"; Virginia Sapiro, "Feminism: A Generation Later," *Annals of the American Academy of Political and Social Science* 514 (March 1991): 10–22; Kim Dill, "Feminism in the Nineties: The Influence of Collective Identity and Community on Young Feminist Activists" (M.A. thesis, The Ohio State University, 1991).

4. Alice Rossi, *Feminists in Politics* (New York: Academic Press, 1982); Lindsay Van Gelder, "Grown Up Children of Feminist Mothers—What They Think of It All," *Ms.*, April 1983, pp. 44–45, 90.

5. Naomi Wolf, "How Does Your Rhetoric Fit Into My Life Now?" *Ms.*, April 1983, pp. 46, 89–90. Ironically, Naomi Wolf later wrote the widely read feminist book *The Beauty Myth* (New York: William Morrow, 1991).

6. Gloria Steinem, "Why Younger Women Are More Conservative," in *Outrageous Acts and Everyday Rebellions* (New York: Holt, Rinehart, and Winston, 1983), pp. 211–218.

7. Suzanne Staggenborg, *The Pro-Choice Movement* (New York: Oxford University Press, 1991).

8. Diane Salvatore, "A Classic Case of Sensory Overload," *Ms.*, April 1983, pp. 43–44.

9. These organizations include Fan the Flames Feminist Bookstore, Women Against Rape, NOW, the Association of Women Students, Women's Outreach for Women, and two offspring of earlier groups: Take Back the Night, which grew from marches organized in the mid-1970s by WAC members and campus activists, and Ohio Women Martial Artists, which rose from the ashes of Feminists in Self-Defense Training. Information in this section is taken from interviews with key informants who were core activists in each of these organizations in the early 1990s. The interviews with members of Association of Women Students were conducted by Kim Dill. See Dill, "Feminism in the Nineties," for a fuller discussion of young feminists.

10. This description of the routes by which college women entered the women's movement is heavily indebted to Dill, "Feminism in the Nineties."

11. After much debate, the male volunteer was not allowed to work, but some members still argued for permitting male staff. At this writing, the issue remains unresolved. One member also reported that the group was considering abandoning their collective structure in order to operate more efficiently.

12. "Take Back the Night" flier distributed at annual march, May 1992.

13. Dill, "Feminism in the Nineties."

14. On the sex wars, see Carole S. Vance, *Pleasure and Danger: Exploring Female Sexuality* (Boston: Routledge and Kegan Paul, 1984); Ann Snitow, Christine Stansell, and Sharon Thompson, eds., *Powers of Desire: The Politics of Sexuality* (New York: Monthly Review Press, 1983).

15. See, e.g., many of the pieces in Arlene Stein, ed., *Sisters, Sexperts, Queers: Beyond the Lesbian Nation* (New York: Plume, 1993).

16. See Erik H. Erikson, *Identity: Youth and Challenge* (New York: Basic Books, 1968); Mathilda White Riley, "Aging and Social Change, and the Power of Ideas," *Daedalus* 107, no. 4 (1978): 31–54; Margaret Braungart, "Aging and Politics," *Journal of Political and Military Sociology* 12, no. 1 (1984):79–98. As I explained in Chapter 3, I do not want to suggest that youth is the "natural" time for rebellion.

17. Wolf, "How Does Your Rhetoric Fit?"

18. Myra Marx Ferree and Beth B. Hess, *Controversy and Coalition: The New Feminist Movement* (Boston: Twayne, 1985); Barbara Ehrenreich, "The Next Act," *Ms.*, December 1988, pp. 32–33.

CONCLUSION

1. On the links between politics, organizational structure, and culture in the New Left, see Wini Breines, *Community and Organization in the New Left 1962–68* (New York: Praeger, 1982).

2. Jack Whalen and Richard Flacks, *Beyond the Barricades: The Sixties Generation Grows Up* (Philadelphia: Temple University Press, 1987); James Max Fendrich and Kenneth Lovoy, "Back to the Future:

Adult Political Behavior of Former Student Activists," *American Sociological Review* 53 (1988): 780–784; Doug McAdam, *Freedom Summer* (New York: Oxford University Press, 1988); Doug McAdam, "The Biographical Consequences of Activism," *American Sociological Review* 54 (1989): 744–760; James Max Fendrich and Robert W. Turner, "The Transition from Student to Adult Politics," *Social Forces* 67 (1989): 1049–1057.

3. Karl Mannheim, "The Problem of Generations," in *Essays on the Sociology of Knowledge*, ed. Paul Kecskemeti (London: Routledge and Kegan Paul, 1952), pp. 276–332.

4. David S. Meyer and Nancy Whittier, "Social Movement Spillover," *Social Problems* 41, no. 2 (1994): 277–298.

5. Most notable of these analyses was Adrienne Rich's "Compulsory Heterosexuality and Lesbian Existence," *Signs* 5 (1980): 631–660.

6. Beth Schneider also makes this point in "Political Generations in the Contemporary Women's Movement," *Sociological Inquiry* 58 (1988): 4–21.

7. The most noted proponent of this view is Alice Echols, *Daring to Be Bad: Radical Feminism in America 1967–1975* (Minneapolis: University of Minnesota Press, 1989). It is shared by Barbara Ryan, *Feminism and the Women's Movement* (New York: Routledge, 1992).

8. See Verta Taylor and Leila J. Rupp, "Women's Culture and Lesbian Feminist Activism: A Reconsideration of Cultural Feminism," *Signs* 19 (1993): 32–61, for another version of this argument.

9. Criticism comes from both the Left and the Right. On the Left, see L. A. Kauffman, "The Anti-Politics of Identity," *Socialist Review* 20, no. 2 (1990): 67–80. On the Right, see Dinesh D'Souza, *Illiberal Education: The Politics of Race and Sex on Campus* (New York: Free Press, 1991).

10. Anthony Giddens, *Modernity and Self-Identity: Self and Society in the Late Modern Age* (Palo Alto, Calif.: Stanford University Press, 1991).

11. J. Craig Jenkins, "Resource Mobilization Theory and the Study of Social Movements," *Annual Review of Sociology* 9 (1983): 527–553.

12. Naomi Abrahams, "Towards Reconceptualizing Political Action," *Sociological Inquiry* 62 (1992): 327–347.

13. This is the conclusion drawn by Echols, *Daring to Be Bad;* and Ryan, *Feminism and the Women's Movement.*

14. See, e.g., Karen Lehrman, "Off Course," *Mother Jones*, September/October 1993, pp. 45–51, 64–68.

15. See Naomi Wolf, *Fire With Fire* (New York: Random House, 1993).

16. John McCarthy and Mayer Zald, "Resource Mobilization and Social Movements: A Partial Theory," *American Journal of Sociology* 82 (1977): 1212–1241; Charles Tilly, *From Mobilization to Revolution* (Reading, Mass.: Addison-Wesley, 1978); Doug McAdam, *Political Process and the Development of Black Insurgency* (Chicago: University of Chicago Press, 1982); Jenkins, "Resource Mobilization Theory"; Sidney G. Tarrow, *Democracy and Disorder: Protest and Politics in Italy, 1965–1975* (New York: Oxford University Press, 1989).

17. Carol Mueller, "Collective Identities and the Mobilization of Women," paper presented at the Colloquium on New Social Movements and the End of Ideology, Sandander, Spain, July 16–20, 1990.

18. Todd Gitlin, *The Sixties* (New York: Bantam, 1987), ch. 4.

19. Aldon Morris, *The Origins of the Civil Rights Movement: Black Communities Organizing for Change* (New York: Free Press, 1984).

20. Leila J. Rupp and Verta Taylor, *Survival in the Doldrums: The American Women's Rights Movement, 1945 to the 1960s* (New York: Oxford University Press, 1987), ch. 8.

21. Verta Taylor, "Social Movement Continuity: The Women's Movement in Abeyance," *American Sociological Review* 54 (1989): 761–775.

INDEX

AA. *See* Alcoholics Anonymous
Abalone Alliance, 166
Abortion rights, 2, 7, 44, 64, 80, 195, 200, 252. *See also* Pro-choice movement; Reproductive rights
Acquired immune deficiency syndrome (AIDS), 109, 126, 155, 158, 160, 169–177, 189, 249
ACT UP. *See* AIDS Coalition to Unleash Power
AIDS. *See* Acquired immune deficiency syndrome; Columbus AIDS Task Force
AIDS Coalition to Unleash Power (ACT UP), 172, 174, 230
Alcoholics Anonymous (AA), 181. *See also* Recovery movement; Women's Outreach for Women
Anarcha-feminism, 167
Animal rights, 98, 155, 167
Ann Arbor, Michigan, 35, 42
Antiapartheid movement, 155, 160, 162
Antifeminist backlash, 2, 20, 40, 80–81, 85, 115, 150, 162–163, 191. *See also* Conservative backlash; Family values; New Right; Religious Right
Antiinterventionism, 155, 158, 160, 162–167, 248
Antinuclear movement, 155, 158, 160, 162, 165–167, 189–190, 228. *See also* Women's Action for Nuclear Disarmament
Antiwar movement, 2, 6, 28–29, 31, 158, 161, 164–166. *See also* Peace movement

Appearance, 2, 7, 116, 120, 141–145, 218–220
Association of Women Students (OSU), 7, 9, 32, 40, 41, 116, 230
Auto mechanics, 34, 42, 63. *See also* Women's Co-op Garage

Battered women's shelters, 1, 19, 37, 89, 197, 204, 247
Boles, Janet, 204
Bookstores, 1, 246. *See also* Fan the Flames Feminist Bookstore
Breines, Wini, 137
Buechler, Steven, 157
Bush, George, 195

CAP. *See* Child Assault Prevention Project
CASA. *See* Committee Against Sexist Advertising
CASSR. *See* Community Action Strategies to Stop Rape
Celeste, Richard, 152
Center for New Directions, 208
Center for Women's Studies (OSU), 9, 33, 41–42, 44, 61, 64, 71, 117, 121, 123–124, 181, 203
Central Ohio Gay Coalition, 170
Central Ohio Lesbians (OSU), 9, 36, 39–40, 65, 67–68, 116, 144, 170, 174. *See also* Stonewall Union
CETA. *See* Comprehensive Employment and Training Act
Chicago, Illinois, 6, 35, 51
Child Assault Prevention Project (CAP), 48, 208. *See also* Women Against Rape

Childcare, 19, 29–30, 37, 196. *See also* Mothers; OSU Childcare Pilot Program; Single Mother's Support Group
Child-In, 30–31
Child rearing, 120, 148–151. *See also* Mothers
Children's literature. *See* Feminist presses and publications
Children's literature interest group, 34
Civil rights movement, 2, 6, 19, 28, 59, 156, 158, 160, 189, 193
Clamshell Alliance, 166
Class, 196, 248; appearance, 145; as feminist issue, 4, 96, 98, 100, 158, 163; as lesbian and gay issue, 188; as WAC issue, 71–73, 76, 93, 163
Clinton, Bill, 243
Coalition for the Implementation of the ERA, 43
Coalition strategies, 3, 4, 21, 42–45, 98–100, 105, 158, 161, 188–190, 207–208, 229, 246
Collective action, 81, 96, 118, 194, 209, 223, 226, 228, 251
Collective identity, 15–18, 23–24, 56–58, 120, 250, 252; of founders, 61–63; generational differences in, 15–17, 24, 194, 222–224, 244, 255, 258; and group boundaries, 100–115; of initiators, 59–61; of joiners, 63–71; lesbian feminist, 65, 72, 77, 107–110, 146, 212, 249; microcohorts, 56–58, 78, 253, 256; political, 120, 250; radical feminist, 14–18, 22–24, 53–54, 82, 100, 113, 115, 152, 194, 196, 211, 226, 248, 252; of sustainers, 71–76
Collective structure. *See* Structure, collective
Columbus AIDS Task Force, 172, 174–175
Columbus-OSU Women's Liberation, 8–9, 28–31, 38, 41, 59–61, 117, 198; and formation of WAC, 34; reorganized as Central Ohio Lesbians, 40; statement of goals, 30; ties to New Left, 77
Columbus Tenants' Union, 168–169

Columbus *Women's Community Calendar*, 170
Committee Against Sexist Advertising (CASA), 47. *See also* Sexism in advertising
Community. *See* Women's movement community
Community Action Strategies to Stop Rape (CASSR), 37–38, 121, 206, 210, 231, 240. *See also* Women Against Rape
Comprehensive Employment Training Act (CETA), 86, 121
Consciousness-raising (CR) groups, 1, 6, 19, 22, 26, 28, 34, 61, 92–93, 136, 138–140, 197, 205, 211, 245
Consensus decision making, 35–36, 128, 167, 197, 231
Conservative backlash, 14, 27–28, 71, 83, 151, 155, 161, 189, 246. *See also* Antifeminist backlash; Family values; New Right; Religious Right
CR groups. *See* Consciousness-raising (CR) groups
Culture: coalitions, 156, 159, 161; and cultural feminism, 51–53, 211, 214–215, 220–222, 250; and essentialism, 216–217, 221; lesbian feminist, 40, 216, 249; political, 16, 21, 23, 26–27, 51–54, 66, 117–118, 161, 187–189, 245, 250, 252; radical feminist, 22, 41–42, 49, 53, 71, 77, 118, 120, 191, 195, 211–222, 245–246; separatist, 62–63, 168, 229–230; survival, 191–192

Daily life, politics of, 13–14, 120, 136–138, 152–154, 188
Daycare center. *See* Childcare
Disabled women, 196
Disarmament. *See* Antiinterventionism
Displaced homemakers, 44, 89, 197, 208
Diversity, 77. *See also* Class; Ethnicity; Homophobia; Racism
Douglas, Carol Anne, 60

Echols, Alice, 51, 220
Ecofeminism, 167–168. *See also* Environmentalism
Education, 29, 163–164, 166, 195
Employment: counseling, 126; and discrimination, 125, 196; environments, 132–136; and the legal profession, 125; nontraditional, 121–122, 140, 197; and politics, 120–137, 202, 228; and professional positions, 145; therapists, 127–131
Environmentalism, 98–99, 155, 158–168, 246, 248, 252
Epstein, Barbara, 167–168
Equal Rights Amendment (ERA), 2, 28, 36, 43–44, 49, 64, 88, 198. *See also* Coalition for the Implementation of the ERA; Ohio ERA Task Force; Ohio Task Force for the Implementation of the ERA
Ethnicity, 11, 71–72, 158, 164
Exposing Nuclear Phallacies, 167

Family Protection Act, 80, 88, 162
Family values, 2, 14. *See also* Antifeminist backlash; Conservative backlash; New Right; Religious Right
Famous Feminist Day, 49, 218
Fan the Flames Feminist Bookstore, 36–37, 39, 66, 69, 151, 171, 212, 230–232, 239; survival of, 51, 196
"Fat Is a Feminist Issue," 46–47
Federation for Progress, 163
Feminist analysis. *See* Theory
Feminist bookstore, 1, 8. *See also* Fan the Flames Feminist Bookstore
"A Feminist Celebration for Life," 162
Feminist consciousness, 84, 91–100, 118, 120
Feminist discussion groups. *See* Radical feminism; Reading and theory groups; Theory
Feminist ideology. *See* Ideology
Feminist Institute, 209–210, 213, 234
Feminist mothering. *See* Mothers
Feminist music. *See* Women's Music Union

Feminist presses and publications, 63, 150. *See also* Children's literature interest group
Feminists in Self-Defense Training (FIST), 39, 48, 231. *See also* Ohio Women Martial Artists
Feminists in the Workplace, 46, 48
Feminist theory. *See* Theory
FIST. *See* Feminists in Self-Defense Training; Ohio Women Martial Artists
Foster Care Network, 208
Foucault, Michel, 22
Founders micro-cohort, 59, 61–63, 77, 209, 253
Funding: cuts, 51, 76, 85–87; federal grants, 37, 63–64; Ohio State, 31–33, 41–42

Gay Activists' Alliance, 169–170
Gay and Lesbian Alliance (OSU), 7, 230
Gay Liberation Front, 169–170
Gay men. *See* Lesbian feminism
Gay Women's Peer Counseling. *See* Lesbian Peer Support
Gender: definition, 22, 251; traditional roles, 148. *See also* Child rearing; Sexism
Generations, 253–254, 258; boundaries between, 3, 106–107; cultural differences between, 220. *See also* Intergenerational relations; Political generations
Giddens, Anthony, 22
Gilligan, John, 27

Habermas, Jürgen, 22
Herizon, 47
Heterosexual feminist group, 46–47
Heterosexuality, 108, 146, 148, 188; and conflicts with leftists, 187–188; and conflicts with lesbians, 107–208, 110, 249
Hierarchy. *See* Structure
Hill Collins, Patricia, 117–118
Hiroshima Day Die-In, 163
Homophobia, 77, 93, 139, 163, 165, 185. *See also* Heterosexuality; Lesbian feminism
Homosexuality. *See* Lesbian feminism

Identity. *See* Collective identity; Individual feminist, identity
Ideology: influence upon coalitions, 156, 159–161, 187, 189; lesbian and gay conflict, 177. *See also* Theory
Imperialism. *See* Antiinterventionism
Individual feminist: actions, 4, 119–120, 153–154, 210, 251; identity, 188, 192; survival, 192, 196, 224
Initiators micro-cohort, 58–61, 77, 253
Intergenerational relations, 18, 222, 225–227, 233, 236–240, 244, 254, 256–257; definition of feminism, 254; politics, 4. *See also* Generations; Political generations
International women focus group, 46–47
International Women's Year, 9, 44–45
Intervention. *See* Antiinterventionism
Iowa City, Iowa, 35, 42

Jewish lesbians, 46, 48
Joiners mocro-cohort, 59, 63–71, 77–78, 209
June 21st Coalition, 162–163

Kent State shootings, 27–28

Labor movement, influenced by feminists, 160
Language use. *See* Sexism in language
Legal Action Group, 35, 39
Leisure time. *See* Culture; Daily life
Lesbian Association on Substance Abuse, 46, 48, 181
Lesbian feminism, 7–8, 20–21, 113, 215, 253; and AIDS, 173, 187; and alcohol and substance abuse. 180–187; coalition, 207; coalitions with gay men, 104, 109, 155, 169–177, 189, 246, 249; coalitions with the New Left, 158–160, 188; community, 14, 212–213; and conflicts with heterosexuals, 4, 104, 107–108, 110, 145–146, 187, 249; culture of, 196–197, 212–214, 221; and International Women's Year, 44–45; and organizing, 40; and relationships with men, 110; relations

of, with gay men, 104, 109; relations of, with men, 65; relations of, with nonfeminists, 108–109; separatist, 62, 66, 146–147, 170, 230; survival of, 196, 249; of sustainers, 71–72; and theory, 146
Lesbianism Study Group, 46–47
Lesbian Peer Support, 37–38, 40, 49, 62–64, 170, 174, 181
Lesbian support group, 47
Lesbians who want children, 46, 48
Liberal feminism, 5, 9, 19–20, 28, 32, 43, 195, 197, 202, 204, 246
Livermore Action Group, 166
Lotta Crabtree, 30. *See also* Women's Music Union

McCarthy, John, 157
Madison, Wisconsin, 35
Male dominance. *See* Patriarchy
Mannheim, Karl, 16, 83, 248
Marriage and motherhood, feminist critique of, 149
Mentors, 235–236
Micro-cohorts, 17–18, 20, 56–58, 62, 70, 75, 77, 81, 82; conflict among, 57, 67–70, 77–79, 81. *See also* Founders; Initiators; Joiners; Sustainers
Militarism. *See* Antiinterventionism
Minneapolis, 35, 42
Monogamy and marriage, feminist critique of, 148
Morris, Aldon, 193
Mothers, 14, 137, 150, 228. *See also* Childcare; Child rearing
Music. *See* Women's Music Union

NARAL. *See* National Abortion Rights Action League
National Abortion Rights Action League (NARAL), 19, 195, 197, 199, 200–201, 204
National Assault Prevention Center, 208
National Gay Task Force. *See* National Lesbian and Gay Task Force
National guard. *See* Kent State shootings; Ohio National Guard; Ohio State student strike
National Lesbian and Gay Task Force, 169–171, 175

National Organization for Women
(NOW), 4, 19–20, 34, 44, 49, 50,
195, 197–200, 202–204, 230
National Woman's Party, 105, 193,
241
National Women's Political Caucus, 51,
198
Native Americans, 166, 178, 180
Near, Holly, 110, 158, 162, 220
Neo-pagan, 177–178, 180. *See also* Religion
Networks, 21, 26, 30, 41, 50, 101,
111–114, 150, 204, 242, 245. *See
also* Women's policy networks
New Jewish Agenda, 164
New Left: coalitions with women's liberation, 158, 160, 166; conflicts
with lesbians and gays, 188; conflict
with women's liberation, 60, 62–64;
critique of separatism, 116; cultural
divergence from women's liberation,
62; influence of women's liberation
on, 161; origins of women's liberation, 6, 8, 19, 26–28, 30–31, 59,
77, 156, 159–160, 245; sexism,
248
New Right, 20, 161, 189. *See also*
Antifeminist backlash; Conservative
backlash; Family values; Religious
Right
New social movement theory, 22
New York City, 6, 51, 169, 219
9 to 5, 166
NOW. *See* National Organization for
Women
Nuclear disarmament. *See* Antinuclear
movement

Office for Women's Studies. *See* Center
for Women's Studies
Office of Women's Services (OSU), 9,
41–42, 170, 232
Ohio Commission on the Status of
Women, 9, 27–28, 43
Ohio ERA Task Force, 198. *See also*
Equal Rights Amendment; Ohio
Task Force for the Implementation of
the ERA
Ohio Human Rights Bar Association,
126

Ohio Lesbian Festival, 182
Ohio National Guard, 27, 29
Ohio State student strike, 28–30, 60
Ohio State University. *See* Association of
Women Students; Center for Women's Studies; Central Ohio Lesbians;
Columbus-OSU Women's Liberation;
Gay and Lesbian Alliance; OSU
Childcare Pilot Program; Rape Education and Prevention Project;
Women in Comfortable Shoes;
Women's Caucus of the OSU Community; Women's Self-Government
Association; Women's Studies Ad
Hoc Committee
Ohio Task Force for the Implementation
of the ERA, 9. *See also* Equal Rights
Amendment; Ohio ERA Task Force
Ohio Women, Inc., 44
Ohio Women Martial Artists, 231–232.
See also Feminists in Self-
Defense Training
Ohio Women's Information Center,
127, 208
Organization, 197–211; and coalition,
6, 11, 62, 187; created by founders,
61, 77; cultural, 249; growth of, in
1990s, 229–230; institutionalization
of, 195–196, 204–206, 208, 229;
lesbian and gay, 59, 60, 64–65,
176, 207; lesbian feminist, 197; liberal feminist, 5, 197–204; and professionalization, 196–198, 204;
radical feminist, 5, 197, 202, 204–
211, 229, 245–246; survival, 192,
224. *See also* Separatism
OSU Childcare Pilot Program, 31
OSU Women's Liberation. *See* Columbus-OSU Women's Liberation

Patriarchy, 92–93, 103–106, 162–163;
definition, 166; and environmental
exploitation, 159; and militarism,
167; and violence, 167, 210
Peace movement, 98, 155, 158, 160,
166–167, 246, 248, 252. *See also*
Antiwar movement
Peer counseling groups, 196
Personal is political, 13, 81, 95, 122,
134, 136–139, 245, 248

Playboy Foundation, 51, 86
Political culture. *See* Culture
Political generations, 15, 16, 24, 81–
85, 98, 111, 192, 194, 210, 222–
224, 241–242, 247, 252, 256,
258. *See also* Generations; Intergenerational relations
Political opportunities: federal, 87–88;
state and local, 88
Pornography, 168, 238. *See also* Playboy
Foundation; Sadomasochism
Pornography Task Force, 46, 48
Postfeminist era, 2, 3, 25, 89–90,
191–224, 226–229, 250, 253
Poverty, as feminist issue, 163–164,
202
Prison Solidarity Group, 35
Pro-choice movement, 7, 201, 228. *See
also* Abortion rights; Reproductive
rights
Progressive movement, 156, 158, 187,
190, 248; coalition, 160–169, 229,
248; conflict over separatism, 168–
169, 187; feminist influence, 189–
190

Queer Nation, 171, 173–176, 230,
238

Race. *See* Women of color
Racism, 162–163, 165–168, 189, 196,
248; appearance of, 145; as coalition
issue, 158, 160; feminist analysis of,
93, 161; as lesbian and gay issue,
175; as WAC issue, 72–73, 76
Radical feminism: agenda, 163, 200,
249, 254; analysis of marriage, 147–
149; analysis of motherhood, 137;
analysis of patriarchy, 166–167;
analysis of rape, 89, 95; analysis of
relationships, 145–146; analysis of
violence, 168; coalition, 29, 98,
100, 155–190; culture, 51–53,
222; definition, 54, 81, 190, 243–
245, 247–248, 251, 253, 258; of
founders and joiners, 75; of joiners,
62, 65–66; organizing, 1, 4, 7–8,
11, 13, 22, 24, 26–27, 34, 82,
155, 197; politics, 21, 42, 195; re-

definition, 98–100, 224–225, 243–
244; relationships with lesbians, 40,
64, 72; relationships with liberal
feminists, 43–45; relationships with
men, 103, 106, 137; relationships
with nonfeminists, 101–104; sexuality, 4, 20; survival, 4–5, 12, 19,
24–25, 85, 115, 151, 154; of sustainers, 75; theory, 2, 26, 92–94,
96, 136–141, 147, 167, 202, 205,
210, 217. *See also* Lesbian feminism;
Liberal feminism; Postfeminist era;
Socialist feminism
Radical feminism study group, 46–47
Rape crisis center, 1, 8–7, 89, 197;
counseling, 19, 42, 247; hotline,
33, 62–63, 204–205; intervention,
207; prevention, 34, 37, 77, 168,
205, 207. *See also* Community Action Strategies to Stop Rape; Women
Against Rape
Rape Education and Prevention Project
(OSU), 87
Rap group. *See* Consciousness-raising
(CR) groups
Reading and theory groups, 46–48,
161, 196, 209
Reagan, Ronald, 2, 80, 85, 86, 161–
162, 195
Recovery movement, 99, 160, 180–
189, 196, 248, 252. *See also*
Women's Outreach for Women
Religion, 71, 158; Buddhism, 177–
179; goddess, 178–180; Method-
ism, 178–179; New Age, 160, 177,
179–180; Sufism, 178; Taoism,
178; Unitarian Universalism, 178;
Yoga, 17, 177–178. *See also* Jewish
lesbians
Religion study group, 46–47
Religious Right, 2, 44–45, 80, 152,
177. *See also* Antifeminist backlash;
Conservative backlash; Family values;
New Right
Reproductive rights, 196, 201, 212. *See
also* Abortion rights; Pro-choice
movement
Resources mobilization theory, 23, 268
Rhodes, James, 27–28
Rossi, Alice, 227

Sadomasochism, 175, 238–239
San Francisco, Calif., 6, 219
SDS. *See* Students for a Democratic Society
Seeger, Pete, 158
Self-defense training, 19, 37, 50, 63, 87, 175, 204–205. *See also* Feminists in Self-Defense Training; Ohio Women Martial Artists
Self-help. *See* Recovery movement; Women's Outreach for Women
Seneca Falls Women's Peace Camp, 166
Separatism, 5, 7, 52–53, 61–62, 66, 77, 104, 110, 114–116, 151, 158, 168, 187, 215–216, 249; and AIDS, 173; conflicts in, 168–169, 187; radical feminist, 65–66, 146
Sexism, 142, 158, 163, 248; analysis of oppression of women, 34–35, 57, 72, 93; analysis of rape, 37; feminist critique, 161, 187; lesbian and gay issue, 175–176; recognition by public, 64, 77, 139, 187
Sexism in advertising, 47, 205
Sexism in language, 56–57, 103, 177
Sex radicalism, 218–220, 238–239
Sexual harassment, 168, 195, 209–210, 247
Sexual orientation. *See* Heterosexuality; Homophobia; Lesbian feminism
Sex wars. *See* Sex radicalism
Share-A-Job Group, 35
Shelters. *See* Battered women's shelters
Single Mothers' Support Group, 36–37, 39, 46, 48
Slightly Older Lesbians, 48
Socialist feminism, 98, 160–161, 195
Social movement: in abeyance, 193–195, 257; continuity of, 4–5, 24–25, 193–194, 255–258; definition, 22–24, 153; participation in, 117–118, 153
Spirituality, 71, 73–74, 76–78, 155, 160, 177–180, 188–189, 196, 216, 248, 252. *See also* Religion
Steinem, Gloria, 228
Stonewall Riot, New York City, 169
Stonewall Union, 40, 170–171, 174–176, 207
St. Paul, Minnesota, 35, 42

Strategies, 21, 23, 27, 30, 32–33, 38–39, 65, 117–118, 153, 160–161, 188, 202, 257; influence of, on coalitions, 63, 159–161, 167, 189. *See also* Tactics
Structure, 5, 240, 248; collective, 35, 68, 206, 230–231; influence of, on coalitions, 156, 159–161; influence of, on lesbians and gays, 175–177
Struggle sessions, 73, 75
Student rights movement, 2, 28, 60, 158. *See also* Ohio State student strike
Students for a Democratic Society (SDS), 31
Study and support groups. *See* Radical feminism; Reading and theory groups
Sustainers micro-cohort, 59, 71–78, 98

Tactics, 24, 30, 33, 38–39, 156, 159–161, 167, 189, 202, 248, 257; militant, 230. *See also* Strategies
Taylor, Verta, 193
Theory, 57, 92–95, 136. *See also* Radical feminism
Therapy, 196. *See also* Employment

Unions. *See* 9 to 5
United Way, 86, 206–207, 247
Urban League, 208

Vietnam War. *See* Antiwar movement
Violence against lesbians and gay men, 171, 175, 207
Violence against women, 60, 89, 93, 125, 168, 196, 205, 210, 212, 232–233

WAC. *See* Women's Action Collective
War. *See* Antiwar movement; Peace movement
Washington, D.C., 6, 199–200, 213, 239
WEBS. *See* Women's Education and Beautification Society
White supremacy, WAC discussion group, 161
Wiccan covens, 177, 178, 252. *See also* Religion

Womansong, 36–38, 46, 48
Women Against Rape (WAR), 35–38,
121, 239–241; coalitions, 208;
funding, 46, 64, 86–87, 171, 205,
207, 232; orientation and training,
69; staffing, 234; structure, 231;
survival, 51, 196. *See also* Child Assault Prevention Project; Community
Action Strategies to Stop Rape
Women and economics study group,
46–47
Women in Comfortable Shoes (OSU),
230
Women in politics and government, 88,
127–131
Women of color, 71, 253; coalition,
100, 158, 207; feminist, 4, 96, 98;
lesbians and gays, 188
Women's Action Collective (WAC), 9,
34–35, 38, 240–241; coalitions,
42–45, 63, 162–163; community
house, 41; conflict with NWPC, 51;
dissolution, 46, 51, 76, 198–199;
founding, 34, 61; funding, 36–37,
64, 86, 90; internal conflicts, 72–
76; by laws, 49–50; organizing by
founders, 77; orientation and training of new members, 66–71, 92;
philosophy, 65–66, 72; reduced resources, 71; staffing, 121; structure,
38–39, 97, 231; study and support
groups, 46–48, 161, 196, 209; survival, 186
Women's Action for Nuclear Disarmament, 166. *See also* Antinuclear
movement
Women's Band, 30. *See also* Women's
Music Union
Women's Broadcasting Group, 36, 38
Women's Caucus of the OSU Community, 32–33, 111, 115
Women's center for Columbus, 45
Women's Center Group, 35
Women's community. *See* Women's
movement community
Women's Community Development
Fund, 35–36, 38, 62
Women's Co-op Garage, 35, 37, 39,
46, 48, 62
Women's Creative Arts Co-op, 35

Women's culture. *See* Culture
Women's Education and Beautification
Society (WEBS), 48
Women's Equity Action League, 19,
86, 195, 197–198
Women's Health Action Collective. *See*
Women's Health Collective
Women's Health Collective, 35, 39, 46
Women's International League for Peace
and Freedom, 166
Women's Liberation. *See* Columbus-OSU
Women's Liberation; Postfeminist
era; Radical feminism
Women's Literature and Publishing
Group, 35
Women's Media Co-operative, 30, 38
Women's movement. *See* Liberal femi-
nism; Postfeminist era; Radical femi-
nism
Women's movement community, 17,
26–27, 66, 111–113, 221, 222,
246, 250; lesbian, 40–42, 77
Women's music. *See* Women's Band;
Women's Music Union
Women's Music Union, 36, 39, 40–42,
49–51, 66–67, 170, 181, 212
Women's Outreach for Women (WOW),
48, 181–184, 186
Women's Pentagon Actions, 166–167
Women's policy networks, 88–89, *See
also* Networks
Women's publishing. *See* Feminist
presses and publications
Women's Publishing Group, 39
Women's Research and Policy Develop-
ment Center, 43–45, 208
Women's Restaurant Collective, 47
Women's Self-Government Association
(WSGA), 31–32, 41
Women's services. *See* Office of Women's
Services
Women's Studies Ad Hoc Committee
(OSU), 32
Women's studies courses and programs,
1, 7–8, 14, 29–30, 77, 195, 203,
212, 217, 230, 234, 247. *See also*
Center for Women's Studies
Women's Support Group, 35
Women Take Back the Night, 219–
220, 232–233

"Womoon Rising," 73–74, 179, 216
Work. *See* Employment
WOW. *See* Women's Outreach for
 Women
WSGA. *See* Women's Self-Government
 Association

Young Women's Christian Association
 (YWCA), 208

Zald, Mayer, 157